"A book like this is an exclamation po[...] [...] [...] t the
Seattle area is a marvelous place to li[...] [...] ooks
and crannies."
—**Patti Pay**

"Takes a visitor behind the scenes of th[...] [...] [...]urce,
opening new windows for visitors to v[...] [...]
—**Tom Ekste[...] [...]ject Administrator, Div. of
Natural Resources & Parks, King County**

"I've always believed the Northwest is best. *Nature Walks* takes one more step toward
helping us all enjoy it even more."
—**Jean Enersen, KING-5 News**

"Hundreds of people I interview every year tell me their delight in discovering our
hilly, watery, woody community. I wish each one could take a copy of this wonderful
book and discover the real Seattle."
—**Jim French, KIRO Midday**

"These are places of simple but extraordinary experiences for all students of nature
...this book should be a resource guide for every teacher who places importance
on a student's appreciation and understanding of our natural heritage."
—**Tony Angell, author, *Owls*; supervisor,
Environmental Education Programs,
State Dept. of Public Instruction**

"A friendly and informative guidebook such as *Nature Walks* is invaluable to anyone
who loves nature and loves Seattle."
—**Carole Beers, *The Seattle Times***

"It is a pleasure to commend this publication. As this book shows, Washington's rich,
accessible natural environment complements our cultural diversity. *Nature Walks* is a
useful tool for all who wish to make the most of the Northwest living experience."
—**Booth Gardner, Governor, State of Washington**

"At last, the key to the treasure—25 Seattle parks where nature lives on. This book
is the best thing to happen to parents of small children since the invention of the
VCR (and, unlike the VCR, you don't have to feel guilty about using it)."
—**Tim Appelo, *Pacific Northwest* Magazine**

"Our area is abundant with wonderful places where Mother Nature has applied her
unique handiwork. *Nature Walks* will be an invaluable resource for those wishing
to explore and learn about those places."
—**Tim Hill, King County Executive**

"Take this guidebook with you and you'll see things you never saw before...it's
difficult to imagine a better companion on the trip..."
—**Jean Godden, *Seattle Post-Intelligencer***

"Seattle offers an accessible, diverse natural environment not duplicated anywhere.
Our area is rich in natural resources and wildlife, and this guide is an excellent
source for anyone who wishes to truly experience the most of the Pacific Northwest."
—**Charles Royer, Mayor, City of Seattle**

Nature Walks

—IN AND AROUND—
SEATTLE

All Season Exploring
In Parks, Forests, and Wetlands

STEPHEN R. WHITNEY

Photographs by James Hendrickson

THE MOUNTAINEERS/SEATTLE

The Mountaineers: Organized 1906 " . . . to explore, study, preserve and enjoy the natural beauty of the Northwest."

© 1987 by the Mountaineers
All rights reserved.

Published by the Mountaineers
306 2nd Avenue West, Seattle, Washington 98119

Published simultaneously in Canada by Douglas & McIntyre, Ltd., 1615 Venables Street, Vancouver, B. C. V5L 2H1

Manufactured in the United States of America

Maps by Nick Gregoric
Edited by Barbara Chasan
Book design by Shawn Lewis
Cover design by Elizabeth Watson
Cover photograph—Washington Park Arboretum, Waterfront Trail
Frontispiece—Old red cedar snag surrounded
  by common native forest plants

Library of Congress Cataloging in Publication Data

Whitney, Stephen, 1942-
    Nature walks in and around Seattle.

    Bibliography: p.
    Includes index.
    1. Nature trails--Washington State--Seattle Region--
Guide-books.   2. Natural history--Washington State--
Seattle Region--Guide-books.   3. Parks--Washington State--
Seattle Region--Guide-books.   4. Seattle Region (Wash.)--
Description and travel--Guide-books.   I. Title.
QH105.W2W48   1987   917.97'78   87-12225
ISBN 0-89886-128-4 (pbk.)

0 9 8 7
5 4 3 2 1

Contents

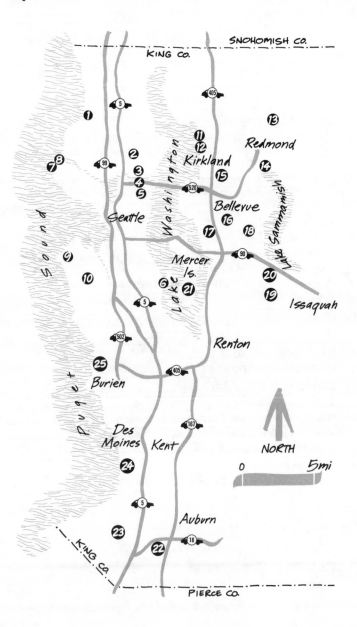

Acknowledgments

I am grateful for the assistance of the following individuals in reviewing and helping to assure the accuracy of the walk descriptions in this guidebook: Paul Frandsen and Lynn Givler, Seattle Department of Parks and Recreation; Roger Hoesterey, Bellevue Parks and Recreation Department; Sandra Bettencourt, Redmond Parks and Recreation Department; Tom Eksten, King County Parks and Recreation Division; Steve Wang, Washington State Parks and Recreation Commission; and Grant Sharpe, University of Washington College of Forestry. I also want to thank Milt Davidson and Doris Thomas, of the Seattle Department of Parks and Recreation, and Dave Enger, of the Sammamish Orienteering Club (P.O. Box 3682, Bellevue, WA 98009), for providing base maps from which final sketches were made. In addition, special thanks are due Roger Hoesterey and Ilene Marckx, who took time out from their busy schedules first to conduct me on guided tours, and then to critique the resulting write-ups. Fred Sharpe also deserves special thanks for checking many of the trail descriptions in the field and making numerous valuable suggestions for their improvement. The book and its author owe much to the skillful editing of Barbara Chasan and the clear, graceful sketch maps of Nick Gregoric. And, of course, I want to thank Jim Hendrickson, my co-conspirator in this project, for slogging with me through mud, rain, and nettle to get the splendid photographs that bring the text to life.

Stephen R. Whitney
Seattle, Washington

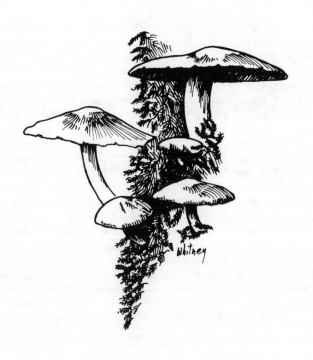

Introduction

Nestled between mountains, forest, and a vast inland sea, Seattle offers the attractions of a lively cosmopolitan center in a natural setting of uncommon beauty. Most Seattleites find the combination irresistible. We like being able to climb a glacier, hike a forest trail, ski down a mountain, fish a wild stream, or sail Puget Sound—and return home in time for a dinner and show.

Even so, there are many times when getting out of town is inconvenient or impossible. Busy schedules, bad weather, unreliable transportation, or the impatience of small children may keep us close to home. We yearn for a whiff of the wild, but we are stuck in town.

Fortunately, lovely patches of forest, meadow, and wetland are preserved in many of the city, county, and state parks that are located in Seattle and surrounding communities. Some were left over from a time when trees outnumbered buildings. Others were created by city dwellers to soften the hard corners of urban life. Today, these pockets of greenery provide our nearest contact with nature. Within minutes we can be off the streets and into the trees.

This book describes twenty-five nature walks within the Seattle metropolitan area—east to Issaquah and south to Federal Way. It also tells a little about the natural features found along the trails.

Eleven of the walks are within Seattle. Most are within fifteen minutes of downtown. The two farthest are only a half-hour away. The walks range from one-half mile to nearly three miles in length. Most are level or nearly so. None are strenuous. Children should have no difficulty completing any of the walks, and the elderly will find many that are admirably suited to their needs

HOW TO USE THIS BOOK

The book is set up like the popular self-guiding nature trails found in many parks. Brief, easy-to-read discussions are keyed by number to obvious natural features found along the trails. The text tells how to find the features, while sketch maps show their approximate locations. Distances along the trails are expressed in yards, where necessary for clarity. The distances, however, are approximations based on pacing the trails and should not be regarded as precise measurements.

Self-guiding nature trails work best with plants, which have the decency to stay in one place, where you can see them. Animals insist on coming and going as they please, which is inconvenient to writers and readers of guidebooks such as this. To circumvent the difficulty, discussions of animals are generally tied to specific habitats in which they can be expected. Some plants, of course, may not be apparent in winter because they have died back to underground bulbs, corms, or rhizomes, or are enduring the cold season as seeds. Deciduous trees and shrubs will be present but may (or may not) prove difficult to identify in the absence of leaves or flowers. A number of the more common plants are shown in photographs, but readers who are serious about identifying plants and animals should consider also carrying one of the field guides listed in Appendix A.

Nine of the walks in this book are along already-established self-guided nature trails. For these trails the descriptions are keyed to numbered stations already in place. Obviously, there is some overlap in information between the discussions in this book and those already written for such trails. Repetition, however, has been kept to a minimum either by expanding existing discussions or treating different topics altogether. For maximum information, refer to both sources while walking the trails.

Since most of the common plants and animals in the region occur along at least several of the trails, some are discussed more than once. By focusing discussions of recurring species on different facets of their life cycles, habits, or places in the environment, however, such repetition is slight. As another way of reducing repetition and cramming as much information as possible within the limited space of a modest guidebook, no walk description attempts to include each and every significant natural feature found along the way. Instead, the information is scattered throughout all the walks. Readers who want more information on a particular plant, animal, or natural phenomenon should consult the topical index at the end of the book.

In the walk descriptions, plants and animals are referred to by their common English names. Exceptions are organisms for which no widely accepted common names exist. While scientific names are more precise and informative, they are also difficult to pronounce, hard to read, and typically regarded with amusement, annoyance, or dismay by the non-scientific public for whom this guidebook is intended. Readers interested in the scientific names of the plants and animals mentioned in this book will find them in Appendix B.

Many of the plants discussed in this book are deciduous and will appear far different in winter than in summer. Others sprout anew each spring from seeds, perennial trailing stems, or underground parts and may not be in evidence at all during the winter. Discussions of such plants assume a spring, summer, or fall outing. Regardless, the majority of walks are worth taking at any time of year.

All together, the discussions in this book amount to an informal natural history of Seattle and its environs. They are not intended, however, to constitute a systematic treatment of that vast subject, which lies outside the scope of a book such as this. Many interesting topics were purposely, if regrettably, omitted because they are too abstract, too complex, or too difficult to peg to natural features actually seen along the trails.

Information blocks at the beginnings of the walks indicate distances, best seasons to go, highlights, and Metro bus connections. Because all the walks are at low elevation, they normally can be done any time of year. Some areas, however, are prettier, easier to walk, or more interesting in some seasons than others. Where appropriate, those seasons have been indicated. Metro bus routes have been provided for people who either do not have cars or would prefer not to use them. For information on schedules or route changes, call Metro information, listed in the white pages.

WHAT TO TAKE

Running shoes or other comfortable footwear are sufficient for all the walks in this book. Hikers accustomed to wearing boots will probably want to do so, but they are nowhere essential. Many of the trails, however, are wet or muddy in spots or during the rainy season. On such trails boots are very desirable if not absolutely necessary.

Binoculars are highly recommended because attempting to observe birds without them is an exercise in futility. A tripod-mounted telescope would be useful on Walks 3, 4, and 22. A small, inexpensive hand lens is invaluable for examining the intricacies of flowers, insects, and other minutiae. Such lens usually magnify objects five to fifteen times.

Field guides exist to the trees, wildflowers, ferns, mosses, mammals, birds, reptiles, amphibians, and invertebrate life of the Pacific Northwest. Some people will want to take one or two such guidebooks. Others will not be happly unless they have all of them on hand. And a few people will not care to take a single one. And that's okay too. For a list of recommended field guides, see Appendix A. Also listed are a number of more general works about the natural history of the Pacific Northwest.

SAFETY

Of all the walks in this book, there is only one where a person conceivably could get seriously lost: Walk 19, Cougar Mountain Regional Wildland Park. The loop is easy enough to follow, and no one is likely to lose the way—but it's possible. Hikers walking that loop or using it as access to the larger network of trails within the park are advised to carry the Ten Essentials: map, compass, extra food, extra clothing, rain gear, matches in waterproof case, flashlight, first-aid kit, pocketknife, and sunglasses.

Most of the trails in this book feature one or more wooden bridges, boardwalks, simple planks, or even logs. When damp, all such wooden structures can be extremely slippery. Everyone should be careful when walking on planks or logs, and children may need several safety reminders.

The most frequent hazard along the trails in this book is stinging nettle. People unfamiliar with this native plant should learn to identify it (see figure below) for their own sakes. Children, in particular, should be taught how to recognize stinging nettle. Although the burning sensation that follows contact with the plant is not serious, and normally lasts but an hour or two, the experience is sufficiently unpleasant that few children will be able to shrug it off. According to herbal lore, the burning can be relieved by rubbing affected areas with juice from coast red elderberry, thimbleberry, or bracken fern. Home remedies include baking soda, alcohol, or meat tenderizer.

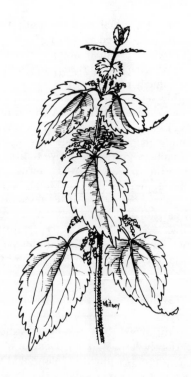

Reference is made to the practices of local Indian tribes in utilizing various native plants for food, medicine, and materials. These descriptions are provided solely for the insights they provide into the role played by plants in native cultures and should not be construed as endorsing the edibility or efficacy of any particular plants. Nor should the fact that animals consume certain plants—such as some poisonous mushrooms—be taken as evidence that they are safe for humans.

Few urban pastimes are safer than walking the trails of our local state, city, and county parks. Nevertheless, the inclusion of a walk in this book does not mean that it will necessarily be safe for you or other members of your party. On some walks, cliffs, ravines, or slippery trails could pose a degree of hazard, especially for untended children. Moreover, in recent years several highly publicized incidents of assault, rape, and kidnapping have occurred in public parks of the region. While the likelihood of trouble in local parks is extremely small, simple prudence suggests, for example, that women should walk with companions and that parents should closely supervise their children. Of course, no one should attempt these walks at night. Complaints about rowdiness, threatening behavior, or destruction of public property should be reported immediately to the police (call 911).

ETIQUETTE

Because the parks are heavily used, their woods and wetlands are especially vulnerable. A few trails and adjacent areas are in places badly eroded and stripped of vegetation. In some instances this is the work of trail bikers who sneak onto the trails in defiance of posted prohibitions against motorcycles. Litter is also a problem in many parks, though by design the trails chosen for this book are largely free of significant litter.

Motorcycles and bicycles are prohibited on all the trails in this book. Dogs are permitted on some trails if they are on leashes. Horses are permitted only in Bridle Trails State Park and Cougar Mountain Regional Wildland Park.

Uprooting, collecting, or otherwise damaging plants for whatever purpose is forbidden in all the parks. Readers are strongly urged to respect this prohibition so that our wild plants may be left for others to enjoy. This restriction does not apply to picking blackberries, huckleberries, and other wild fruits, but people who do so should be certain that the berries they pick are in fact what they think they are. Mushroom picking is allowed in some parks but not others. In either case it is not recommended for untrained collectors. Mushrooms as a group are probably no more poisonous than plants as a whole, but distinguishing between certain poisonous and edible species can be very difficult.

Walkers can help maintain the beauty and utility of our parks by staying on the trails, not cutting across switchbacks, packing out litter, following posted regulations, and respecting plants and wildlife.

1

SEATTLE

Carkeek Park

Distance: 1 - mile loop
Season: best spring through fall
Highlights: Olympic Mountain views, stream
Metro: 28 (½-mile walk to trailhead)

Carkeek Park offers wooded trails and a fine stretch of Puget Sound beach, as well as picnic tables, rest rooms, archery range, play area, and model airplane field. But, alas, what was formerly the best walk in the park, down the wooded canyon of Piper's Creek, has been ruined. Today, that once lovely slice of semi-wildness is blighted by an enormous concrete

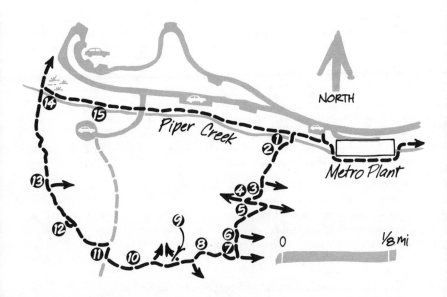

Western red baneberry bearing fruit in early summer

15

retaining wall built to keep houses perched on the brink from sliding down into the creek. The need may have been clear, but the resulting scar is a terrible loss for the park. You can still walk along the creek (see below), but the solitude and illusion of wildness are gone.

The walk described here follows a different route. It is a pleasant loop, with much to recommend it, but for all who remember the Piper's Creek Trail as it once was, this alternative will always seem second best.

Drive 3rd Avenue N.W. to N.W. 110th Street and turn west, toward Puget Sound. The street turns right and plunges into the Carkeek woods, here dotted with homes. In just over a curvy one-half mile, turn left into the park proper. Drive another two-tenths of a mile to a trail sign and small parking lot on the left, near the Metro sewage plant. Park here.

Metro riders should get off the 28 bus at 100th Place N.W. and walk to the grassy field at the end of the short stub of road with the grandiose name 6th Avenue N.W. Cross the lawn and follow the Piper's Creek Trail, which plunges into the woods. In one-half mile come to the trail sign and parking area.

The trail sign, erected by the Steve Crouch Troop 167 of the Boy Scouts in the fall of 1985, shows the general layout and trail system of the park. It is a fine, informative sign, but some of the details are sketchy and hikers should not rely exclusively on it when attempting to negotiate the maze of paths found in the park.

To begin the walk, cross the lawn to an obvious bridge over Piper's Creek.

(1) The creek is named for A. W. Piper, a candy manufacturer who lived in the canyon. A dirt road ran past his house to a sawmill near the mouth of the stream. The mill closed in the 1920s, when the last old-growth western red cedars and western hemlocks were cut down. The city of Seattle purchased "Piper's canyon" in 1928 with the help of a $25,000 gift from Morgan J. Carkeek, an English-born building contractor who came to Seattle in 1875.

At the end of the bridge, where the trail turns right, the large shrub on the right is Indian plum. Directly across the trail from it is a coast red elderberry. The bank on the left is covered with waterleaf.

Follow the broad trail uphill into the woods. Where the trail curves left, about fifty yards beyond the bridge, notice the fallen tree on the right.

(2) Out of death comes new life, as English ivy, sword fern, and fringecup have established themselves on the dead root mass of the fallen tree. Where light and moisture are sufficient, as here, plants are quick to invade habitats newly created by natural or human disturbance. Birds and wind are the chief agents by which seeds and spores are carried to new areas.

The trail continues uphill in a corridor of salmonberry beneath good-sized bigleaf maples and red alders. On the left, fifty yards beyond the

Young family at trailhead in Carkeek Park

turn, you will see a bigleaf maple with a long, straight trunk and several dead branches. Just beyond, pass a side trail and continue uphill. Look for candyflower, false Solomon's seal, and bleeding heart, along with young western red cedars that have been planted by the Seattle Parks Department. The trail bends right and in twenty-five yards passes an old western red cedar stump with lady fern, wood fern, and bleeding heart growing on it.

(3) Big western red cedars once dominated the hillside forest. Since red cedar prefers moist ground, the presence of large stumps on this slope indicate that it is well watered despite the presence of an obvious stream. Today, dense thickets of salmonberry, elderberry, and stinging nettle have replaced the red cedar as indicator of abundant moisture on this slope—an inglorious substitution.

The trail makes a broad switchback left. At the head of the switchback a side trail heads right, down into a shallow draw.

(4) The tree to the right of this side trail is a Douglas fir in the process of ridding itself of nonproductive lower branches, which are shaded by

the forest canopy. Douglas firs are intolerant of shade and require full sunlight for growth. They also require bare mineral soil for germination. Failure to burn logging slash may inhibit or prevent the germination of Douglas fir seeds. Such appears to have happened on this slope, where there are only a few scattered Douglas firs.

The trail heads uphill and in fifty yards switchbacks right. A side trail heading left marks the turn. Twenty yards beyond, pause by an old western red cedar stump with a handsome young western hemlock growing on top.

(5) Western hemlocks commonly sprout atop old logs and stumps. Young hemlocks are able to continue growing even in the deep shade. As the relatively short-lived alders on this slope die off, the hemlocks will replace them. Pure stands of western hemlock may be so thick with trees that they produce more lumber than equivalent acreage of the much larger, but sun-loving, Douglas fir.

Twenty-five yards beyond the stump, the trail bends left. Then, where the trail turns right, pass another path heading left. Keep right. Stinging nettle is thick along here but soon gives way to sword fern. Twenty yards beyond the side path watch for a western red cedar on the right side of the trail. There are several other cedars and a few Douglas firs in this area. This is a good place to consider the forest as a whole.

(6) Thousands of individual plants, from trees to tiny mosses and herbs, grow on this hillside. Together, they form a plant community. Each species has its own requirements for sunlight, moisture, and nutrients. But since resources are never plentiful enough to permit unlimited growth, competition among individual plants is intense. The dominant plants in the community are those that, by virtue of sheer numbers or greater size or both, are able to command a disproportionate share of the available resources. In forests, of course, the dominant plants are always trees. By blocking the sun and hogging both water and nutrients in the soil, trees place firm restraints on the development of vegetation beneath them. Plants that can tolerate these conditions will be found growing in forests. Those which can't will be restricted to treeless places.

The trail swings left and, forty yards beyond the red cedar, turns right. Yet another side path on the left marks the turn. The trail dips into a shallow draw and in ten yards comes to an old snag with a number of holes made by woodpeckers. There is also one much larger hole that could well serve as a nest or resting place for an owl, raccoon, or squirrel.

(7) Since winters are mild in the Puget Sound lowlands, virtually all birds and mammals remain active throughout the cold months. During especially frigid or stormy periods, however, animals temporarily seek shelter from the elements. Abondoned woodpecker holes provide such refuge. Without them, many small birds and mammals might well perish.

From the snag the trail descends gradually and in sixty yards, as it bends left, look for a badly diseased but still living bigleaf maple on the right.

(8) This tree has lost the bark and much of the wood on one side of the trunk yet still supports a healthy crown of leaves. The plant's life is being conducted up one side of the trunk, which is flattened and less than a foot thick. The trunk probably will succumb to wind and break before fungi and insects are able to completely destroy the living wood. Should the tree be gone when you arrive, look for its remains sprawled in the undergrowth.

The trail swings left, drops slightly, and passes a trail leading to houses visible on the left. On the right are the remains of a tree house. The trail tops a small rise, then descends to a prominent fork. Between the forks is a large shrub with droopy clusters of white flowers in the spring.

(9) The shrub is ocean spray, or creambush. It is most common on well-drained forest sites, often in the company of salal. The Indians valued ocean spray for its hard wood, which they used for making a variety of tools. Today, we appreciate it more for its clusters of creamy flowers, which appear in June and July. Hundreds of flowers make up the clusters.

The right fork heads downslope to the park's model airplane field. Instead, keep left and within thirty yards pass two side trails that head downslope to join the right fork a few yards past the junction. The main trail continues its more or less level traverse and in sixty yards turns left, then right. Much of the slope to the right, all the way down to the bottom of the ravine, is covered by a dense shrub thicket consisting mostly of salmonberry but also containing coast red elderberry, and Indian plum.

(10) The salmonberry thicket provides food and cover for resident birds such as song sparrow, rufous-sided towhee, and Bewick's wren. In late April or May, Wilson's warbler arrives at the thicket to set up house for the summer. The male has a bright yellow breast and belly, an olive green back, and a black cap. The female lacks the cap but is otherwise a duller version of the male. When either bird is sitting on the nest, the yellow underside is obscured and the green back provides camouflage from the sharp eyes of curious predators.

The trail drops to an old skid road, which heads straight downhill to the model airplane field.

(11) The great conifers that once grew on this slope were skidded down this old road to the sawmill, which stood at the site of the model airplane field. Half-buried logs laid at intervals across the road served as skids, preventing the trees from nosing into the mud on their journey to the mill.

Turn right on the skid head road and pass the elevated sewer manhole. About twenty yards farther, turn left on a side trail. The trail traverses the slope and in about forty-five yards bends right and runs along the top of the ridge. The trail gradually descends beneath large red alder, with views of Puget Sound and the Olympic Mountains through the foliage on the left. About seventy-five yards from the skid road the trail forks. Turn left and come to a large bigleaf maple sitting on the edge of the bluff. The tree has a broad, buttressed base that has been hollowed out by fire. Except that the tree is right next to an oft-frequented trail, it would provide excellent shelter for a family of coyotes.

(12) Carkeek Park is a known refuge for coyotes, and hollowed-out trees such as this one could serve as dens. Coyotes also have been sighted in other Seattle parks and neighborhoods, much to the surprise and consternation of residents. Coyotes, however, pose no danger to humans and may even provide a valuable service as rat catchers. On occasion, coyotes may attempt to kill a small cat or dog, but more often they enter backyards to score a bit of dog chow or raid garbage cans. Coyotes hunt small mammals and birds but also feed on insects, carrion, and garbage, as well as a variety of fruits. In Seattle coyotes are not restricted to parks but may occur wherever a bit of woods or otherwise undeveloped land exists—even beneath freeways! Coyotes also have been observed on city streets in broad daylight.

From the tree the trail bends right and drops down the crest of the ridge. In about thirty yards come to an overlook of Puget Sound and the Olympics. Now the trail drops steeply, levels out, swings left and descends to the railroad tracks running along the shore. The view of Puget Sound and, in clear weather, the distant Olympic Mountains is here unobstructed.

(13) The Olympic Mountains began about fifty-five million years ago as an accumulation of basalt lava that was erupted from rifts and fissures deep beneath the sea. Sediments derived from the nearby continent, which then lay east of its present position, piled up on both sides of the volcanic pile. Between about thirty million and twelve million years ago, these rocks were jammed into the continent by eastward movement of the Juan de Fuca plate, one of many mobile plates making up the earth's crust. Further pressures from within the earth caused the rocks to rise, forming the range we see today. The sharp peaks and jagged ridges of the Olympics are the work of glaciers, which buried much of the range at least four times during the last Ice Age, between 2.5 million and 10,000 years ago. Small glaciers still mantle the upper slopes of most of the higher peaks in the range.

From the southwest corner of the model airplane field, walk on the grass along the chain link fence to where Piper's Creek flows through a culvert beneath the railroad tracks. Just across the creek, turn right on a broad path. (This path becomes quite muddy after a rain. Hikers who wish to avoid the goo can continue walking along the chain-link fence to the beach parking lot and then walk back alongside the park road to their cars.) Immediately upon turning onto the path, notice the large old broken tree on the right.

(14) This is Pacific willow, which frequents streambanks and other wetlands along the Pacific Coast. Pacific willows and red alders form the canopy of this streamside woodland.

Aging Pacific willow leaf in late autumn

About seventy yards beyond the willow, a narrow trail heads right toward the creek.

(15) Damp thickets are the favored haunts of two mammals unique to the northwestern corner of the continent. One is the aplodontia, or mountain beaver, a reclusive rodent that feeds on grasses, wildflowers, and the tender young shoots and bark of shrubs and trees. The other mammal is the shrew-mole, which digs tunnels beneath the forest humus but emerges aboveground to hunt for spiders, worms, and insects. The shrew-mole is barely four inches long, of which about one inch is devoted to tail. The aplodontia is considerably larger, measuring twelve to seventeen inches from tip of nose to base of its tiny tail.

About forty yards beyond pass a leading left to the park road and beach parking lot. To return to the trailhead parking area, keep straight, cross the road leading to the model airplane field, and walk the length of the lawn back to the car. Bus riders will need to continue from there back up the Piper Creek Trail to 100th Place N.W.

2

Ravenna Park

Distance: ¾ - mile loop
Season: all year
Highlights: stream, forest
Metro: 48, 71, 72, 73, 74, 78

Tucked in a narrow ravine below the level of surface streets, Ravenna Park is Seattle's hidden treasure. Thousands of people have driven across the 15th Avenue N.E. bridge without realizing that a splendid woodland park, complete with babbling brook, lies beneath the span. Others have played soccer at the lower end of the ravine, or frolicked in Cowen Park at the upper end, without bothering to take the walk from end to end.

University students and district residents, however, know the fifty-two-acre park well and use it often. If solitude is a requirement, the best times to visit are during foggy or drizzly weather (or perhaps on days so incredibly warm and sunny that the entire student population is sprawled out on the lawns of Green Lake).

Rest rooms and picnic tables are located near the trailhead, off 20th Avenue N.E.; by the soccer field, off N.E. 55th Street; and in Cowen Park, which adjoins Ravenna Park on the west. Children's play areas are located at Cowen Park and near the soccer field. Ravenna Boulevard provides end-to-end access.

From downtown Seattle drive north on I-5. Leave the freeway at exit 170, Ravenna Boulevard. At the light turn right on Ravenna and after about three-fourths of a mile turn left on 20th Avenue N.E. The street dead-ends in one block at the bridge over Ravenna Park. The unmarked park entrance is on the right, just left of the alley. From the parking lot, walk past the rest rooms toward a large trail sign at the edge of the woods.

The sign has a map of the trail and a box for interpretive pamphlets. If you take a pamphlet, be sure to return it. Pamphlets are also available through the Seattle Parks Department. The following discussions attempt

Shiny needles of a Pacific yew in Ravenna Park

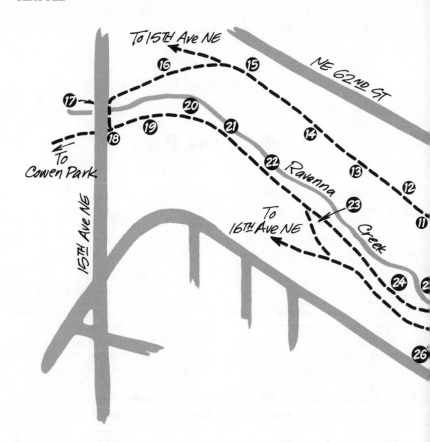

to supplement those in the interpretive pamphlet, not to replace them. If possible, it is recommended that the two publications be used together.

The trail begins just behind the sign. Take the right-hand path to signpost 1 on the left.

(1)   The original conifer forest in the narrow valley of Ravenna Creek had been logged off by 1930. Today's woods are a mixture of conifers and deciduous trees, of native plants and exotic (foreign) ornamentals. The wooded portions of the valley are pleasant. Most of the forest openings, however, have been taken over by nonnative plants.

The trail descends steeply into the ravine. Signpost 2 is on the right, about halfway down.

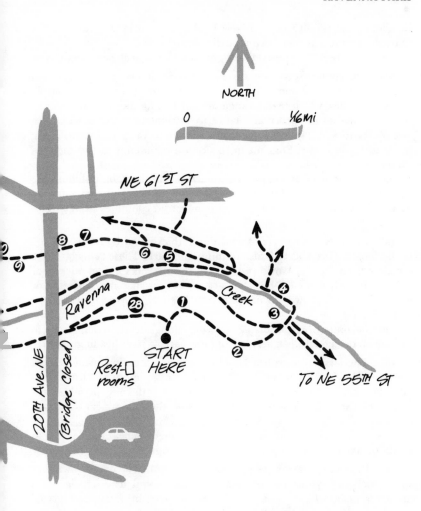

NORTH

0   1/16mi

NE 61ST ST

⑧ ⑦
② ⑥ ⑤
⑨
Ravenna   Creek   ④
28 ①   ③
②
20TH Ave. NE
(Bridge Closed)
Rest-□ START
rooms   HERE

To NE 55TH ST

(2)   This Douglas fir has a "pistol butt" trunk, aptly named for the way in which it grows out and then turns abruptly upward, like the handle of a pistol. The downward creep of soil on this steep, moist slope causes the trunk to lean outward. The tree's search for light causes it to bend upward.

The trail levels out in the bottom of the valley and intersects the broad track connecting Cowen Park, to the west (left), with the soccer field and N.E. 55th Street to the east. Signpost 3 is on the left, just before the bridge over Ravenna Creek.

(3)   The metal cap here seals a sulfur spring. Sealing this spring was one of several projects undertaken in the park during the 1930s by the

Civilian Conservation Corps, a New Deal public works program. At the time, the spring was said to be a public hazard.

Cross the creek. The post on the right points straight ahead to signpost 4.

(4) The conifer is Norway spruce, a widely planted park and garden tree that is rather common along this trail. The tree's short, stiff, sharply pointed needles, which tend to angle forward along the twig, are distinctive. Two species of spruce are native to Washington state: Sitka spruce (see Walks 16 and 23) and Engelmann spruce. Sitka spruce grows along the Washington coast; Engelmann spruce, on mountains east of the Cascade crest.

Keep to the main track, passing a narrow path heading uphill on the right. Directly ahead, the track curves left and another, broader side trail on the right, marked by a signpost with an arrow, continues straight. Follow this trail uphill to signpost 5.

(5) Evergreen blackberry forms dense thickets on both sides of the trail. Himalaya blackberry is also found in the park. These two aggressive invaders from the Old World provide Northwesterners untold buckets of tasty fruit each summer, but they are obnoxious in semi-wild settings, where they often crowd out native plants. Even so, they do provide food and cover for wildlife.

Just beyond a bigleaf maple growing alongside the trail, come to signpost 6 on the left, just across from the narrow path heading uphill.

(6) The large tree with a knobby trunk is a London planetree, an ornamental hybrid cross between the American sycamore and the Oriental planetree. The beautiful California sycamore is the only planetree native to the Pacific Coast, where it reaches its northern limit near San Francisco.

The trail climbs gradually beneath a canopy of bigleaf maple. Just as the 20th Avenue bridge comes into view, find signpost 7 on the right.

(7) Distinct soil layers are evident on this bank. The dark brown topsoil is rich in organic matter—naturally composted leaves, twigs, and animal remains. Below it is a gray-brown layer of weathered glacial till—unsorted rock debris deposited in the Puget Sound region by the Vashon Glacier, which reached its greatest extent about 15,000 years ago. Out of sight beneath this layer is unweathered glacial till. Weathering is the process whereby water breaks down minerals to form clay. Soil is therefore a mixture of weathered inorganic materials and decomposed organic materials. Both are essential ingredients of good soils.

The trail now passes through an open area where the slopes are covered with blackberry. Signpost 8 is on the right, just before reaching the bridge.

(8) Beneath the large bigleaf maple are English holly and a couple of small horsechestnut seedlings. Both trees are European natives that are widely planted in Seattle. Eastern gray squirrels fancy the large horsechestnut seeds, which they have carried from nearby neighborhoods and buried here in the park. These two seedlings probably sprouted from some squirrel's forgotten seed cache. Birds eat the red holly berries and deposit the undigested seeds in their droppings.

The 20th Avenue bridge is Seattle's oldest steel arched span. Designed in 1913, it was closed to vehicles in 1975. Pass under the bridge to signpost 9 on the left.

(9) Here are second-growth Douglas fir, western red cedar, and western hemlock, the three conifers that dominated the original forest along Ravenna Creek. The trees in this damp ravine were once so large that people paid a small admission to see them. Although the city obtained the ravine for a park in 1910, pioneer lumber baron Henry Yesler, with city connivance, began logging the giant trees. The last ones were gone by 1930.

The trail continues level, skirting an open area on the left. As the trail bends right come to signpost 10.

(10) Here, a scrawny Pacific madrona (or madrone) is struggling to establish itself, but its prospects don't look good. A larger madrona is located across the trail and some forty-five feet away. Birds relish the red berries, which appear in the fall, but most people find them bland and mealy. Some local Indian tribes brewed a cold remedy from the leaves, bark, and berries.

Continue straight ahead, avoiding side trails left and right. Signpost 11 is on the left.

(11) The trees with the smooth, dark reddish brown bark are bitter cherries. The highly astringent fruits are sought by birds, though rarely

Fifteenth Avenue Bridge marking the Cowen Park entrance of Ravenna Park

by people. Bitter cherry occurs widely in the West, but throughout most of its range it is a shrub. Only west of the Cascades does it normally grow as a good-sized tree.

The trail enters another opening, with pleasant views across the ravine. Signpost 12 is on the right.

(12) The woods on the right-hand side of the trail and the open area on the left are two distinct habitats. The boundary separating them is a transitional zone in which plants from both habitats can be found growing together. Such zones are called ecotones. Because they attract animals from adjacent habitats, they are among the best places to seek wildlife.

Pass by a maple growing alongside the trail and come to signpost 13 on the left.

(13) Evergreen blackberry has nearly taken over this open slope. Since tree seedlings find it nearly impossible to become established within the dense thickets, such berry wastelands can persist for decades. Although eradication is difficult, removal of the vines and replacement with native trees and shrubs would be a worthy goal for all local park authorities.

The trail continues skirting the open area. Come shortly to signpost 14 on the left.

(14) Trees that grow on this moist open slope are particularly vulnerable to wind. Wet, unstable soils provide poor footing, and the openings expose trees to the worst gusts.

Signpost 15 is on the right, where the slope is densely covered with English ivy.

(15) English ivy is taking over this area, though it has died back on some of the tree trunks. Birds have dispersed its seeds throughout the greater Seattle area, where it competes vigorously with native ground covers.

The trail now descends gently, as the 15th Avenue bridge comes into view. The side trail on the right heads uphill to the avenue; keep left and come to signpost 16 on the right.

(16) The trees here are bigleaf maples, which dominate the second-growth woods of Ravenna Park. Eventually, conifers will overtop and shade out most of the maples. Local Indians used maple wood for dishes, cooking utensils, paddles, and other implements.

At the 15th Avenue bridge turn left, downhill, and come to signpost 17 on the right. From here, you have a good view up the valley to Cowen Park and down the valley to near 20th Avenue.

(17) The Ravenna Valley was carved by ice and water. The Vashon ice sheet gouged out the trough now occupied by Lake Washington and deposited the excavated rock debris in ridges on either side. One of those ridges forms the bluff now cut through by Ravenna Creek. The University of Washington campus is perched on this bluff where it extends southward along Montlake Boulevard.

Exposed root system of large Douglas firs in Ravenna Park

The trail descends the broad track running the length of Ravenna Park. Turn right to exit at Cowen Park, left to continue the loop. But first, signpost 18 is located directly across the track.

(18) Behind the post is Pacific dogwood, a common understory tree throughout the region. Studies have shown that dogwoods are able to grow in dense shade because they can carry out photosynthesis with as little as one-third the sunlight of plants growing in open areas.

Follow the main track left and find signpost 19 next to the creek.

(19) The low, round-leaved plant growing in the stream is water-cress, a delicious salad green from Europe. Ravenna Park's watercress is unfit for consumption, however, because the creek is polluted with coliform bacteria from human and animal wastes.

As the track curves right, come to signpost 20 on the left.

(20) This great sprawling tangle of a tree is English yew, whose wood was—and is—highly valued for making bows and other implements. Yew is a conifer without a cone. Instead, it bears a single naked seed in a fleshy red cup called an aril. Birds eat the aril and scatter the undigested seeds in their excrement. It is uncertain whether the fleshy red cup is toxic to humans, but since all other parts of the yew are poisonous, the aril may be as well.

Passing a trail heading upslope on the right, come to signpost 21.

(21) The white-trunked trees in the opening are European white birch, a widely planted ornamental. It closely resembles the native paper birch, which is on display in Bellefields Nature Park (Walk 18).

Ravenna Creek is noticeably more energetic than it was even a few yards back. Woods border the trail on the right. Come to signpost 22 on the left.

(22) The trees here are western larches, which are native to mid-mountain forests of eastern Washington. Unlike other conifers, larches have deciduous leaves. In winter their branches are bare. In spring the new needles are bright yellow-green like new leaves of a deciduous tree; in fall they turn gold before dropping. Evergreen conifers also drop their needles, but not all at once.

Pass a broad trail heading uphill on the right. As the track begins to curve left, come to signpost 23 on the right.

(23) The numerous small holes in these trees were made by the red-breasted sapsucker. This bright woodpecker drills rows of holes in a variety of trees, though it prefers cottonwoods and alders. It returns later to drink the running sap and feast on the small insects attracted to it.

The trail swings left, passes one stand of redwoods, and comes to a second one, where signpost 24 is next to a split-log bench.

(24) California redwoods are native to coastal forests from central California to extreme southwestern Oregon. These magnificent trees achieve heights of more than 380 feet and trunk diameters in excess of twenty feet. Fifty million years ago, when the climate was warmer and more humid, they occurred in a diverse subtropical forest that covered most of North America. Today, they are confined to a narrow coastal strip where summer fogs and winter rains combine to create a mild, humid climate year-around.

Just before the track crosses Ravenna Creek, come to signpost 25.

(25) Ravenna Creek is the original outlet for Green Lake. Today, however, sewers carry away most of the water. Originally, the creek formed a large, marshy delta where it flowed into Union Bay. The delta was later filled to make way for University Village and other real estate wonders.

Turn right here and cross the creek on an elegant plank bridge. On the left is a huge mossy boulder.

(26) This boulder is a glacial erratic—a rock plucked by moving ice from one region and unceremoniously plopped down in another. As the Vashon ice sheet moved south into the Puget Sound region, it brought with it tons of rock quarried in Canada. This boulder is some 200 miles from its place of origin in British Columbia.

On the other side of the creek, climb a set of steps to signpost 27, next to an old western red cedar stump with red huckleberry growing on it.

(27) Feel the exposed wood on this stump. It is soft and crumbly from the work of fungi and bacteria, which busily break down its indigestible fibers into substances of use to plants. In effect, the fungi and bacteria predigest the wood.

The trail now passes once more under the 20th Avenue bridge and begins to gradually descend. A signpost with an arrow points the way uphill on a steep side trail. About half way to the top, look for signpost 28 on the right.

(28) The slim tree here is Pacific, or western yew, a native cousin of the English yew. The two are very much alike, though the English yew has longer needles, which have two green bands on their undersides. The Pacific yew grows in moist, shady forests along the Pacific Coast from California to British Columbia. Although its wood is as good as that of the English yew, there are too few yews to make it commercially attractive.

From here the trail climbs to the trailhead.

Bank covered with sword fern in Ravenna Park

31

3

SEATTLE

Montlake Fill

Distance: 1 - mile loop
Season: best fall through spring
Highlights: good birding, bay views
Metro: 25, 30, 32, 75

Montlake Fill is a homely name for a special place—a broad field dotted with ponds and fringed with marsh, with long views west to the University of Washington, south across Union Bay to the Arboretum, and east to Laurelhurst.

The area lies between the university parking lots along Montlake Avenue and the new Center for Urban Horticulture at the corner of Union Bay Place N.E. and N.E. 41st Street. Connecting the two is a broad gravel path dubbed Wahkiakum Lane. Student traffic along the lane is regular but never intrusive. South of the lane lies a maze of narrow foot-beaten paths that poke about ponds, marshes, lakeshore, and berry thickets.

This is one of Seattle's birding hot spots, so bring binoculars or a telescope if you have one. Also wear boots, or shoes fit for tromping through mire and goosh. The field is like a saturated sponge. Press it and water oozes to the surface. Although most of the area dries out by midsummer, there are a few low-lying places that remain soggy year-around. Rest rooms are located at the Center for Urban Horticulture or across N.E. 45th Street at University Village. Picnicking is free-lance.

From downtown Seattle drive north on I-5, then east on SR 520. Leave the freeway at the first exit, Montlake Boulevard. At the light turn left onto Montlake. In about a mile keep right as the highway curves eastward to join N.E. 45th Street. Pass University Village (left) and turn right on Union Bay Place N.E. If street parking is available, park as near to the end of the block as possible. If not, turn left on N.E. 41st, then immediately right into the visitor parking area for the Center for Urban Horticulture.

One of many paths winding through the Montlake Fill wildlife refuge

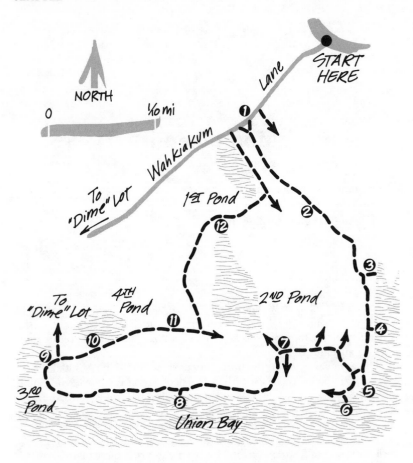

From wherever you park, walk to the west side of the center and find a broad gravel track heading across the open field toward the university. This is Wahkiakum Lane.

The lane runs alongside a chain link fence and thicket of Himalaya blackberry. Just beyond the end of the fence, pass a faint path on the left and come to another trail heading in the same direction. Straight ahead is a shallow pond that often dries up in late summer. Turn left here and survey the terrain.

(1) Originally, this entire field lay beneath the waters of Union Bay, which extended from the stadium northward to just beyond University Village and east over to Laurelhurst. In 1916, with the completion of the Chittenden Locks in Ballard, the level of Lake Washington and Union Bay dropped nine feet, exposing most of this area. Gradually, marsh plants invaded the new ground. After World War II, much of the area

was filled for real estate development, and the land immediately north of Wahkiakum Lane was used for dumping garbage. When Harry W. Higman and Earl J. Larrison's classic, *Union Bay: The Life of a City Marsh,* appeared in 1951, most of the area south of the lane was still given over to marsh. Later this too was filled—for parking lots and athletic fields. In recent years, the university had planned to use the remaining area as a research arboretum for the new Center for Urban Horticulture. Local conservationists persuaded school officials to manage the former marsh as an ecological research area instead.

On the left are cottonwoods, red alders, and European white birch. In the distance you can see bare snags rising over the marsh.

(2) The tall weedy plants growing abundantly in this field are Queen Anne's lace, or wild carrot. This European immigrant is indeed the wild plant from which garden carrots were developed. It presumably got its name from the lacy pattern formed by the flat clusters of tiny white flowers. Within the center of some clusters, or umbels, there may be a single red, brown, pink, or purple flower that perhaps serves as a bull's-eye for insects. In fall, when Queen Anne's lace has dried up, the bright blue daisylike flowers of chicory, another European import, brighten the field.

As the trail approaches a dense berry tangle, a faint path heads left, through the shrubbery, to the edge of the cattail marsh. In winter and spring the way is clear. By midsummer, however, the path may be overgrown.

(3) This is an excellent place to find rails—both the Virginia rail and sora—if you have the patience to wait for these reclusive marsh dwellers to emerge from the cattails. Rails feed on invertebrate animals and the seeds of marsh plants. The best chance of luring them into the open is to play a recording of rail calls, though only dedicated birders are likely to take the trouble.

Back at the main trail, come to another side trail on the left, just before the first large cottonwood. Turn left here and again follow a short, narrow path to the edge of the marsh.

(4) In spring the marsh is filled with the chattery songs of long-billed marsh wrens. Males are polygamous and may set up two or more females in adjacent territories. The nest is a globular affair woven from wet vegetation and lashed to the cattail stalks a foot or two above the ground or water. Although the males loudly and persistently assert their territorial claims, the tiny birds are difficult to spot.

The trail skirts the Himalaya blackberry jungle and comes shortly to an overlook of Union Bay. This is a good place to scan the water for ducks, coots, gulls, and other aquatic birds.

(5) The bird you are most likely to see is the American coot, which many people mistake for a duck. The dark gray to black plumage, red eye,

White water lilies in bloom, Montlake Fill

and white, pointed bill, however, easily distinguish this cousin of the rails from any sort of duck. A year-around resident, the coot nests among the cattails in summer and moves into open water in winter. It feeds mainly on underwater vegetation, which it obtains by diving or dabbling on the surface. Coots may also venture on land to feed on seeds and invertebrates.

Enter a small grove of cottonwoods. Where the trail angles right, a short side trail on the left leads to the water's edge. On the right, near the tall cottonwood with an obsolete "trail closed" sign posted on the trunk, look for a couple of gnawed stumps. These are the remains of young cottonwoods felled by beavers. The log lying here with one end in the bay would appear to have been one of the victims.

(6)　The beaver is the largest North American rodent, reaching almost three feet in length, not counting the tail. Nearly hunted to extinction for its fur during the nineteenth century, the beaver has made a remarkable comeback throughout its range. Beavers still occur in Lake Washington proper, here at Union Bay, and even in Lake Union. Young poplars (including cottonwoods), alders, and maples are among their favorite construction materials. When local supplies are exhausted, the rodents move elsewhere.

Backtrack to the main path and turn left. Cross the field and come to a four-way junction where your faint trail meets three others. Take the one that turns ninety degrees left (west). The path continues across the open field, tops a gentle rise, and comes to another junction and a small pond. Keep left along the edge of the marsh and berry thicket. This area can be very wet in winter. Hook up with another narrow path and come to a berry hedge, where a small path turns left. From here you have a good view of the largest of the several ponds scattered through the field.

(7) The ponds of the Montlake Fill attract a remarkable variety of shore birds and waterfowl, including species rarely seen elsewhere in the region. In late summer and early fall numerous migrating shore birds frequent the ponds. As autumn progresses, waterfowl and rain both begin to arrive, and by winter the greatly enlarged ponds may be thronged with ducks of many kinds. In spring look for migrating green-winged, cinnamon, and blue-winged teals, small fresh-water ducks that whistle rather than quack. Mallards and gadwalls are present year-around.

Turn left on the little path that follows a berry hedge south toward Union Bay. As the narrow path approaches the edge of the bay and bends right to skirt a narrow channel separating the fill from a line of marshy islets. In winter look for ducks, gulls, and great blue herons. In spring, as many as six different kinds of swallows may be seen overhead. Marsh wrens, red-winged blackbirds, green-backed herons, and Canada geese all nest in the area.

(8) Nesting boxes for Canada geese have been erected in the marshes on both sides of Union Bay. Our resident population was apparently introduced to the city from eastern Washington. During spring and fall, they may be joined by migrating geese from other areas. There are several geographic races of Canada geese, which vary greatly in size and somewhat less in coloration. During migration, it is not unusual to see geese of two or three races foraging together in the fields. This shore is a favorite feeding area, judging by the abundance of goose droppings hereabouts.

After a bit the trail bends away from the water and comes to another pond, this one surrounded by cattails.

(9) Muskrats utilize cattails as food and as a primary material for use in constructing their large dome-shaped lodges. Sedges, rushes, water lilies, and other aquatic plants are also eaten, along with fish, frogs, and crayfish. Muskrats are superb swimmers that are able to remain submerged for many minutes. They are primarily nocturnal but from time to time are seen during the day.

Straight ahead is the so-called "dime" parking lot, an alternative starting point for the loop. Off to the right is a large clump of Scotch broom and a low, damp area. Keeping this side of the broom, head east toward shrubs and small trees and pick up a faint trail. (You can't really get lost in this big, open field.) Come to a small pond on the left, a backwater of a still larger pond almost completely surrounded by a dense hedge of purple loosestrife.

(10) Most of the marshes in western Washington support nesting colonies of red-winged blackbirds. Colonial nesting offers birds a number

Scouler's willow buds indicate the coming of spring

of advantages. For example, red-winged blackbirds benefit from security in numbers. One adult can alert the entire colony, and mobs of adults can—and do—act in concert to repel invaders, including people. Another advantage derives from synchronizing the breeding cycle. The proximity of neighbors seems to get the whole colony in the mood at one time. Synchronized breeding, egg laying, and raising of chicks restricts the period during which all species of birds are most vulnerable to predators.

The path winds between the pond on the left and berry bushes on the right, then heads across the open field.

(11) This weedy field provides excellent cover for birds. Although ring-necked pheasants are rather large, they are able to keep hidden even in the short grass. To flush a pheasant is an unforgettable experience. The bird remains in place, perfectly motionless, until it is almost stepped on. Then it explodes into the air, flies swiftly across the field, and drops out of sight again. Other field residents include common snipe and California quail. Water pipit and savannah sparrow are regular migrants in the area.

As you top a low rise, the largest pond once again comes into view. Where the path forks, keep left, skirting the pond and staying far enough away not to spook whatever birds may be there. Follow the curve of the pond and pick up a little path heading toward the Urban Horticulture Center. The trail passes a solitary tree.

(12) This tree is Scouler's willow, one of the two tree-sized willows commonly growing in and around Seattle. It sprouts readily from seed following fires and is often among the young trees found in recent clearcuts. The male and female flower clusters—called catkins or, more popularly, "pussy willows"—are an important source of early spring nectar for bees.

Beyond the willow, the trail skirts the south end of the first (seasonal) pond and shortly returns to Wahkiakum Lane. Turn right on the gravel path to return to the parking area.

4

SEATTLE

Washington Park Arboretum: Waterfront Trail

Distance: 1 - mile round trip
Season: all year
Highlights: marsh, views across Union Bay
Metro: 25, 43, 48, 68, 77, 243 (⅓-mile walk to trailhead)

The newly refurbished Waterfront Trail is a gem. It takes you into the lush and watery heart of the largest wetland remaining in Seattle, a blend of marsh, woodland, and open water. In short—duck heaven. And from fall through spring, waterfowl are here in abundance, both in variety and in sheer numbers. The trail also provides panoramic views across Union Bay to the University of Washington campus, University Village, and resplendent Laurelhurst. The parade of pleasure and other craft plying the waters between Lake Washington and the Montlake Cut also provides distraction.

The original trail was built in 1967 through the cooperation of the University of Washington and the U.S. Department of the Interior. It was managed by the University, but years of heavy use caused extreme deterioration. For well over a year the trail was closed for safety reasons, and for a time it was not clear that the funds would be forthcoming to rebuild it. In 1985, however, the state Department of Natural Resources came up with $75,000, and the city of Seattle park bond issue financed the remainder. Reconstruction at last began in the spring of 1986 and was completed in July. Formal dedication of the trail took place the following October. Today the trail is managed by the Seattle Department of Parks and Recreation.

The new trail essentially follows the course of the old one but has been improved throughout. The entire trail has been resurfaced, and an elevated platform has been added for observing wildlife and enjoying the

Waterfront Trail—west entrance

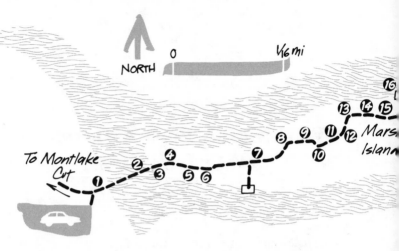

scenery. Children will particularly enjoy the platform, as well as the floating walkways, little bridges, side trails, and abundant bird life. The level grade and frequent benches for resting also make this an ideal trail for the elderly.

The trail has twenty-seven numbered posts corresponding to discussions contained in an interpretive pamphlet. A copy may be available at the west entry of the trail (see below). Otherwise, get one from the Arboretum visitor center or the Museum of History and Industry. The following discussions are keyed to the same numbered posts. They attempt to supplement those in the interpretive pamphlet, not to replace them. It is recommended that the two publications be used together, if possible.

The trail can be walked in either direction, but the numbered posts progress from west to east, from the parking lot of the Museum of History and Industry to Foster Island. From there a broad lane leads southward to the Arboretum visitor center. It is also possible to do the walk backwards, beginning at the end of Foster Island Road, which runs between the Arboretum duck pond and the Broadmoor Golf Course. Follow the gated road (no motor vehicles) across the channel onto Foster Island. Pass under SR 520 and follow the path to the east entry of the Waterfront Trail.

Rest rooms are available at the Arboretum visitor center and the Museum of History and Industry. While there are no formal picnic facilities, Foster Island and the Arboretum offer an abundance of choice spots.

Bicycle riding, jogging, and dogs are prohibited on the Waterfront Trail, which crosses a fragile nature sanctuary and is intended for the quiet contemplation, study, or enjoyment of the marsh environment. Although bicycles, jogging, and dogs are all wonderful in their place, their place is not here.

From downtown Seattle drive I-5 north and SR 520 east to the Montlake Boulevard exit. At the stoplight, go straight onto E. Lake Washington

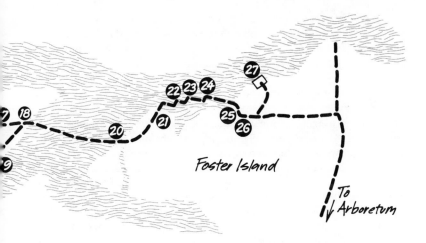

Foster Island

To Arboretum

Drive. In a block turn left on Park Drive, cross over the freeway, and continue into the parking lot of the Museum of History and Industry. Park at the far end. To begin the trail from the eastern entry, continue on E. Lake Washington Boulevard until the intersection with Foster Island Road. Turn left at the stop sign and drive to the end of the road, near the Arboretum duck pond, actually a backwater of Union Bay.

From the northwest corner of the Museum of History and Industry parking lot, follow the wood-chip path to the west entry of the Waterfront Trail. A large sign features a map of and background information on the trail. An interpretive brochure may be available here, but don't count on it. Next to the sign, on the right, is signpost 1.

(1) A Pacific willow growing in the damp, low ground behind the sign has an almost horizontal trunk, as if this route toward the sun were the most reliable under the circumstances. In fact, shallow-rooted trees in wet places often lean at odd angles because their footing is not firm enough to securely hold their weight upright. High winds reinforce this horizontal tendency.

From signpost 1, the path heads into the marsh and crosses a small bridge onto a floating walkway. This is the first of several good areas along the trail for observing ducks and other marsh birds. Signpost 2 is located atop the second small bridge, just before coming to Marsh Island.

(2) The combination of marsh and open water makes this area one of Seattle's prime wintering grounds for ducks. Nearly a dozen species can be expected, and others may be present on occasion. Most of the species nest far to the north, arriving some time in the fall and leaving in spring.

Step onto Marsh Island and immediately come to signpost 3 on the right.

(3) The marshes around Lake Washington have been evolving since the close of the last Ice Age, about 13,000 years ago. Marsh Island is a floating mat consisting mostly of peat that has built up as generation after generation of marsh plants has died and accumulated on the shallow lake bottom.

Only a few steps beyond, signpost 4 is located on the left side of the trail.

(4) Except during winter months, the water here is covered with a dense growth of white water lily, an imported beauty from eastern wetlands. The showy white blossoms appear in early summer. To a plant, the main advantage in growing in standing water is that the precious liquid is always abundant. The main disadvantage is that oxygen is not. Like land plants, water lilies obtain some of their oxygen directly from the air through microscopic openings, or stomates, in the leaves. In water lilies, the stomates are located on the tops of the leaves rather than on the bottoms, as in land plants. Oxygen obtained in this way is then transported down the stems to the roots, which are anchored in the muck.

Now look for signpost 5 next to a bench on the right.

Waterfront Trail—east entrance

(5) With the completion of the Hiram M. Chittenden ("Ballard") Locks in 1916, the level of Lake Washington was lowered nine feet. Before then, this area was all under water.

The trail continues through a corridor of European yellow iris on the left and willows on the right. Signpost 6 is on the right.

(6) Behind the signpost is Pacific willow and next to it, on the left, is Scouler's willow. Pacific willow has long, slender leaves tapering to a point; Scouler's willow has broader, shorter leaves that are more or less oval, though usually broadest toward the tip. Throughout their range, willows are commonly associated with water. When their roots are flooded, they rapidly grow new ones filled with oxygen. Flooding also stimulates the development of openings in the bark, called lenticels, through which oxygen can be obtained from the air.

The trail jogs left, then comes to a bench and a path on the right leading to an observation platform and another bench—a good place for observing birds or the migratory patterns of East Side commuters on SR 520. Just beyond this path, on the left, is signpost 7.

(7) The long, slender leaves of the European yellow iris resemble those of cattails. In spring, however, when the large, showy blossoms appear, there can be no mistaking the two. Yellow irises here and along other fresh-water shores throughout the city are probably garden escapees.

A few yards down the path, on the left, is signpost 8.

(8) Another European import is purple loosestrife, a tall plant with four-sided stems and lancelike leaves in pairs. The elongated clusters of pink, star-shaped flowers brighten the summer marsh. In fall the plants turn a rich, dark red.

In several more yards come to signpost 9, also on the left.

(9) Cattails are readily told by the familiar, brown, sausage-shaped clusters of tiny female flowers. Dense stands of cattails, however, develop mainly by sprouting from creeping underground stems, not from flower seeds. The roots are starchy and a favorite food of muskrats, which may "eat out" large sections of the plants.

The trail jogs right to another bench, then left, right, and left again. Signpost 10 is on the right.

(10) The small, white-trunked trees growing on both sides of the trail are European white birch, a common garden and street tree throughout the area. Their seeds have been carried into the marsh by wind. The native American paper birch is very similar and may be seen growing wild in Bellefields Nature Park in Bellevue (Walk 17).

Just before the trail turns left, look for signpost 11 on the left.

(11) In back of the sign are young red alders, which can be identified from this distance by the straight, parallel ribbing and toothed margins of their leaves. Alders are one of the most common trees of our region. On

the opposite side of the trail is common rush, another characteristic wetland plant. Look for clumps of round, hollow, dark green, grasslike stems that taper to a sharp point.

The trail turns left. Signpost 12 is on the right.

(12) Red-winged blackbirds are the most conspicuous nesters in the marsh. Marsh wrens often go unseen, but in spring and summer their rough, chattery song is one of the common sounds of the marsh.

Signpost 13 is beneath the tall cottonwood trees straight ahead.

(13) In the arid Southwest cottonwoods are well-known indicators of water. Our black cottonwoods are a different species from the Southwestern cottonwood, but they too are a sign of abundant water at or near the ground's surface. Cottonwoods help to stabilize riverbanks and lake shores.

The trail turns right here and comes shortly to signpost 14, on the left.

(14) In late summer hardhack, a member of the rose family, glorifies the marsh with showy pink plumes of flowers. This tall, slender wetland shrub forms dense thickets, through which early settlers found it "hard" to "hack."

The trail jogs right and meets a path leading left to a bench and signpost 15.

(15) Himalaya blackberry, the common blackberry of Seattle vacant lots, can be seen among the foliage here. As much of a nuisance as this vine can be, its berries are a valuable food resource for urban wildlife. Song sparrows, for example, which frequent dense, moist tangles such as this, consume numerous berries every year.

The side trail continues to an observation platform, another bench, and signpost 16.

(16) The view across Union Bay is panoramic, stretching from the Montlake Cut and the University of Washington in the west to Laurelhurst in the east. Notice the cattail fringe along the distant shore of the bay. This is the Montlake Fill, an ecological study area (Walk 3).

Return to the main trail and turn left. The trail bends right and comes to another bench and signpost 17.

(17) According to the interpretive brochure, the ground beneath your feet, from here to the next bridge, lies on a foundation of debris. Prior to 1967, the city engineering department and the Army Corps of Engineers used this end of Marsh Island to burn logs, derelict boats, and the like.

Continue to signpost 18 on the left. Across the trail from it, another side trail leads to an observation platform.

(18) This somewhat higher, drier section of the marsh supports a number of plants not found in the wetter portions. These plants, in turn, attract a variety of birds that otherwise are uncharacteristic of marshes — for example, bushtit, American goldfinch, and song sparrow.

Signpost 19 is located at the observation platform at the end of the side trail across from signpost 18.

Marsh reeds along the Waterfront Trail

(19) The backwaters and channels of the marsh are popular with canoeists. Canoeing is an excellent way to explore the marsh at water level and to see corners of it that are accessible no other way. Canoes may be rented for a modest fee at the University boat house.

Return to the main trail and turn right. Come to the floating walkway connecting Marsh Island to Foster Island. Just before reaching Foster Island, look for signpost 20 on the left.

(20) Look down at the water. The feathery leaves of European water milfoil can be seen suspended just below the surface. This invasive aquatic

Ducklings, Waterfront Trail

plant spreads rapidly to form dense tangles. It first appeared in Lake Washington in 1975 and since then has become a nuisance to boaters, swimmers, and water skiers.

The trail turns left to a bench, then wanders along the edge of the water. Signpost 21 is located on the right, just before steps leading to the longest floating walkway of the trail.

(21) The tall grass that resembles small bamboo is reed canary grass, which grows commonly in wetlands throughout the region. It spreads by sprouting from creeping underground stems.

Step onto the floating walkway, which jogs this way and that as it snakes over the shallow water here at the northern fringe of Foster Island. The walkway first turns right, then left, where there is a bench and signpost 22.

(22) This walkway is an excellent place to observe marsh birds. On the open water, look for coots and pied-bill grebes swimming among the ducks. Canada geese are also commonly seen in this area, nesting on nearby wooden platforms set up specially for them. The great blue heron, American bittern, green-backed heron, and Virginia rail also frequent the marsh. The American bittern and Virginia rail are retiring birds that often go unnoticed even where they are fairly common. The bittern attempts to escape detection—and usually succeeds—by holding his long,

48

Great blue herons frequent the marshes along the Waterfront Trail

The Waterfront Trail can be enjoyed by people of all ages

spearlike bill upright, as if to mimic the cattails and marsh grasses. The green-backed heron is an uncommon but regular summer breeder in western Washington, where it was first recorded nesting in 1939, here at Union Bay. A pair is believed to still nest in the area.

The walkway turns right and before crossing a small bridge comes to signpost 23 on the left.

(23)   Lake Washington occupies a trough scoured out by the Vashon Glacier, the last continental ice sheet to invade western Washington. Before the ship canal was created, the lake drained southward by way of the Black River, which joined the Green River to form the Duwamish. With the opening of the canal and lowering of the lake, drainage shifted away from the Black River, which is now merely a backwater slough of the Green. The Cedar River, which once emptied into the Black, now drains directly into Lake Washington.

The walkway turns right and comes to signpost 24, on the left.

(24)   Chinook (king), coho, and sockeye salmon, along with steelhead and ocean-going cutthroat trout, all migrate up the ship canal and through Lake Washington to reach their spawning streams, which empty into the lake. Frequenting the warmer, shallow margins of the lake are fish such as large-mouth bass, carp, and pumpkinseed sunfish, which feed off the plankton, insect larvae, and algae that are abundant in the marsh. These fish in turn provide meals for birds such as the belted kingfisher and great blue heron.

Cross a small bridge and come to a little sign pointing to signpost 25 ahead. Not far beyond, the floating walkway comes to an end, replaced by wood chips and the semisolid ground of Foster Island. Signpost 25 is on the right.

(25)   The moss carpeting this damp ground is sphagnum, which is characteristic of cold wetlands such as this. Partially decayed sphagnum and other bog plants are collectively called peat moss, which is valued by gardeners for its soil-improving qualities. Mats of sphagnum often expand outward from existing shores, providing a foothold for later plants. In this way lakes are gradually reduced to ponds, and ponds to wet meadows.

The trail bends to the left and comes to signpost 26 on the right.

(26)   Beaver and muskrat both live in the marsh. Muskrat scat is oval and about one-half inch long. Look for clusters deposited on logs, rocks, and banks. Beaver scat is usually deposited in water and therefore seldom seen. It is about one inch long and resembles compressed sawdust. Beavers more often betray their presence by gnawed tree stumps and massive stick lodges.

Come to a narrow path on the left. This leads to an elevated platform and signpost 27, the last one along the trail.

(27)   This platform provides an overview both of the marsh and Union Bay, a fitting end to the walk.

Those who wish to continue on to the wooded section of Foster Island, or all the way to the Arboretum visitor center, can return to the main trail and turn left.

5

SEATTLE

Washington Park Arboretum: Native Plant Walk

Distance: ½ - mile semiloop
Season: best spring through fall
Highlights: native trees and shrubs labeled for easy identification
Metro: 43, 48 (½-mile walk to trailhead)

Seattle's Washington Park Arboretum is a spectacular place to walk at any time of year, but for maximum glory visit it in April and May for spring flowers, or in October for fall color. True, it is not a natural area but, instead, a large, wonderful, carefully tended garden. No matter. The Arboretum is just too beautiful to keep out of this book. Besides, it is a great place to get acquainted with a variety of native plants.

The following walk is a short semiloop through the Winter Garden, where native plants are labeled for easy identification. Some of the trees featured on this walk are still seedlings or saplings as of fall 1986 and therefore may not display all the characteristics of mature specimens. Even so, the walk provides a good opportunity to get acquainted with these plants.

Follow Lake Washington Boulevard north or south to the Arboretum. At the northern end of the park, turn onto Foster Island Road and then right on Arboretum Drive. The visitor center is on the left. Park here. If the lot is full, park along Foster Island Road and walk to the visitor center.

The only convenient rest rooms are at the visitor center. The Arboretum's vast lawns provide a wide choice of picnic sites.

The walk begins directly across the street from the visitor center. Cross the grass and follow a broad path heading westward toward Azalea Way. In a few yards, just before reaching the lane, come to a junction with another path. Turn left here.

A crabapple tree begins the Native Plant walk at the Arboretum

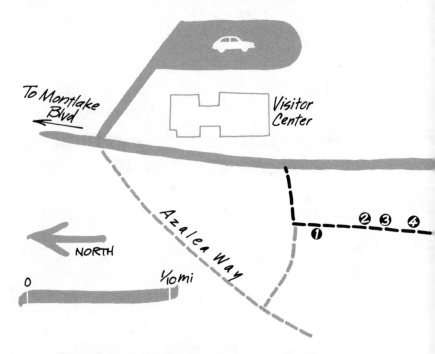

The posts identifying native plants are low to the ground and spaced only a few yards apart. They should not be difficult to locate. Their positions on the left- or right-hand side of the path are indicated in italics at the beginning of each discussion. Because the posts are so closely spaced, other directions are given only as needed.

(1) *Right:* Oregon crabapple grows along the Pacific Coast from northern California to south-central Alaska. In the wild it prefers bottomlands and streamsides, where it occurs with red alder, Oregon ash, black cottonwood, willows, bigleaf maple, and cascara.

(2) *Left:* This is a young lodgepole pine, which is distinguished from all other native pines by having two, rather than three or five, needles in a bundle. Two forms of the lodgepole pine grow in Washington. The typical form is a straight, slim tree that mainly occurs east of the Cascade crest. The second form, the shore pine, grows along the coast and in parts of the Puget Sound region on rocky or damp, gravelly ground where other conifers do not fare well.

(3) *Left:* Ponderosa pine is the only native pine in Washington with three needles per bundle. In western Washington it occurs only in a few scattered locations. East of the Cascade crest, however, it is abundant from lower to middle elevations in the mountains, often in the company of Douglas fir. Mature ponderosa pines have handsome rusty golden bark broken into large plates.

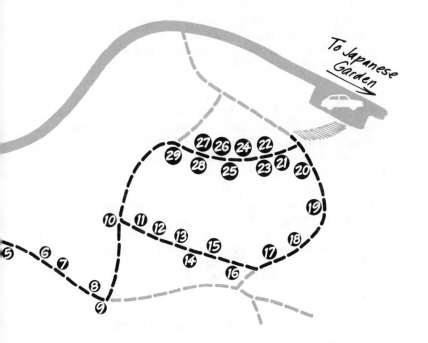

(4) *Left:* Alaska cedar ranges from northern California to southeastern Alaska. In Washington it is a subalpine tree that grows most commonly at and just below timberline. Compare the foliage of this young Alaska cedar with that of the same-sized western red cedar on the right. Both have tiny, flat, scalelike leaves that overlap one another and lie tightly pressed to the stem. The leaves of the Alaska cedar, however, have sharp, flaring tips, while those of red cedar are rounded, smooth, and more closely pressed to the stem. Note, too, how the foliage of the Alaska cedar is noticeably droopy while that of the red cedar is not. Moreover, the bark of mature Alaska cedars is gray and, unlike that of red cedar, does not peel off in long strips. Neither tree is actually a cedar; rather, both are members of the cypress family, which also includes junipers and incense cedars.

The next post is directly opposite the young red cedar.

(5) *Right:* The Columbia hawthorn is a shrub or small tree that grows sparingly in the ponderosa pine belt east of the Cascades. It has slender thorns one to two inches long and deep red berries, which appear in the fall. The more common Douglas hawthorn, which occurs on both sides of the Cascades, has dark purple berries and shorter thorns.

(6) *Left:* Vine maple is a familiar understory shrub or small tree in the forests of western Washington. In fall the leaves turn a variety of colors, from pale yellow to fiery red and bronze-purple.

(7) *Left:* Just beyond the vine maple, is a bigleaf maple. Bigleaf maples growing in damp ravines around Seattle and its suburbs usually have trunks padded with moss and festooned with growths of licorice fern. This tree lacks those adornments because it grows in an open, relatively dry environment.

The next two posts are located on either side of the path, just before the junction with the Winter Garden loop.

(8) *Left:* Behind the red cedar is a California hazelnut, a member of the birch family. This large shrub is common in local forests, where it prefers moist but well-drained soils. The deciduous leaves have toothed margins and feel like soft paper.

(9) *Right:* Indian plum, or osoberry, is another common shrub in local forests. The plant is unmistakable in late February and early March, when clusters of hanging white flowers appear, usually ahead of the leaves. Unlike the hazelnut, male and female flowers are borne on separate plants. Clusters of red berries appear from June through August on the females.

Turn left. A sign identifies the Winter Garden.

(10) *Left:* Western larch does not grow naturally in western Washington, but it is common in mid-elevation forests on the eastern flank of the Cascades. A relative, alpine larch, grows near timberline in the eastern Cascades south to near Leavenworth.

The route leaves the gravel path here, turning right and following the edge of the woods. The next post, marking a western hemlock, is located along this edge, just a couple of yards from the gravel path.

(11) *Left:* Western hemlock is probably the most abundant conifer in western Washington. Its distinctive leaves and cones make it easy to identify. The needles are short, flat, stubby, and loosely arranged in two ranks on opposite sides of a twig. The underside of each needle has two white lines. The cones have papery scales and are less than one inch long.

Follow the edge of the woods.

(12) *Left:* Most Washington natives recognize Douglas fir. Anyone unfamiliar with the tree can identify it by its distinctive cones. They are about two inches long and have three-pronged bracts (known to many children as "monkey tails") that protrude from between the woody scales. The yellowish green needles radiate from all sides of the twigs, producing a bottle-brush effect.

(13) *Left:* Grand fir is the only *true* fir to grow commonly in the lowlands of western Washington, particularly in the broad river valleys. It is not, however, particularly common in or around Seattle. Unlike Douglas fir—which, by the way, is not a true fir—grand fir has barrel-shaped cones that grow upright on the tree's uppermost branches, where they disintegrate in place. The needles are also distinctive: one and one-half to two and one-fourth inches long, flat, blunt, shiny green above, and splayed out flat in two rows on opposite sides of a twig.

(14) *Right:* Western red cedar is readily identified by its shaggy red bark; sprays of flat, overlapping, scalelike leaves; and small woody cones shaped something like the French fleur de lis. Most of the parks in this book occupy lands that once supported old-growth forests dominated by giant red cedars. Today, in all but a couple of places, only the stumps remain to remind us of that vanished magnificence.

Follow the narrow gravel path that begins hereabouts.

(15) *Left:* Evergreen huckleberry has thick, waxy, green leaves that remain on the plant throughout the year. The several other species of huckleberry growing in Washington, including the ubiquitous red huckleberry of lowland forests, are deciduous. Evergreen huckleberry prefers somewhat drier conditions than typically exist in the forests in and around Seattle, where it is far less common than red huckleberry.

(16) *Right:* Thimbleberry is a common shrub in damp, open places within or at the edge of the forest. The combination of soft maplelike leaves, large white flowers, red "raspberries," and lack of thorns serves to distinguish it from all other members of the blackberry tribe growing in our region.

Turn left on the wide gravel path.

Western hemlock cones

(17) *Left:* Two kinds of Oregon grape grow in our area. Low Oregon grape, the one growing here, prefers shady places within the forest. Tall Oregon grape, the state flower of Oregon, is usually found in sunnier places, often growing among rocks. The two species are similar. Perhaps the easiest way to tell them apart is by examining the leaflets. Those of tall Oregon grape are shinier and have a single main vein; those of low Oregon grape are duller and have three or more principal veins. The two species also differ in the number of leaflets per leaf: five to nine for tall Oregon grape; nine to twenty-one (usually fifteen to nineteen) for low Oregon grape.

(18) *Left:* Red alder is easy to identify. The leaves have strongly toothed margins and straight, parallel veins. In the fall they fade slightly before dropping but (alas) do not turn color. The fruit is a small woody cone called a strobile. The bark is smooth and light gray, though often mottled or splotched with nearly white growths of lichen. Red alder is named for the reddish inner bark and heartwood.

The path begins bending toward the left.

(19) *Left:* Pacific silver fir is the dominant conifer in mid-elevation forest on the west slope of the Cascades. On the Olympic Peninsula and in the northern Puget Sound region, however, silver firs occur sparsely in lowland forests. The needles resemble those of grand fir (see above), but they are rarely more than one inch long and include some that are bent forward so as to hide the twig.

(20) *Left:* Subalpine fir grows near timberline, often in tree "islands" scattered over vast parklands in the Cascades and Olympics. It is common in the eastern Cascades, but also occurs in rain-shadow areas such as the northeastern Olympics and around Sunrise on Mount Rainier. The subalpine fir's slender, symmetrical, spirelike shape is distinctive. The branches grow in whorls, and the blunt one-inch needles brush upward to obscure the stems.

Come to a set of steps on the left. Go up the steps and along a narrow path.

(21) *Left:* Sitka mountain ash is a common shrub on avalanche slopes and in moist sunny forest openings at mid- to high elevations in the Cascades and Olympics. So is a similar species, Cascade mountain ash. Both are related to the European mountain ash, or rowan, a common street tree in our region. Mountain ashes belong to the rose family, while *true* ashes, like Oregon ash, are members of the olive family.

(22) *Right:* Scouler's willow grows either as a tall shrub or, as in this instance, a tree. It is often found growing with other willows in damp bottomlands or near water. But unlike the others, it also grows well away from water, as it does here.

(23) *Left* (opposite Scouler's willow): Oregon white oak (or Garry oak) is the common oak in Oregon's Willamette Valley. It also forms open

woods in the Fort Lewis–Steilacoom area south of Tacoma and, sparingly, in dry places northward to southern British Columbia.

(24) *Right:* Red huckleberry is the more common of the two lowland huckleberries in our region (see evergreen huckleberry above). It is easy to recognize by its green twigs, its delicate foliage, and its late-summer crop of bright red berries. In addition, the twigs in cross-section are angled rather than round, a characteristic at once apparent to anyone attempting to roll one between thumb and forefinger. Red huckleberry tolerates deep shade and of all the forest shrubs is the one most often found growing on old stumps and logs.

(25) *Left:* Mountain hemlock is the main timberline tree in western Washington, seldom growing below 3000 feet elevation. Unlike western hemlock (see above), mountain hemlock has plump needles growing in clusters from all sides of each twig, and cones that are usually one and a half to two inches long.

(26) *Right:* Pacific (or western) dogwood is a small forest tree common throughout the Puget Sound region. Its large white "flowers" appear in spring (and sparingly in fall) and rival those of its close cousin, the eastern dogwood, a garden favorite. Actually, what appear to be white petals are bracts (modified leaves) that surround a central cluster of small green flowers.

(27) *Right:* Oregon ash is a tall, slender tree of riverbanks, lake shores, and moist bottomlands. It is readily told by its leaves, which have five or seven lance-shaped leaflets. The undersides of the leaves are hairy. Unlike the mountain ash encountered earlier, the Oregon ash is a *true* ash of the genus *Fraxinus.*

(28) *Left:* (The sign and the shrub are located about a yard back from the trail and may be obscured by other vegetation.) Snowberry is a deciduous shrub that is easily recognized during fall and early winter by its conspicuous white berries, which persist on the plants for some weeks. After the berries have dropped, the thin green twigs, which grow in pairs, are distinctive. The leaves are also easy to recognize: light green, oval or irregularly lobed, very thin, and arranged on the stem in pairs.

(29) *Left:* Madrona is easy to recognize by its thick, shiny, evergreen leaves; thin, reddish, peeling bark; and clusters of red berries. It is the region's only broadleaf evergreen tree and is confined to the driest forest sites.

Just beyond the madrona, rejoin the Winter Garden loop path near the young western larch. From there you can either return the way you came or cross the lawn to the road and follow it back to the visitor center.

6

Seward Park

Distance: 1¾ - mile loop
Season: all year
Highlights: big trees, lake views
Metro: 39 (½-mile walk to trailhead)

Seward Park, in southeast Seattle, occupies the entire Bailey Peninsula, which juts into Lake Washington like a giant thumb. This is a busy multi-use park with several picnic areas, a playground, amphitheater, art studio, Japanese garden, and fish hatchery. A shoreline road (closed to motor vehicles) is popular with walkers, joggers, and cyclists. On a warm, sunny weekend, Seward Park is always packed with people. Fortunately, most of the action is in the developed southern third of the park and on the shoreline road. Even on busy weekends the forested north-central upland offers a measure of tranquillity. The best time to explore this forest, however, is during the week when school is in session.

Here are Douglas firs six feet in diameter and western red cedars nearly as big. Of the handful of big trees left on public lands in Seattle, those at Seward Park are the only ones found on an upland rather than within the depths of a ravine. Seattle owes their preservation to the foresight of Park Commissioner E. O. Schwagerl, who proposed in 1892 that the city buy the then remote peninsula for a park. The Olmsted brothers, who completed their plan for Seattle's city parks in 1903, supported this idea. The city purchased the peninsula in 1911. Despite extensive development of Seward Park over the next several decades, most of the northern two-thirds of the peninsula was left in its natural state.

Several designated picnic areas, complete with shelters and grills, are located in the southern third of the park. Rest rooms are situated near the entrance, at the first parking area along the loop drive, and at the north end of the peninsula slightly east of where the forest trail described below intersects the shoreline road.

Fallen bigleaf maple leaves

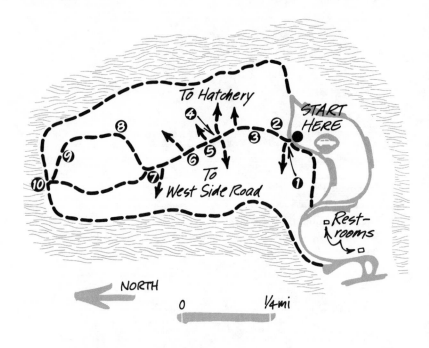

Drive Lake Washington Boulevard south to the park entrance. Turn left and follow the park loop road one mile to a parking area on the left. Park here, cross the road to the grassy strip on the other side, and backtrack a few yards to where a broad path enters the forest. A sign warns people with motorcycles, bicycles, and other "wheeled vehicles" to stay off the trails.

Bus riders can walk alongside the park road to the first parking area at the top of the hill. Across the road from the parking area a signed trail heads into the woods, emerging at the trailhead parking area in about a quarter mile. Follow the grassy strip as described above to the trail.

At the beginning of the trail, on the left, is a Douglas fir.

(1) The forest of Seward Park is dominated by Douglas fir. Western red cedar, western hemlock, and bigleaf maple are also common. Red alder, cascara, and madrona are somewhat less numerous but by no means scarce. The shrub layer is varied and well developed, containing most of the species characteristic of conifer forests throughout the region: Oregon grape, coast red elderberry, salal, Indian plum, ocean spray, salmonberry, thimbleberry, and California hazelnut. Sword fern often forms dense stands over large areas. While this forest shares most plants in common with local ravine forests, it is drier overall.

Pass a side trail heading left. Red alder, Douglas fir, and western red cedar grow at the junction. Oregon grape is the common understory shrub. Keep straight and pass a fair-sized red cedar on the right, growing amid clumps of sword fern, Oregon grape, and thimbleberry. Then come to an even larger, slightly charred red cedar, with a big, moss-draped maple nearby.

(2) Western red cedar was the most important tree in the economy of the Northwest Coast Indian tribes, from Oregon to Alaska. The wood was used for house posts and siding, roofing planks, canoes, boxes, cradles, spindles, and numerous other household items. The fibrous bark was shredded and woven into napkins, towels, baby blankets, and clothing. Unwoven strips were plaited to make bowls, plates, and mats. Red cedar roots were used to weave baskets. Various parts of the tree were also used for medicinal purposes, including remedies for colds and tuberculosis.

Pass by more red cedars and a large Douglas fir. The forest here is quite lovely: the trees are large, the understory rich and varied. Continuing, look for a large, double-trunked bigleaf maple on the left. Oregon grape and sword fern grow at the base.

(3) The Northwest coastal forest ranges from Alaska to northern California and east to the Cascades. For most of that range the main species of trees are western hemlock, Douglas fir, western red cedar, and Sitka spruce. Other conifers may be present, even locally common. Deciduous trees, however, are few and generally restricted to specialized habitats such as wet soils, logged or burned ground, or openings within the forest. Among the world's temperate forests, the Northwest coastal forest is unique for the size and longevity of its trees and the overwhelming dominance of conifers.

The trail bends left and drops very gradually, passing a side trail on the right. Fringecup, youth-on-age, creeping buttercup, and thimbleberry grow along the path. Not far beyond is a four-way junction with a path that heads right toward the fish hatchery and left to the shoreline road on the west side of the peninsula. Here, well away from the park road, the only noises likely to break the forest quiet are the songs and calls of birds.

(4) In fall and winter the forest is usually silent. Occasionally, a medley of high chirps, cheeps, buzzes, signals the presence overhead of a wandering winter flock of golden and ruby-crowned kinglets, black-capped and chestnut-backed chickadees, red-breasted nuthatches, brown creepers, and sundry other small birds. Bird song reaches a crescendo in spring and early summer, when males sing to proclaim their territorial boundaries and to attract females looking for mates. The best time to hear the songs and see the singers is near dawn, which at this latitude comes dreadfully early in late spring. As you walk through the woods, listen for the bubbly melody of the winter wren, the high trill of the rufous-sided towhee, the rising and falling cadences of the American robin (and its near-sound-alikes, the western tanager and black-headed grosbeak), and the distinctive "Hip, three cheers" call of the olive-sided flycatcher.

Beyond the junction there is another side path on the right. The leaning tree on the left is a madrona. Another grows next to it.

Seward Park trail

(5)   The madrona is the only broadleaf evergreen tree in the Puget Sound region (and except for a couple of widely separated stands of golden chinquapin, in all of western Washington). All our other broadleaf trees are deciduous, and all our other evergreens are conifers. Several native shrubs, however, are broadleaf evergreens, including salal, manzanita, and Pacific rhododendron, evergreen huckleberry (all, like madrona, members of the heath family), and Oregon grape. The leaves of broadleaf evergreens, like those of conifers, are covered with a resinous substance called cutin, which gives them a leathery or waxy texture. This coating provides insulation against cold and reduces water loss during times of stress. Madrona not only tolerates dry soils; it prefers them. In wet soils the tree rapidly succumbs to root rot. The presence of madrona in a conifer forest indicates soils that may be seasonally moist but that drain rapidly.

Not far beyond the madronas, walk under a Douglas fir leaning out and over the trail. Passing side trails left and right, come shortly to a great bigleaf maple with seven upright trunks, all mantled in mosses and adorned with ferns.

(6)   Bigleaf maple is the only truly tree-sized maple that grows along the Pacific Coast, where it ranges from southern California north to northwestern British Columbia. It is one of the most beautiful trees in our region, especially in autumn, when the leaves turn yellow. Reaching a

Sword ferns grow throughout the upland forest of Seward Park

height of seventy to eighty feet, with a crown nearly as broad, bigleaf maple is readily told by its deeply lobed leaves, which commonly are eight to twelve inches across. Maples achieve their greatest size on deep, rich bottomlands, but they also are among the first trees to colonize talus slopes in the mountains. They can be found growing somewhere or other with virtually every tree species native to the Puget Sound region, from madrona to red cedar, indicating a tolerance for a wide range of environmental conditions.

Pass a faint, primitive trail on the right and, as the main trail bends slightly right, come to another one on the left. Here grows a large maple with sword fern and Oregon grape at its base and hazelnut beside it.

(7) A common but seldom-seen inhabitant of the forest floor throughout our region is the Trowbridge shrew, an appetite on four legs that measures barely five inches from tip of snout to tip of tail. Because of their size, shrews lose heat rapidly and must eat almost constantly to maintain their high metabolic rates. The Trowbridge shrew eats insects, worms, and just about any other animal it can subdue. It also eats Douglas fir seeds and other plant materials when necessary. Shrews are hunted in turn by owls, weasels, and other predators.

The trail again curves slightly right, again passing another primitive trail on the left. Thimbleberry is common here. Also look for black twinberry twined among the shrubbery on the right-hand side of the trail. Enter a small opening with abundant hazelnut. Beyond the opening, the trail bends more sharply toward the right and begins to gently descend. Purple pea grows here among the thimbleberry and salal. As the trail bends leftward, there is a dense growth of stinging nettle on the right.

(8) In our region, stinging nettle is the principal food for the larvae of three attractive species of butterflies. The most common of these in local parks is the satyr anglewing. Milbert's tortoiseshell and the red admiral are seen less often. Butterflies are relatively few in number and variety throughout most of the western Washington lowlands. As a group, they are creatures of warm, sunny habitats, which are scarce west of the Cascades. Butterflies increase in both number and kind in mountain meadows and are downright abundant in sun-drenched eastern Washington.

As the trail continues bending left, it passes a side trail on the right. The junction is marked by red cedar stumps, one with sword fern, salal, and red elderberry growing on it. Beyond the junction the trail straightens out but continues to descend. Off to the right now, Lake Washington is barely visible through the trees. The trail passes a western hemlock on the left, bends left, and enters a more open area. As the trail continues curving left, watch for the largest tree encountered thus far.

Lakeside view, Seward Park

(9) This tree, a Douglas fir, is at least six feet in diameter and free of branches for the first twenty feet or so. Its trunk, like that of most Douglas firs of this size, is charred by fire. Over the centuries, Douglas firs may survive numerous relatively cool ground fires thanks to their thick, corky bark. Western red cedar and western hemlock have thinner bark and are more susceptible to fire.

The trail comes shortly on the right to a bigleaf maple that is a mass of knobby burls. Why such burls form is unknown, but they are apparently harmless, though they make the tree appear rather grotesque. The trail continues to descend gently, passing other large trees. Curving left, it enters a small, parklike open area where madronas and bigleaf maples rise above a grassy understory clumped with salal and sword fern. The trail continues dropping and soon meets the road at the edge of the lake. In the distance is the Mercer Island bridge and the high-rise buildings of downtown Seattle.

(10) Lake Washington is the largest body of fresh water in western Washington—eighteen miles long and about four and a half miles across at its widest point near the Mercer Island bridge. It reaches a maximum depth of 210 feet near the Evergreen Point bridge. It occupies a long topographic depression that extends southward some thirty miles beyond the lake to the town of Orting. Several rivers occupy portions of this trough but it was scoured out by the Vashon ice sheet, which predates them all. The ice reached its maximum extent about 15,000 years ago, then slowly retreated northward to Canada. Seattle's hills, Mercer Island, and the Overlake Highlands are ridges of glacial debris left behind in its retreat.

This is the end of the nature walk proper. To complete the loop, turn right on the shoreline road for a walk down the east side of the peninsula. In roughly one-half mile, the road crosses the fast stream flowing from the trout hatchery on the right. Beyond the stream, it skirts the lake, then bends right, uphill, to the loop road. From the junction walk less than a quarter mile alongside the loop road back to the trailhead parking area. (Unless you plan a long, roundabout walk back to the car or bus stop, do not follow the jogger's path that continues along the lake from where the shoreline road heads uphill.)

One alternative route back to the trailhead is to return along the forest trail. A second (and for bus riders, the quickest way back to transportation) is to turn left on the shoreline road and follow it down the west side of the Bailey Peninsula back to the main road, art center, and park entrance. Along the way, side paths branch left into the woods and back to the main forest trail. It is also possible to follow the park loop road back to the trailhead.

7

SEATTLE

Discovery Park: Loop Trail

Distance: 2¾ - mile loop
Season: all year
Highlights: forest, Puget Sound views, beach access
Metro: 19 (South Parking Lot), 33 (visitor center)

Discovery Park is the jewel in the crown of Seattle's park system. It is not only the city's largest park (535 acres), but the most varied, featuring forest and meadow, cliffs and beaches, and perhaps the finest Puget Sound views in town. The 2.8-mile Loop Trail samples all these delights and is the best way to become acquainted with the park.

When the secretary of the army announced in 1964 that eighty-five percent of Fort Lawton, on Magnolia Bluff, would become surplus, there was immediate and nearly unanimous sentiment in Seattle to acquire the land for a park. The federal government transferred 391 acres to the city in 1972. The new park was named Discovery, after Captain George Vancouver's flagship, the H.M.S. *Discovery*. Discovery Park was opened to the public in 1973. The remaining acreage was added in 1975.

From the beginning, Discovery Park was conceived as a nature sanctuary within the city, a place where one could go for peace and solitude and to experience and learn about the natural environment of the region. Today, the park has a full-time interpretive staff and offers a wide variety of programs for the entire community (for more information, see Walk 8).

At Discovery Park it is possible to combine walking, beachcombing, biking, picnicking, sunbathing, jogging and other activities in one long-day's outing. Picnic tables are located near the visitor center, the Daybreak Star Arts Center, North Bluff, and West Point. Rest rooms are found at the visitor center, North Bluff, West Point, and South Meadow. Telephones are at East Gate. A children's play area is located just south of the visitor center.

A lookout point along the Discovery Park Loop Trail

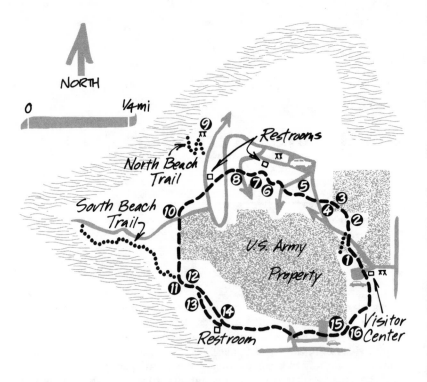

Because Discovery Park is a nature sanctuary, pets must be on leash at all times. They are not permitted at all on the beaches or the Wolf Tree Nature Trail (Walk 8). Motor vehicles are permitted only on designated park roads. Bicycles must be walked on unpaved trails.

From downtown Seattle follow Elliott Way and 15th Avenue W. to the Dravus Street exit and turn left at the stop sign. Turn right on 20th Avenue and follow the arterial (which becomes Gilman Avenue, then Government Way) to the park entrance. From Ballard, cross the ship canal bridge and immediately turn right on the Emerson Street/Nickerson Street exit. Drive to Gilman Street, turn right and proceed as above. Just inside the park, take the first left into the visitor center parking area.

A large sign, near the entrance to the parking area, features a good map of the park, a summary of attractions, and a short history. Cross the closed-off road to the beginning of the trail, which is marked here by a pair of small signs. The one on the left, showing the silhouette of the hiker, is the official Loop Trail sign.

The trail, a broad gravel path, enters an open woodland of bigleaf maple, with scattered shrubs and a grassy floor. Several kinds of nonnative plants grow here, including Scotch broom, Himalaya blackberry, European mountain ash, and English ivy. Native plants in addition to bigleaf maple, include salal, sword fern, Oregon grape, Douglas fir, and western red cedar.

(1)   Upon entering the forest, the most obvious change in the environment, even on a foggy or overcast day, is a sharp reduction in sunlight. On warm, sunny days, the drop in air temperature within the forest is also pronounced. Winds and raindrops are slowed down by the trees. Because air temperatures and wind speeds are lower in the forest than in the open, moisture evaporates more slowly from soil and plants. At the same time, the humidity within a forest is typically higher than outside because the canopy of branches tends to trap much of the moisture in the air. Finally, because the dominant trees withdraw so much water and nutrients from the soil, plants growing beneath them may experience shortages of either or both. These are the main environmental conditions to which plants growing within the forest must adapt.

Just before reaching the park road, the Loop Trail passes an alternative route heading back sharply left. This path sticks to the woods above the visitor center area, rejoining the main Loop Trail not far from the South Parking Lot. Keep straight ahead here and carefully cross the road leading to the North Parking Lot. On the right is the Fort Lawton Cemetery, which was opened in 1902 for army personnel and their families.

The trail enters the woods and descends gradually in forest, passing European white birch, western red cedar, bigleaf maple, and Douglas fir. Just beyond where the path curves right come to a large western hemlock on the right.

(2)   Before the coming of whites to the Pacific Northwest, western hemlock was probably the most common tree in a forest that spread virtually unbroken from the Cascades to the coast and along the coast from northern California to southern Alaska. In the absence of large-scale disturbance such as fire or logging, western hemlock is able to maintain its dominance indefinitely. Today, however, most old-growth stands of western hemlock have been logged. Though hemlocks remain common, the dominant position in today's young mixed forests usually belongs to alder, maple, or Douglas fir.

The woods take on a more natural appearance as native sword fern, bracken fern, salmonberry, and Pacific blackberry join nonnatives such as English ivy and English holly. As the trail continues to descend, pass numerous multi-trunked bigleaf maples.

(3)   The vegetation of Discovery Park is a blend of native and exotic — that is, nonnative—plants, a legacy of some 120 years of continuous human occupation. From the beginning, settlers not only on Magnolia Bluff but throughout the region have brought with them favorite garden plants from back East, Europe, and other parts of the world. Other plants were brought inadvertently, as seeds "hitchhiked" here on people or animals, or among household goods or commercial cargoes. Over the years, birds, mammals, people, and winds all helped carry the seeds of exotic plants into adjacent wild areas. Most of the aliens were unable to compete with

Steep steps lead to the water in Discovery Park

West Point Lighthouse in Discovery Park

native plants. Some, such as Scotch broom and Himalaya blackberry, were mainly successful in areas where disturbance had removed or greatly reduced competition. A few, such as English ivy and English holly, became naturalized in the lowland forests of the region. Other introduced plants found along the Loop Trail are horsechestnut, European mountain ash, Portuguese laurel, and English hawthorn.

Shortly, the path passes a leafy track on the right and, after a brief, gradual ascent, levels out and enters an opening overgrown with Scotch broom and Himalaya blackberry.

(4) In summer the bright rose-colored flowers of fireweed are conspicuous along the right side of the trail. Fireweed and bracken, which also may be found here, are native "weeds," that is, plants that often grow where people do not want them. What else is a weed, after all? Bracken and fireweed are both distributed worldwide. In the wild they are among the first plants to colonize areas denuded by logging, fire, or other disturbance. That same hardiness and opportunistic quality also allows them to invade city lots and gardens. The cottony seeds of fireweed and the invisible spores of bracken fern are carried far and wide by the wind.

The trail soon passes a path on the left (signed "The Uplands") and again crosses the main park road, which leads to the North Parking Lot. Just beyond the road, a pair of paths join and lead down to the North Parking Lot and Daybreak Star Arts Center. Keep straight. The trail skirts

73

woods for a short way, then vegetation begins to crowd in on both sides. Young alders grow on the left; bigleaf maple, western red cedar, and Douglas fir on the right.

(5)   Magnolia Bluff was originally covered by conifer forest. A few bigleaf maples and red alders would have been scattered here and there through the forest, and small deciduous trees such as vine maple, Pacific dogwood, and cascara would have grown in the understory. But the dominant trees would have been conifers—western hemlock, Douglas fir, and western red cedar. These, of course, were the trees the early loggers sought. Many of the deciduous trees growing at that time are still standing. Many more have sprung up since then on lands opened up by the saw. As the remaining conifers continue to grow, they will gradually crowd out and shade out the deciduous trees.

The trail climbs gradually passing a western hemlock, then curves right in a salmonberry-Himalaya blackberry corridor. The path intersects a paved service road, used mainly by bicyclists, which heads downhill to the North Parking Lot. The trail continues through an opening crowded with Scotch broom, bends left, and plunges into the woods again. On the left is a giant knobby maple with several trunks, one of the survivors alluded to above. The way then descends in mixed forest with alder, maple, and hemlock. Salmonberry and coast red elderberry are the common shrubs.

(6)   The greatest variety of bird life in Discovery Park occurs in mixed woods like this, where conifers and broadleaf trees grow together. Why? Because such woods attract birds such as Steller's jay, golden-crowned kinglet, chestnut-backed chickadee, brown creeper, winter wren, purple finch, and red-breasted nuthatch, which are typical of conifer forests as well as ruby-crowned kinglet, black-capped chickadee, bushtit, downy woodpecker, house finch, and Bewick's wren, which are adapted to broadleaf habitats.

The trail bends right, crosses a culvert draining a shallow draw, climbs a short way, then levels out. Now bordered on each side by walls of salmonberry and elderberry, it passes between the sawed-off remains of a fallen log that once lay across the path, then curves left, passing an old red cedar stump with salmonberry and wood fern growing on it. Just beyond the stump, the path turns sharply left and begins to descend, traversing the slope of a deeper ravine. At the bottom, just before turning sharply right, the trail passes between the two sawed-off ends of what was once a single log. Next to the log on the right is an old stump with salal, red huckleberry, and a young western hemlock growing on it.

(7)   The stumps and logs scattered through the woods are reminders of the magnificent conifer forest that once covered Magnolia Bluff. The bluff was first logged in the 1860s, then again in the 1890s, before the coming of the army. Horses and oxen were used to haul the logs over skid roads, which consisted of half-buried logs laid crosswise in the ground.

These skids prevented the logs being hauled from nosing into the mud. The last wave of old-growth logging was carried out by the army in 1907.

The trail bends right and crosses to the opposite side of the ravine. In summer the bottom of the ravine is lush with salmonberry; in winter it is nearly bare of shrubbery. Even in winter, however, evergreen Oregon grape and sword fern keep the trailside lush. The path climbs gradually and bends to the left, passing a red alder with an elbow-shaped branch, where an old horizontal trunk broke off and a new limb grew upward to replace it. A bit beyond, the trail leaves the woods to cross a third road, which like the two before it also leads to the North Parking Lot. The park maintenance yard is on the left, across the road. Follow the trail to the right of the yard and across an open, grassy area. The trail plunges back into the forest. The first tree on the left, whose boughs hang over the path, is western hemlock. The slender tree about ten yards beyond it, and also on the left, is bitter cherry.

(8) Bitter cherry is easily recognized by its bark, which is smooth, deep reddish brown, and marked by rougher, darker rings. The rings, called lenticels, are actually collections of pores that permit the passage of air into the trunk. In spring, when covered with blossoms, bitter cherry provides a splashy white accent to the prevailing forest green.

The path turns left, passing a side trail on the right, where a multi-trunked bigleaf maple marks the junction. Keep left. The trail climbs, turns right, emerges into the open, and comes to the fourth road. This one leads north to the Daybreak Star Arts Center.

Veer left, cross the old road, skirt the abandoned parking area, and follow the gravel track back into the woods. After a brief descent, the trail comes to a fifth road (also leading to the arts center) and the grassy North Bluff area. Rest rooms and drinking fountain are to the right. To reach the North Bluff overlook and picnic area, follow the paved road past the rest rooms to a pair of park signs on the left. A grassy path through the open field leads to the overlook, which is visible in the distance.

(9) North Bluff was once the site of barracks and the noncommissioned officers' club. To the north are views of Shilshole Bay, Puget Sound, and Bainbridge Island. On a clear day, the Olympic Mountains can be seen in the west. Until early in this century, the section of coast below the bluff and to the north and south was inhabited by the Shilshoh people, who thrived on abundant shellfish and salmon.

To the left of the picnic area a set of stairs leads downhill into the woods. As the sign indicates, this is the trail leading to North Beach. North Beach offers perhaps the best tidepooling in Seattle. It is the rockiest section of city shore and the least exposed to waves generated by southerly storm winds. At low tide, look for crabs, sea stars, sea anemones, sea urchins, mussels, and other intertidal life (but please don't remove or otherwise disturb them).

Return to the paved road and back to the Loop Trail. Turn right and follow it through a weedy field filled with Scotch broom and Himalaya blackberry. Visible not far ahead are the homes of personnel still stationed at what remains of Fort Lawton. Please keep out of the residential area. The trail follows the chain link fence to a crossing of the road leading down to West Point, the westernmost jut of land in Seattle.

(10) West Point is renowned among birders as perhaps the best place in Seattle for viewing marine birds. The greatest number and variety occur in the fall, when gulls, terns, jaegers, loons, grebes, cormorants, alcids (i.e., auks), and ducks can all be expected. West Point beaches also offer fabulous views of the Sound and mountains and are probably the loneliest stretches of public sand in the city. To reach West Point, continue walking the Loop Trail to South Bluff overlook, where a signed trail leads down to South Beach.

Beyond the West Point Road the Loop Trail follows the fence alongside the military housing, then leaves it behind and shortly arrives at South Bluff overlook. (Despite the guard rail, this is a good place to keep a tight rein on children. The bluff is steep here, and a slip could result in serious injury or death.) The view of Puget Sound and the Olympics is among the best in Seattle. Look down and sharply right to see the West Point Light House. A signed path to the right of the overlook winds down the bluff to South Beach and West Point. This is a good side trip for the energetic.

(11) Puget Sound is a deep glacier-carved valley that was invaded by the sea after the ice had retreated. Great continental ice sheets have moved southward into the Puget Sound region at least twice, and probably four times, during the last million years. The last advance began about 18,000 years ago, when the area now occupied by Puget Sound was a broad coastal flood plain crossed by meandering streams. Advancing south from Canada the Vashon ice sheet eventually covered the entire region to a depth of nearly 3500 feet. The ice sheet reached its maximum extent, just south of Olympia, between 15,000 and 13,500 years ago. The ice carved the deep, narrow valleys now occupied by Puget Sound, Lake Washington, Lake Sammamish, and the Hood Canal. It also deposited great mounds of rock debris that today form these bluffs, as well as the lines of hills separating the valleys. By 13,000 years ago, the ice had retreated from the region and the Puget Sound shoreline had acquired its basic form. Since then, ongoing processes of erosion and deposition have created deltas, beaches, spits, necks, and other shoreline features. The most dramatic alterations of the shoreline, however, are the result of human activities, such as dredging, filling, and the construction of jetties, piers, and other structures.

From the overlook the Loop Trail enters a thicket.

(12) The dense tangle of vegetation provides cover from predators for birds that nest or forage on the ground. The rufous-sided towhee,

Looking toward South Bluff in Discovery Park

song sparrow, and Bewick's wren all nest and forage within the thicket. California quail nests in the thicket and returns to it when frightened, but otherwise feeds in adjacent fields. All the above birds are year-around residents. In spring they are joined by two additional nesting species—the white-crowned sparrow and rufous hummingbird.

The trail leaves the thicket and emerges into the vast opening called South Meadow. Here the Loop Trail forks. The right-hand path skirts the bluffs; the left-hand path crosses the meadow. The two rejoin beyond the sandy bluffs, near the South Meadow rest rooms. A sign at the fork asks visitors to stay behind the guard rails and avoid climbing, walking, or carving on the bluffs. Take the right-hand fork.

(13) The sands here have developed atop a thiry-foot layer of unsorted rock debris dropped here by the Vashon ice sheet. Beneath the debris lie a hundred feet of yellowish sand deposited by streams as the glacier began to advance into the area. Below that layer are eighty feet of dark clay and silt that settled out of an enormous fresh water lake that formed when the ice sheet, still well to the north, dammed the Strait of Juan de Fuca. The bottom layer consists of seventy feet of lake and stream sediments from a time before the last glacial advance. These layers can be seen on the face of Discovery Park's bluffs, which are as much as 250 feet high.

The two forks of the Loop Trail rejoin and continue to skirt the south edge of the meadow.

A closeup look of leathery madrona leaves

(14)   South Meadow was cleared and maintained as an athletic field for military personnel. Today, it is managed as a natural area. The tall grasses provide food and shelter for small mammals such as shrews, moles, and mice. These attract predators such as hawks, owls, and coyotes. If the field were left alone, it would be invaded first by shrubs and eventually by trees. This succession of communities represents the natural course of events, yet if it were allowed to proceed, the diversity of habitats and wildlife within Discovery Park would be diminished.

As the Loop Trail approaches W. Emerson Street, it enters groves of bigleaf maples and madronas, then runs along the entry road to the South Parking Lot. From the lot, the Loop Trail is the gravel path to the right (south) of both the information sign and the blocked-off paved road next to it. The familiar Loop Trail sign is located a few steps down the path.

(15)   The tall, slender trees forming a line on the left are Lombardy poplars, which are widely planted in the United States as street trees or wind screens. This cultivated variety of the European black poplar is related to black cottonwood and quaking aspen, the Northwest's two native poplars. Lombardy poplar is readily told from the natives by its narrow crown of short upturned branches and by its broadly triangular leaves.

The Loop Trail curves left and enters woods. At the first junction keep left. At the second, you have a choice, depending on where you started the hike. If you began the walk at either the North or South parking lots and wish to bypass the visitor-center area, keep left at the junction. If you began at the visitor center, take the right fork and follow the trail downhill through alder woods.

(16) The swift-flying sharp-shinned hawk is an efficient predator on forest song birds. It flies fast enough to run down any small bird, and its short wings enable it to maneuver agilely among the trees. So long as small birds are present, sharp-shinned hawks are not choosy as to what types of trees make up the forest. This hawk is very aggressive in defending its own nest, however, and will not hesitate to dive at intruders.

The trail emerges from the woods at the children's play area. The visitor center is in the distance on the left (north).

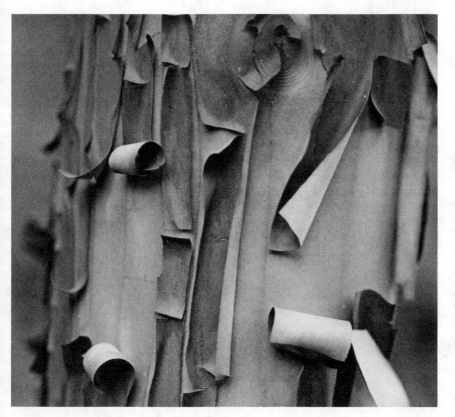

Madrona sloughing its bark

8

SEATTLE

Discovery Park: Wolf Tree Nature Trail

Distance: ½ - mile loop
Season: all year
Highlights: forest, wetland, stream
Metro: 33

Discovery Park serves not only as a sanctuary for urban refugees but also as an educational center specializing in the natural history of the Puget Sound region. A full-time interpretive staff conducts a variety of programs for schools, groups, individuals, and the community at large. These programs include guided nature walks, classes and workshops, lectures, exhibits, and the self-guiding Wolf Tree Nature Trail.

The Wolf Tree Nature Trail offers a half-mile stroll through a lovely ravine forest of both conifers and deciduous trees. Though logged in the 1860s, this area is perhaps the least disturbed in Discovery Park. And except when patient rangers are guiding bands of school children along the trail, it is also among the quietest.

Numbered posts designate points of interest along the trail. An interpretive booklet, with discussions keyed to the signposts, can be purchased at the visitor center. A guidebook especially for children is also available. The following discussions—also keyed to the signposts—are meant to complement rather than replace those in the booklets.

Drive to Discovery Park as described in Walk 7. From the East Gate follow the park road to the North Parking Lot. At the southwest corner of the lot there is an information sign with a map of the park. Picnic tables and rest rooms are nearby. The Wolf Tree Nature Trail begins at the northwest corner of the lot, next to the gated road leading to the Indian Center. A signpost shows the way.

Entrance to the Wolf Tree Nature Trail, Discovery Park

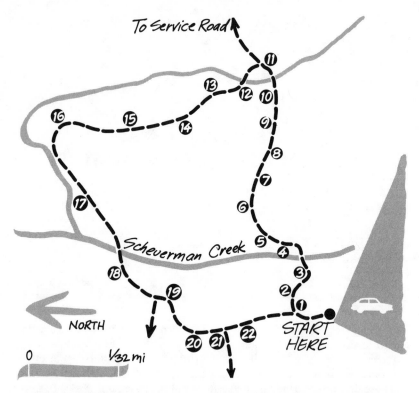

The path descends beneath maple and alder to an information sign. There is a box here for interpretive booklets, and because the staff at Discovery Park is conscientious about keeping it stocked, you may actually find one here when you arrive. Naturally, there is some overlap in information between the following discussions and those in the booklet. They are different enough, however, to warrant using both when walking this trail. When finished with a booklet, be sure to return it to the box so that others may use it as well.

Take the right-hand trail, which crosses a short boardwalk to the first signpost, on the right.

(1) This alder stand has grown up since the removal of World War II army barracks in 1956 and 1957. Alders improve the physical and chemical characteristics of the soil beneath them. Their leaves break down much more rapidly than conifer needles to form a rich humus, and bacterial nodules on their roots add nitrogen to the soil. This partly accounts for the lush vegetation that usually develops beneath red alders and probably explains why young Douglas firs grow faster on lands pioneered by red alders.

The trail bends right. Then, as it curves left, look for signpost 2 on the left side of the trail.

(2) The lush undergrowth in this moist, wooded ravine is dominated by salmonberry. This cousin to the blackberry is one of few forest plants to have pink, rose, or red flowers. Such plants tend to attract hummingbirds or butterflies, but not bees because they are unable to distinguish the color red. In this case, the attracted feeder is the rufous hummingbird, which visits the flowers from March through June.

The trail traverses the side of the ravine. Four different species of fern grow on the bank to the right. The trail descends to a set of steps and a small bridge over Scheuerman Creek, which was named for an early settler. Signpost 3 is on the left, at the foot of a large bigleaf maple leaning out over the ravine.

(3) This fine old tree provides habitat for a variety of plants and animals. Mosses and lichens grow in moist crevices on its trunks and limbs. Bees are attracted by its flowers, while other insects feed on its bark, wood, and leaves. All provide food in turn for many of the birds that nest and forage in its broad crown. Raccoons spend the day resting high in its branches. Squirrels, chipmunks, and mice consume its seeds. Children enjoy the winged fruits—known as double samaras—which flutter to the ground like tiny helicopters.

Signpost 4 is on the left, just across the plank bridge.

(4) The flow of Scheuerman Creek provides a clue to our climate. During the winter, the creek is normally vigorous, sometimes torrential. As rainfall tapers off through the summer, the creek may be gradually reduced to a trickle. This concentration of rainfall in the "winter" months (actually, October through April in most years) becomes increasingly pronounced southward along the Pacific Coast. This type of climate favors cold-tolerant conifers in the Northwest and drought-tolerant broadleaf evergreens in California. Both types of evergreens are able to temporarily shut down operations during summer droughts yet remain active during the cool, moist winter months.

Climb a short set of steps and find signpost 5 at the base of a western red cedar on the left.

(5) Western red cedar occurs along the coast from southeastern Alaska to northern California. It also occurs on the western slopes of the northern Rocky Mountains in Idaho, Montana, and British Columbia. Red cedar favors wet soils and does best in coastal valleys where rainfall ranges between sixty and one hundred twenty inches a year. On such sites, red cedars eight to ten feet thick, 200 feet high, and more than 1000 years old were once common. Because the wood is so highly valued, relatively few big old red cedars remain outside Olympic National Park and other protected areas.

The trail turns right and comes to a decayed stump and signpost 6 on the left.

(6) Red huckleberry is one of the most common forest shrubs in western Washington, where it often, though not always, grows atop logs or

Mushrooms along the Wolf Tree Nature Trail

stumps. This one has sprouted from the stump of a Douglas fir. Although red huckleberry loses its leaves in the fall, its square, green twigs are recognizable any time of year. The color of the twigs is due to the presence of chlorophyll, the pigment that allows plants to capture sunlight for use in synthesizing carbohydrates. This increase in the amount of plant surface available for photosynthesis may be one reason that red huckleberry is able to grow in deep shade.

Pass a bench on the right and come to signpost 7, also on the right, at the base of a double-trunked bigleaf maple.

(7)   The hollylike plants at the foot of the maple are Oregon grape, an abundant shrub in local conifer forests. The leaves consist of individual leaflets arranged in pairs along the stem, with a single one at the tip. Leaves consisting of two or more leaflets are called compound. When the leaflets are arranged symmetrically along a common stem, the compound leaf is said to be pinnate.

The trail bends right around the maple and in several yards comes to signpost 8 on the right.

(8)   Common sword fern (which also has pinnate leaves) is probably the most common and widespread fern in the Pacific Northwest, where it often covers entire slopes within the forest. Actually, there are several species of sword fern, but this is the only one you are likely to see in the greater Seattle area.

Where the trail turns left, find signpost 9 at the foot of a tall, columnar Douglas fir about three feet in diameter.

(9)   Discovered in 1791 on Vancouver Island by the Scottish physician Archibald Menzies, Douglas fir has long puzzled taxonomists, the scientists whose business it is to classify plants and animals. Early botanists thought the tree was a pine, and some lumbermen still know it as Oregon pine. John Muir called it a spruce, and most people think it is a fir. Even its scientific name, *Pseudotsuga menziesii*, which means Menzies' false hemlock, is misleading. Douglas fir is none of the above. It actually belongs in a genus of its own, one it shares with only one other tree in the western hemisphere, the so-called bigcone Douglas fir of southern California.

Signpost 10 is on the left side of the trail, about thirty feet beyond the Douglas fir.

(10)   At least five different species of mosses grow on this fallen red alder. Although mosses don't contribute directly to the decomposition of dead wood, they do help maintain a moist environment that speeds up the process.

The trail descends gradually, bends to the right, and crosses a tributary of Scheuerman Creek. Beyond, on the right, is signpost 11.

(11)   This western red cedar has begun to grow around the remains of an old pole that was part of a military drill area to practice loading troops into boats. Across the trail, look for a low herbaceous plant called youth-on-age, or piggyback plant. Both names refer to the plant's habit of growing new leaves from the bases of old ones.

The trail turns left here and comes to a junction. Keep left and cross the tributary once again on another wooden bridge. Signpost 12 is on the left, at the bridge.

(12)   This toppled red alder began as an upright branch on an earlier fallen tree. Overhead, the opening left when the tree fell still remains unfilled. It represents an opportunity for plants that are unable to reproduce beneath the forest canopy to gain a foothold in these woods.

The trail bends right and comes to signpost 13, at the foot of a pair of alders with a decaying Douglas fir log wedged between them.

(13) The bark is missing from this end of the log but is still present on the other. Bark so effectively insulates a tree from the outside environment that before decomposition can begin it must be penetrated. This is usually accomplished by wood-boring beetles, who feed on the sapwood. The beetles create openings for the invasion of fungi spores, which are the principal agents of decomposition in conifer forests.

The trail crosses a boardwalk and comes to signpost 14 at the base of a big old red alder on the left.

(14) This is the "Wolf Tree" for which the trail is named. A wolf tree, in forester's jargon, is one that seems to take up more than its normal share of space in the forest. The great spreading branches of this alder indicate that it once grew in the open, with little or no competition from other trees. The Wolf Tree grew up some time after the land was cleared in the late 1860s. Since red alders rarely live more than a century, this is an old one indeed. The tree may already be in decline, as evidenced by the dead upper portion of the trunk.

The trail shortly comes to signpost 15 on the right.

(15) The odd cluster of branches directly overhead in this western hemlock is a witch's broom, a deformation usually caused by infestations of dwarf mistletoe. This tree began life as a seedling on top of a nurse log. As it grew, its roots extended around the log and down to the soil. When the log finally crumbled away, the tree was left perched on stiltlike roots.

The trail turns right, around the hemlock, and comes to a boardwalk that winds through a low, poorly drained area.

(16) Water is always at or near the surface here. The soil is black Seattle muck, which is high in acid and low in oxygen. As a result, the area supports a different *community* of plants than the surrounding forest. The main trees here are Pacific willows. Growing with them are Cooley's hedgenettle, water parsley, skunk cabbage, lady fern, and horsetail. Some of these plants also grow in damper areas within the adjacent forest, but only in the wetland do they all grow together.

The trail turns sharply left here. Look for signpost 17, on the right.

(17) Skunk cabbage is an indicator of soggy soils throughout our region. Its small greenish flowers grow tightly clustered on a stalk called a spadix set within a showy yellow bract, or modified leaf, called a spathe. The flowers appear as early as February or March, when little else blooms. Skunk cabbage is related to taro, from whose root Hawaiians make the sour porridge called poi. Local Indians cooked and ate the root of skunk cabbage and used the leaves both as medicinal plasters applied to the skin and as wrappings or platters.

The trail crosses Scheuerman Creek again and comes to signpost 18 on the right.

(18) This small pond was created when water filled a hole left behind when a Pacific willow was uprooted. Eventually, the hole will be filled by

Skunk cabbage

decaying organic matter contributed by the plants growing around it.

Climb out of wetland on wooden steps. The trail then passes a bench on the left, opposite a leafy track leading into the woods. Keep left and come to signpost 19 on the left.

(19) The alders here are in the process of losing their lower branches. Only a few years ago, there was enough light here for the trees to support limbs nearly to the ground. As the canopy gradually closed, shading the lower limbs, the trees began to divert water and nutrients to the functional upper limbs.

The trail turns left and comes to signposts 20 and 21.

(20) The "manhole" cover here provides access to the large pipe that carries sewage to Metro's West Point treatment plant.

(21) Scotch broom has invaded open areas and waste places up and down the Pacific Coast, but nowhere so extensively as in the Pacific Northwest. Its membership in the legume, or bean, family is evident by the shape of the flowers, which often completely cover the plants, and by the pealike seed pods, which appear in the summer. Like other legumes, its roots host bacteria that convert atmospheric nitrogen into compounds useful to plants.

Just beyond the signpost, a side path leads right. Keep left. The final signpost is on the right.

(22) Opposite the signpost, on the left side of the trail, is a slender, toppled tree with smooth, dark reddish brown bark. This is bitter cherry. The tree snapped near the base but, judging by the stout upright limbs, the still-rooted trunk remained alive for a time. At some point, however, the connection was severed because the entire tree is now quite dead.

Beyond the signpost the trail bends left, then right, and climbs the hill to the information sign and the completion of the loop.

9

SEATTLE

Schmitz Park

Distance: ½ - mile loop
Season: all year
Highlights: big trees, stream
Metro: 56

Schmitz Park preserves some fifty acres of modified old-growth forest tucked into a ravine slicing through a quiet West Seattle neighborhood. Most of the land was donated to the city in 1908 by Park Commissioner Ferdinand Schmitz and his wife Emma, who wished to preserve some of the original forest that greeted the first white settlers. Schmitz Park is by no means pristine. Large stumps are scattered through the park, and English Holly—a garden escapee—is in several places one of the more conspicuous understory plants. Nevertheless, Schmitz Park features Douglas firs up to eight feet across and western red cedars perhaps half as thick.

The Schmitz Park loop is the premium forest walk in Seattle. The main trail is a broad track that leads up one side of the stream and down the other for a total circuit of one-half mile. Numerous secondary paths wander away from the main trail, some exiting on neighborhood streets. The route described below follows both the main trail and selected side paths.

To reach Schmitz Park take the West Seattle bridge to S.W. Admiral Way. Follow Admiral Way uphill, through the business district, and downhill to S.W. Stevens (watch for the "rainbow" park sign on the left, just before Admiral Way crosses a bridge over the ravine). Turn left at the sign and keep right, following the road down to the parking area.

From the south end of the lot, facing upstream, a walker has the choice of three main trails. Take the one on the right. Almost immediately, turn left on a small trail leading across a plank bridge. Left of the bridge is a

Deer fern

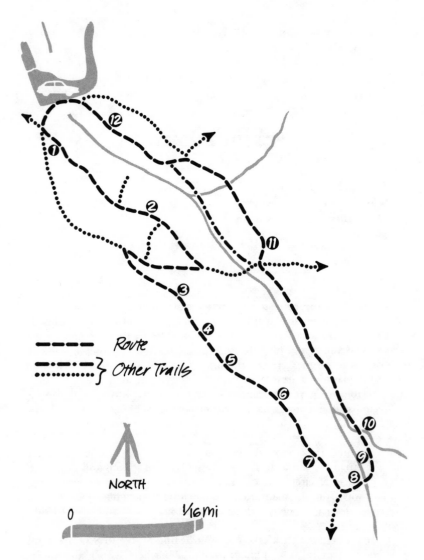

western red cedar about three feet in diameter. To the right are a couple of large Douglas firs. After crossing the bridge, the trail bends right and arrives at three large fallen trees on the right.

(1) These toppled Douglas firs are excellent examples of "nurse logs," so called because they provide a fertile, organic rooting medium, or "nursery," for young trees and shrubs. The closest log supports western hemlock and red huckleberry, along with a single English holly seedling. The log in the rear is densely covered with young hemlocks. Both logs

support several types of moss. Plants growing on nurse logs are spared the need of competing for water and nutrients with those already established on the forest floor. In old-growth forests of the Pacific Northwest, the forest floor is often so densely covered with vegetation that young trees and shrubs have difficulty getting started. As a result, virtually all conifer reproduction in these forests occurs on nurse logs or stumps, both of which may be seen throughout Schmitz Park.

Continuing up the path, notice a log bridge crossing the creek on the left. This is an excellent bridge to keep children off of. Beyond the bridge, the trail enters an open area overgrown with shrubs and ferns. A few steps farther, on the left, at the end of a short path, stands a Douglas fir some five feet in diameter.

(2) Douglas fir cannot tolerate shade and if overtopped would disappear from the forest. It prevents this by growing faster and taller than all the other trees in the forest. Periodic fires create openings in which the seeds of Douglas fir can germinate and seedlings can thrive. At the same time, the thick, corky bark of old Douglas firs, such as this one, provides mature trees with excellent protection from all but the hottest fires (note the blackened places on the trunk).

Follow the path to where it reconnects with the main trail. Turn right and backtrack about a thirty yards to a narrow path heading sharply left up the hillside. Follow the path as it makes an ascending traverse of the slope. In about 80 yards, where the trail first levels out, look on the left for a large, multi-stemmed shrub leaning out over the canyon.

(3) This large shrub is a California hazelnut, a cousin of the commercial filbert. Note the soft, broad, serrated leaves and, in season, the hard-shelled nuts sheathed in two or three greenish bracts (modified leaves), which extend to form a fringed tube. In February and March, before the leaves appear, the drooping yellow catkins of pollen-bearing male flowers are distinctive. California hazelnut is a common understory shrub on moist, well-drained sites in the lowland forests of western Washington. Note here that it is growing from the mounded root clump of a fallen tree, which is lying downslope. Also growing on the clump is a young western hemlock.

The trail climbs up over a rise and bends right. Uphill on the right look for a Douglas fir about six feet in diameter.

(4) Opposite the Douglas fir, several large red alders rise out of the bottom of the canyon. Red alder is perhaps the most common deciduous broadleaf tree in the Pacific Northwest. Intolerant of shade, it is an opportunistic species that quickly invades places where fire, logging, or other disturbance has opened up the forest. Red alder also grows, as here, in damp places within the forest, such as streamsides, lake shores, and swamps.

The trail dips down and swings left, then drops down to a rivulet, which dries up in summer. Just uphill from it is some prominent downed

Lush sword ferns in Schmitz Park

timber. The trail climbs and turns toward the right, then levels out. Look for a burnt-out snag growing downslope on the left.

(5)   Snags are characteristic of old-growth forests. Douglas fir snags, such as this one, typically decompose from the top down, while snags of western red cedar and western hemlock usually remain more or less entire until, finally, they rot away at ground level and fall. The primary ecological role of snags is as wildlife habitat. Woodpeckers excavate nesting holes in large dead snags, and the holes are later used by many other birds and mammals for nesting, overwintering, and temporary shelter. The most impressive hole driller in the Pacific Northwest is the large, red-crested pileated woodpecker, which lives only where tall snags are present.

The trail traverses the slope and enters an open area.

(6)   This entire section of trail is good for birding because it permits you to look directly into the treetops. Notice woodpecker holes in the alders. Listen to the scolding call and see dark blue gliding form of Steller's jay. Watch for brown creepers spiraling up the trunks of conifers in search of insects. In spring and summer, look for warblers; in winter, for varied thrushes.

The trail dips, then curves left. Between here and where the trail bends right around a corner, look for evergreen huckleberry on the right, just opposite a large, moss-covered bigleaf maple. You can recognize it by its rows of small, shiny, dark green leaves, which particularly stand out in midwinter.

(7)   The small, nearly round black berries of evergreen huckleberry were prized by coastal Indians from northern California to British Columbia. This cousin of the store-bought blueberry is relatively scarce on the Seattle side of Puget Sound, but grows abundantly on the Kitsap Peninsula and other areas in the rain shadow of the Olympic Mountains.

Round the bend and follow the trail to a side-trail on the left. Turn here. (The trail leading straight ahead continues up the canyon through tall, arching maples and alders to a residential street.) From the junction the trail enters the shrubby thicket lining the small stream.

(8)   The most prominent shrub making up the thicket is salmonberry, which is common and nearly universal in Northwest forests below about 4000 feet elevation. The fruits resemble boysenberries but are yellow, orange, or light red and—alas—rather watery and bland in flavor. The showy, dark pink flowers appear March through June. Indians not only ate the fruits but also the tender young canes. Thimbleberry, willow, salal, and red huckleberry are also growing in this stream-bottom thicket. Birders will find rufous-sided towhees, black-capped chickadees, and song sparrows amid the tangle of vegetation. Aplodontias—also known as mountain beavers—lurk in the damp tanglewood.

As the trail swings left to parallel the tiny stream, there is a splendid western hemlock on the left and next to it a fair-sized western red cedar.

Loop trail in Schmitz Park

(9) Western hemlock is able to tolerate dense shade better than any of its conifer companions. As a result, its seedlings are usually the most numerous—and sometimes the only—young conifers found in shady forests. In the absence of any disturbance that would open up the forest, western hemlocks would eventually dominate old-growth stands on most sites. Western red cedar is somewhat less tolerant of shade but lives much longer and thrives in soils that are too wet for western hemlock.

The trail crosses a wooden bridge over a small creek.

(10) In summer, the showy red flowers of Cooley's hedgenettle brighten this crossing. The tubular blossoms are one inch long and grow in whorls atop the tall, four-sided stems. The leaves occur in pairs, each set at right angle to the ones above and below. A member of the mint family, Cooley's hedgenettle is common in damp places from sea level to mid-elevations in the mountains. Other plants growing with it in this small creek community include skunk cabbage, deer fern, and water parsley.

The trail passes a large Douglas fir and fair-sized western red cedar on the left before coming to a second red cedar perhaps four feet in diameter. From there it is a short way to a junction with the main trail, where there are four choices. Take the second trail on the right to continue the route. The slopes to the right of the trail are covered with sword fern and deer fern.

Large fallen red cedar in Schmitz Park

(11)   Deer fern has two types of fronds: sterile ones that lie flat on the ground and fertile, spore-bearing ones that grow upright from the center of the clump. The sterile fronds are evergreen; the fertile ones wither at summer's end. Why the fern should have two types of fronds is uncertain. The flat rosette of sterile fronds, however, is certainly well suited to gathering sunlight in a shady forest, while the delicate fertile fronds are more exposed to summer breezes that serve to broadcast their spores.

At the next junction take the left fork along the stream, passing a trail heading left down to the stream and a wooden bridge. A California hazelnut marks the junction. Keep right. When a wooden bridge comes into view, look on the left for an old nurse stump. Directly across the trail, on the right, is a bigleaf maple with numerous knoblike burls on its trunk.

(12)   It is not clear why these burls develop, but they do not appear to harm the tree, and the beautiful swirly grain of their wood makes them prized for carving. Bigleaf maples and red alders are the principal understory trees both in Schmitz Park and throughout western Washington.

Pass between the now separate ends of a fallen tree that extends downslope into the creek bottom. Then cross the bridge and wind down to the parking area.

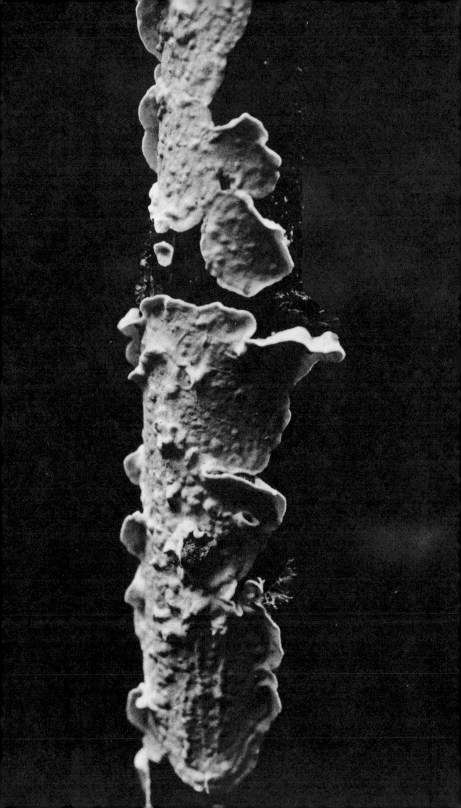

10

SEATTLE

Camp Long

Distance: ½ - mile loop
Season: best spring through fall
Highlights: woods, stream
Metro: 21

For many years the Seattle Park Department operated sixty-eight-acre Camp Long exclusively for organized groups, who could reserve the lodge or outlying cabins for day or overnight use. Today, however, Camp Long is open to the general public as well as groups. The park's active interpretive program offers nature walks, and classes for children, teenagers, and adults in natural history, rock climbing, compass use, and outdoor skills. Camp Long also has a wheelchair trail—the Rolling Hills

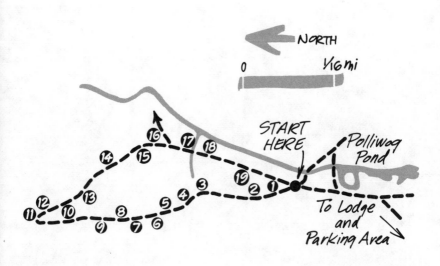

Lichens

Trail—which begins at the south end of the parking lot and provides access to three wheelchair-accessible cabins.

The Animal Tracks Nature Trail is a self-guiding nature trail featuring fiberglass casts of animal tracks. An interpretive booklet keyed to numbered posts may be purchased at the park lodge. The following discussions are meant to complement those of the booklet, not to replace them. It is recommended where possible that both publications be used together.

To reach Camp Long, take the new West Seattle bridge to Fauntleroy Way. Turn left on 35th Avenue S.W. and in just over a half mile turn left on Dawson Street, which is marked by a rainbow park sign. The lodge is the stone building directly ahead, through the gates. Turn right and park.

Follow the broad path leading downhill from the lodge to the large grassy Parade Ground. Turn left on the service road and pass Polliwog Pond on the right. At the north end of the pond, where the service road curves right, leave the road and follow a wood-chip path past the large flat, stone compass set into the ground to the covered sign marking the start of the Animal Tracks Nature Trail.

The trail forks here. Take the left fork past the trail sign. You will return to this point via the trail on the right. On the left-hand trail signpost 1 is located on the right less than ten yards from the start.

(1) The small, badly decayed western red cedar stump to the left of the post is covered with mosses and a dusty apple-green lichen. Its insides

Trailhead of the Animal Tracks Nature Trail, Camp Long

have been invaded by fungus, which consists of cottony, threadlike strands called hyphae. The fungus breaks down complex organic compounds found in the wood into carbon dioxide, water, and other simple substances. In the process the fungi liberate nutrients bound up in these molecules and return them to the forest. While the stump stands, colonies of mosses and lichens benefit from the water created in the course of decomposition.

From signpost 1 the trail very gently descends a hundred feet or so to signpost 2 on the right.

(2) Scouler's willows grows just to the right of the signpost. While often growing as a tree, the willows here are shrubby. Scouler's willow is one of the more common and widespread willows growing in the Northwest, ranging from sea level to well up into the mountains. It is also the only one in the region that regularly occurs away from water. Indians all over North America used tonics derived from willow bark to treat headache, fever, sore throat and other ailments. As it happens, acetylsalicylic acid, or aspirin, is a derivative of salicin, the active ingredient in willow bark. The name salicin is derived in turn from the generic name for willows—*Salix*—whose root is an old Celtic word meaning "near water."

The trail continues straight, jogs slightly right, then angles more sharply to the left. Signpost 3 is located on the right, at this left turn.

(3) The trees here are red alder, the most common species in these woods. The alder woodland at Camp Long has grown up in the wake of logging that occurred here more than one hundred years ago. Originally, western red cedars must have dominated the forest, but there are few conifers in the woods today. On this site the scarcity of young conifers allows young alders to replace their dying elders.

Look for signpost 4 on the right, only a dozen or so yards up the trail. An English holly tree, which bears the familiar red holly berries in winter, grows just left of the signpost.

(4) In winter, robins greedily gobble the red berries of English holly, which has been planted widely in parks and gardens throughout the area. The seeds pass through the birds' digestive tracts and are transplanted to new locations in their droppings. The young holly tree here began in this way. Native to Eurasia, English holly has become naturalized in many parts of the Puget Sound region.

Passing a Lombardy poplar on the right, next to the holly tree, the trail continues about fifteen yards to signpost 5 on the right. Signpost 5 is the first of several along the trail to bear fiberglass casts of animal tracks, for which the trail is named. The cast here is of raccoon tracks.

(5) Like humans, raccoons will eat almost anything. For that reason—and because they are both intelligent and more than a match for most dogs—raccoons have been able to live alongside people (and dogs) in city and suburbs. During the day they commonly rest high in the trees, either in holes in the trunks or on broad limbs. At dusk they descend to prowl parks and backyards for food. Look for raccoon tracks in muddy spots along the trail.

Beyond signpost 5, pass a large Lombardy poplar on the right. Behind it are several western hemlocks and red cedars, forming the first stand of conifers encountered along the trail. About twenty yards beyond, come to signpost 6 on the left.

(6)   English ivy is growing on the trunks of these trees. Like holly, it has been able to invade woodlands throughout the Puget Sound region largely through the agency of birds, who feed on the berries. Individual ivy stems may exceed thirty feet in length. They attach themselves to trees, rocks, fences, or whatever by means of "holdfasts" on the stems.

In another twenty yards come to signpost 7 on the left.

(7)   Look overhead. You can see sky here. There is no canopy of branches and foliage shading this spot. The opening was created when the tree that once occupied this spot was cut down, as evidenced by the sawed-off stump to the right of the post. Thus far, no other trees have filled the void. In future years, however, the competition among young trees to oc-cupy this valuable piece of solar real estate is likely to be fierce. Eventually one, perhaps two trees will win out, fill the opening, and shade out their competitors.

Signpost 8 is located about fifteen yards down the trail, on the right. It bears a cast of the tracks of the common crow.

(8)   Crows seem to be everywhere in the Puget lowlands and, like hu-mans and raccoons, their success is due in part to their willingness to eat just about anything. Crows actively defend their own nests while raiding those of smaller birds. Owing to their large size and aggressive behavior, crows have few predators. One notable exception in the Seattle area is the great horned owl, which probably swoops down on them as they sleep high in the trees.

The trail drops gently and in about twenty yards comes to signpost 9 on the left.

(9)   Moist thickets of nettles, ferns, and wild berries, like the one across the trail from the post, provide ideal habitat for the aplodontia, or mountain-beaver. The increase in such habitats following the logging of old-growth timber has allowed aplodontia populations to swell beyond their original numbers. Although aplodontias occasionally cut down small saplings and seedlings, they are incapable of felling larger trees as true beavers do.

In some forty yards, come to signpost 10 on the right. The post bears a fiberglass cast of the tracks of a red fox.

(10)   The red fox is the wily character of fable and folklore, a testi-mony to the intelligence of this wild canine. With luck you may see a fox as you walk this trail. Or perhaps you will smell its musky scent, which is pro-duced by anal glands and is used to mark the animal's territory. The Euro-

pean red fox is an opportunistic hunter, feeding on small mammals, birds, amphibians, reptiles, insects, worms, and a wide variety of fruits and nuts. It helps keep populations of rodents and rabbits under control. All red foxes in the Puget Sound region were introduced, either for hunting or fur farms.

In another ten yards or so enter an opening with a viewfinder set in the middle, next to signpost 11. A bench sits in front of a side trail leading to the West Seattle golf course.

(11) Just rotate the top plate of the viewfinder until the sighting notch lines up with the letters on the base. Then look through the tube to see: A—bigleaf maple, B—Scouler's willow, C—western red cedar, D—California hazelnut, E—Douglas fir, F—western hemlock, G—red alder, H—Pacific dogwood, and I—Pacific madrona.

The clearing marks the halfway point of the trail. Follow the trail right as it descends gradually for about ten yards to signpost 12, which bears the fiberglass cast of coyote tracks.

(12) All over the West, coyotes have penetrated city and suburb, where they find cover in parks, fields, and greenbelts. Coyotes have even pushed eastward to the Atlantic Ocean, well beyond their former range. What is more, despite concerted trapping campaigns, their numbers and range continue to grow. The reasons for the coyote's great success in expanding its territory are several. First, the removal of the wolf from virtually all of its former range in the lower forty-eight states left the large-canine-predator niche empty and waiting for the coyote to fill. Second, coyotes are highly intelligent and very careful. Third, they eat just about anything. They prey on birds and rodents when available, feed on traffic kills and other carrion if necessary, and enter backyards to raid trash cans and pet-food dishes.

The trail bends right and passes through a thick stand of stinging nettle (not evident in winter) en route to signpost 13, which bears the fiberglass cast of the tracks of the eastern cottontail rabbit.

(13) The eastern cottontail occurs throughout the eastern two-thirds of North America and ranges naturally as far west as northern Arizona. Though not native to the Pacific Northwest, introduced populations are now well established in King County and other parts of the region. Its chief predators include coyotes, foxes, bobcats, and great horned owls. When attempting to elude predators it runs in a zigzag pattern.

The trail continues downhill through moist woods for perhaps fifty yards to signpost 14. Look for the telltale dirt mounds of the coast mole.

(14) Like other moles, the coast mole burrows through the soil searching for worms, sowbugs, insects, and other small creatures. Though nearly blind, the mole is able to sense the location of prey through the sensitive whiskers—called vibrissae—on its snout. It also has excellent hearing and can detect extremely faint vibrations in the earth. Moles have a number of anatomical adaptations to life underground. For example, their forepaws are relatively large and are attached at right angles to the body for more effective digging. The animals' streamlined profile and fur that can be stroked comfortably in either direction are both ideal for scooting down narrow tunnels.

The trail bends right and in about fifty yards enters a small stand of conifers and comes to signpost 15 on the right.

(15) The three species making up this stand are western hemlock, Douglas fir, and western red cedar. Western hemlock has stubby needles and branches that droop at the tips. Western red cedar has flattened overlapping scales for leaves, and the tips of the branches characteristically turn upward. Douglas fir has flattened needles that are twisted at the base and grow from all sides of a twig. In the absence of further disturbance, hemlock and cedar will eventually replace Douglas fir, alder, and maple on this hillside.

Just before reaching a broad side trail heading left down to a bridge, come to signpost 16, which bears the fiberglass imprint of the tracks of the eastern gray squirrel.

(16) The eastern gray squirrel is the common backyard squirrel found throughout Seattle. Introduced into this area from the deciduous forests of the eastern United States, the gray squirrel has benefited from the widespread replacement of conifers with deciduous trees in city and suburban parks and gardens. Favored foods include hazelnuts and the seeds of maple, horsechestnut, and conifers. The native Douglas squirrel, or chickaree, and the northern flying squirrel, still persist in scattered stands of conifers within the metropolitan area. In some parks, where mixed forests occur, all three squirrels may coexist.

Keep right at the junction and climb shortly to signpost 17 on the left, just before the bridge overlooking the ravine.

(17) Two types of ferns are conspicuous here: sword ferns (evergreen) on the moist slope and lady ferns (deciduous and therefore not apparent in winter) in the even moister soil along the watercourses. The resulting distribution of these two ferns illustrates an ecological principle: The occurrence of plants and animals is determined by the condition for which they have the least tolerance. Lady fern, for example, tolerates a wide range of light conditions, from full sun to full shade, but it requires a reliable supply of moisture throughout the growing season. Sword fern, however, requires less moisture but rarely grows in sunny places. Where their light and moisture requirements converge, the two ferns may grow side by side.

Beyond the bridge the trail turns left, then right, then climbs gently, with the help of a few steps, to signpost 18 on the left beside a large stump.

(18) Townsend's chipmunk is the only chipmunk to inhabit the lowland forests of western Washington. It is a large, dark, rather secretive chipmunk. Watch for it in brushy areas and listen for the rustle of leaves

Taking notes along the Animal Tracks Nature Trail

as it forages in the undergrowth. (Of course, that rustle also could be that of a rufous-sided towhee or song sparrow poking about in the leaf litter.)

The trail bends right as it continues climbing gradually to signpost 19 on the right. Directly in front of the post is what appears to be a dense hedge of western red cedar.

(19) The cedar hedge is actually a single young tree which is bent over parallel to the ground. What seem to be individual young cedars are really branches that have adopted an upright habit of growth. Nothing seems to be holding the tree down except perhaps the weight and vigor of its own aspiring limbs. The young tree originally may have been held down by the weight of a fallen tree or limb that is no longer there.

From signpost 19 walk uphill to the end of the Animal Tracks Nature Trail. A set of unlabeled animal casts is located on the right. You may want to take a stab at identifying them. From here, you can extend your walk by following other trails. Park maps are available at the lodge.

11

EASTSIDE/KIRKLAND

Saint Edwards State Park

Distance: 1 - mile loop
Season: all year
Highlights: lush woods, wild Lake Washington shoreline
Metro: 260 (¼-mile walk to trailhead)

Saint Edwards State Park in Kirkland offers some of the most pleasant forest walking in the greater Seattle area. But that's not all. This 316-acre park protects the last remaining wild, undeveloped, forested section of Lake Washington shoreline—nearly three-quarters of a mile in all!

Until 1977, the land occupied by the park was home to a seminary for the Supplican Order of Catholic priests. Upon closure of the seminary, the Seattle diocese sold the land and the buildings thereon to the state for use as a park. In June 1978 the grounds were open to the public.

Facilities include a gymnasium, tennis courts, swimming pool, soccer field, picnic areas, trails, and a grassy "beach" for lolling about. Rest rooms are located in the gymnasium. Pit toilets are provided at the "beach." The park is open 6:30 A.M. to 10:00 P.M. from April 1 to October 15, and 8:00 A.M. to 5:00 P.M. the rest of the year.

Pets are to be on leashes at all times. Motorcycles, bicycles, and horses are prohibited on trails. Bottles and cans are allowed in the picnic areas but not on the trails.

From Seattle, drive I-90 or SR 520 east to I-405. Drive north on 405 to exit 20A, N.E. 116th Street. Drive west on 116th to 98th Avenue N.E. in Kirkland. Cross the intersection and continue on Juanita Drive. In about 4¾ miles turn left on N.E. 145th Street, where signs announce the Saint Thomas Center and the Milham Recovery Center. Don't look for a state park sign on Juanita Drive; as of early 1987 it doesn't exist. A state park sign *is* noticeable on the right *immediately after* you make this turn, but not before. In two-tenths of a mile turn right. In another two-tenths arrive at

The Beach Trail winds among salal and cottonwoods

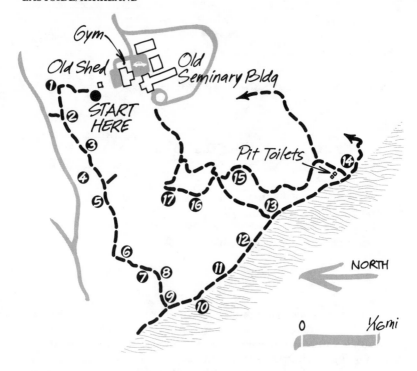

the parking lot. The largest building is the old seminary; the building to the right is the gymnasium.

There are five miles of trails in the park. The route described below combines three trails—the Gym Trail, Waterfront Trail, and Beach Trail—to form a one-mile loop that samples ravine jungle, upland forest, and lake-shore woods. To find the Gym Trail, the first leg of the loop, walk around either end of the gymnasium to the parking lot (usually closed) on the north side. The Gym Trail heads into the woods behind a small shed that is located at the edge of the woods on the opposite (north) side of the parking area from the gym. The trailhead is unmarked.

The path meanders on the level through the forest for about 100 yards, then drops steeply but briefly to a set of steps with a western red cedar stump on the right. Two shrubs—salal and red huckleberry—are among the plants growing on this stump.

(1)   Plants become established on a stump or log when their seeds or spores are carried there by birds, small mammals, or the wind. Like most forest plants, those growing on stumps or logs require the assistance of certain beneficial fungi that, depending on the fungus species, either sheathe or invade the roots of the young plants to form compound structures called mycorrhizae. These structures enable the host plants to provide the fungi with the products of photosynthesis, and the fungi to provide their hosts with certain otherwise unobtainable nutrients, vitamins, and growth regulators. The relationship is an example of symbiosis, an intimate, mutually beneficial association between unrelated organisms.

Beyond the steps, the trail descends steeply through a luxuriant mixed forest of big Douglas firs and western hemlocks, with sword fern, lady fern, bedstraw, candyflower, and salmonberry flourishing along the way. In some thirty yards descend more steps and come to a side trail on the right that angles back and down to the stream.

(2) Opposite the side trail, on the left side of the main path, is a good-sized western hemlock with a second, somewhat smaller one growing next to it. The flaring, stilted base of the larger tree indicates that it, at least, began its life as a seedling on a fallen log that has since rotted away. Just down the trail from here (see following paragraph), is a log with two young hemlocks thriving on it. As evidenced by the numerous tiny cones hanging from the branchlets and littering the ground beneath the trees, western hemlocks produce cones in profusion, each containing thirty to forty tiny seeds. Each of the seeds has a wing, which allows it to ride the wind for great distances. Even a light breeze will carry seeds as much as one-half mile from the parent tree.

Passing a fern slope in mossy woods, the trail comes to a large stump on the right with a couple of western hemlocks growing on top. Compare the roots of the larger of these two hemlocks with those of the mature tree you just left. About twenty yards down the trail is a triple-trunked bigleaf maple decorated with mosses and ferns. More maples, as well as alders, grow upslope on the left. Young conifers are scattered among the deciduous trees. Past the maple, the trail is graced in spring and summer with the beautiful green plumes of lady fern. In winter, only the evergreen sword fern will be in evidence. Where the trail begins a short, gradual climb, look for vanilla leaf.

(3) Each vanilla leaf plant consists of one leaf and one flowering stalk. The leaf consists of three roughly triangular leaflets arranged in a whorl at the end of a wiry stem about a foot long. The cluster of minute white flowers is held above the leaf on a second slender stalk that often pokes up between two of the three leaflets. Each plant sprouts from an underground runner, so that if you see one you will probably see many. When dried, the leaves have a mild vanillalike fragrance. In the early days, bundles of the leaves were hung in rooms as an air freshener or placed with laundered clothes and linens to sweeten their smell.

The trail levels out, traverses a steep slope, and passes more stumps. Along this section of the trail, the ravine supports a lush garden made up mainly of salmonberry, lady fern, and exceptionally tall devil's club.

(4) Devil's club and lady fern in particular are indicators of water at or just below the surface. The dampness of the ravine is largely the result of gravity, as both surface runoff and underground water move downhill.

A view through the forest at St. Edwards State Park

The gradual shift in available moisture from the upper slope to the bottom of the ravine is mirrored by a corresponding change in vegetation.

About fifty yards past station 3 above, keep an eye out for a western red cedar that is riddled with woodpecker holes, on the right, immediately next to the trail. About sixty yards beyond the cedar, where a very steep, narrow trail comes downslope on the left, the good-sized conifer on the right is Douglas fir. Thirty yards beyond is a western red cedar three to four feet in diameter growing right next to the trail. The trees downslope, with lush blue-green foliage, are western hemlocks. As you walk along the trail in spring and summer, you may catch sight of one of the most beautiful songbirds in the Pacific Northwest—the western tanager.

(5) From late spring through early autumn the western tanager is one of the more common residents of both mixed and coniferous forests throughout the region. The male has a bright red head, yellow body, and black back, wings, and tail. He looks like—and, in fact, is—a visitor from the tropics, a gay caballero in the somber northern forest. The female is a plain yellow green—perfect camouflage while tending the nest. Even the male tanager is seldom noticed, partly because tanagers spend most of their time high in the forest canopy, and partly because the bird's bright

colors blend into the bold lights and shadows of the foliage. The bird is perhaps best detected by listening for its seemingly incessant *pet-er-ick* call. The tanager's song, less often heard, resembles that of a robin, but is lower, hoarser, and less exuberant. Flying insects, which are caught on the wing in flycatcher fashion, are the chief item in the bird's diet.

The trail levels out among big firs, hemlocks, and occasional cedars and, in about ninety yards, passes through a damp area with abundant shrubs and ferns. Descend beneath red alder and bigleaf maple into more open woods, and walk under a tree that lies across the trail (it may be cleared away by the time you get there). The trail bends left and begins to drop steeply, turning left again and passing a stump with a young hemlock growing on it. Just beyond a sharp S turn there is a large red alder on the right with a double trunk, one of which is dead and broken off about twelve feet above the ground. Directly across the trail from the alder is a red cedar with woodpecker holes.

(6) The large size and more or less rectangular shape of these holes indicate that they are the work of the pileated woodpecker. This grand bird is nearly the size of a crow and sports a flashy red crest. It feeds on carpenter ants, bark beetles, and other insects found in dead or decaying trees, logs, and stumps. Old-growth conifer forests are its favored haunts, but in the Northwest it also frequents second-growth woods where residual snags provide suitable nesting and feeding sites.

Beyond the cedar, the grade eases and passes among large western hemlocks on the right. Western trillium is also common along this part of the loop. Off to the right, Lake Washington is just visible through the trees. Twenty yards past the woodpecker tree, the trail curves right, begins to descend, then levels off. Seventy yards beyond the woodpecker tree, the trail crosses a pair of fallen logs, then goes alongside one of them.

(7) Although a variety of insects, fungi, and bacteria labor diligently to decompose fallen trees, a large log may take 300 years or more to waste away. This gradual process of decay helps to stabilize the forest community by ensuring a reliable long-term source of essential nutrients.

From the log the trail drops fairly steeply (this stretch is slippery when muddy) and enters a beautiful second-growth Douglas fir forest. California hazelnut, ocean spray, and cascara form a well-developed understory layer. A bench provides a welcome place to rest and enjoy the beauty of the woods.

(8) The most noticeable difference between forests and other plant communities is the vertical dimension: forests are taller than other communities, and that is not a trivial distinction. The ample space beneath the canopy formed by the tallest trees allows the development of several layers of plants, each with its particular opportunities, or niches, for various types of animals. Animals such as squirrels and birds are able to move freely from layer to layer and may even use one layer for feeding and another for nesting. Other animals are confined to only one layer or perhaps a couple of adjacent ones.

About ninety yards downhill, the Gym Trail ends at the lakeshore, where it intersects the Waterfront Trail. This next leg of the loop offers a special treat duplicated nowhere else in the region—a walk along the last remaining stretch of wild, wooded Lake Washington shoreline! No Sunday magazine dream homes, no docks, no manicured lawns, no tennis courts . . . just unruly forest and gently lapping water.

For a short side trip, turn right at the junction and in forty yards, among a ground cover of periwinkle, a cultivated perennial, look on the right for the scant brick remains of an old homestead. Just beyond it, an old Douglas fir, girdled by a cable and dying on the landward side, leans precariously out over the water. From this point return to the junction with the Gym Trail and meet the three most common trees along this shoreline.

(9) The shoreline forest consists mostly of black cottonwood, red alder, and Oregon ash, all three of which grow here at the junction. The cottonwood and ash grow side by side in the middle of the trail. As you face the trees so that the lake is behind them, the cottonwood is the one on the left; the ash, on the right. Alders are leaning over the lake. In summer the three deciduous trees are most easily distinguished by their leaves. The cottonwood and alder both have leaves that grow alternately on the stems. The cottonwood's leaves are triangular; the alder's are more or less oval, with straight, parallel veins and doubly toothed margins. The ash's leaves are compound, that is, they consist of five to seven individual leaflets arranged in opposite pairs along the stem, with one odd leaflet at the tip. What's more, the leaves, as distinct from their leaflets, also grow in pairs on the twigs, unlike those of the cottonwood and alder. In winter the trees are most easily distinguished by their bark: The alder's bark is smooth and blotchy; the ash's is closely furrowed and cross-hatched; the cottonwood's is deeply furrowed.

Turn left (south) on the Waterfront Trail and in about forty yards come to an open area with a good log for sitting and viewing the lake. About a hundred yards farther, the trail swings down to the water's edge.

(10) Submerged just offshore is a "petrified forest" of Douglas fir. About a thousand years ago, a massive mudslide pushed the entire stand of trees en masse and upright across a bed of slick clay and into the lake. Because of the dark, silty environment, the trees just don't disintegrate. When the opening of the Ballard Locks in 1916 caused the lake level to fall, the tops of several of these firs were exposed, and these trees had to be blown up to make the area safe for navigation.

In about eighty yards, the trail jogs left. Salmonberry and thimbleberry are abundant. Notice here, and for that matter all along the trail, the numerous leaning and fallen trees, including cottonwoods, alders, ashes, maples, and even madronas.

(11) The tilting and toppled trees so prominent along the lake shore are victims of soggy ground combined with southwesterly storm winds,

Woodpecker holes in western red cedar

which hit this exposed shore with full force. Cottonwoods and alders are especially vulnerable. And while Oregon ash has a massive spreading root system and is considered to be fairly wind-firm, this double jeopardy is more than even it can withstand.

After passing through a stand of large cottonwoods, the trail meanders along the water's edge, arriving at an open area where two madronas lay toppled in the lake (at least as of January 1987).

(12)   Notice how the steep slope on the east side of the trail stops short of the water's edge, while the Waterfront Trail follows the level bench that lies between that slope and the lake. This bench appears to be an old, formerly submerged, wave-cut terrace that was exposed when the lake was lowered in 1916. Before then, the slope must have dropped directly into the water. Each winter the lake level is lowered to reduce erosion, exposing a succession of delightful, sandy pocket beaches along this shore.

The trail runs right along the water, with views west across the lake to

Seattle. Orange honeysuckle and cascara grow on the left-hand side. About seventy yards beyond the opening, the trail veers left and crosses a damp area with common horsetail, Himalaya blackberry, and Indian plum conspicuous in spring and summer. The lush growth of ferns on the adjacent slope suggests that springs surface on that hillside and that they are responsible for the dampness of the flat as well. Eighty yards past the area, just beyond a path entering on the left, look in spring and summer for Cooley's hedgenettle and skunk cabbage.

(13) Like skunk cabbage, Cooley's hedgenettle is an indicator of well-watered soil. Its leaves superficially resemble those of the unrelated stinging nettle, but its square stems and spectacular spikes of showy magenta flowers make identification easy in summer. The flowers bloom from June through August, when they are visited regularly by rufous hummingbirds. In the process of extracting nectar from deep within the throat of the flowers, the hummingbirds brush against both the pollen-bearing anthers and the pistil. In this way the birds pick up pollen from one plant and deposit it at another. Salmonberry and orange honeysuckle also depend on hummingbirds for pollination; both plants are common along the trail.

In some sixty yards the trail moves back to the water's edge. After passing another path on the left, it rises a little above the water, crosses a small log, and bangs up against a huge, uprooted cottonwood that kids will love to climb over but adults will prefer to walk around. A small path leads around the left end of the fallen giant and regains the main trail. Not far beyond, at the edge of an open, grassy area known as "the beach," there is a huge black cottonwood that has been hollowed out, but not killed, by fire. This is a good place to pause (pit toilets nearby) and enjoy the lake view.

(14) During the spring and summer, troops of swallows swoop back and forth over the water, hawking for insects from dawn to dusk. Barn swallows forage close to the water, or ground, for their deeply forked tails make them among the most acrobatic of fliers. Less agile violet-green swallows feed at higher levels. Since flying insects are scarce during the winter, both species migrate southward each fall and return north in the spring to nest. Violet-green swallows arrive in March; barn swallows, about one month later.

At "the beach" leave the Waterfront Trail and turn left on a broad track heading away from the lake into the woods. This is the Beach Trail, which winds back up the slope to the parking area. On the left are pit toilets. On the right a narrow side path provides an alternative route back up to the old seminary grounds. Shortly beyond the pit toilets the trail begins to ascend and then turns left to begin a series of broad, well-graded switchbacks up the hillside. At the turn, there is another second side trail on the right; like the one before, this too leads to the top.

The trail ascends moderately amid maples and red cedar. Sword fern is common on the slopes. Candyflower, fringecup, youth-on-age, and large-leaved avens line the path. Where the trail bends right, there is a bench on the left. Just beyond, the entire slope is covered in summer by a dense stand of stinging nettle. Continue climbing beneath a canopy of maple, scattered Douglas fir and red cedar, and a few madrona. Down in the bottom of the ravine, some hundred yards beyond the bench, is a huge old bigleaf maple with large colonies of licorice fern on the trunk and branches.

(15) Named for the flavor and scent of its rhizome, or rootstalk, licorice fern can be seen in abundance on every forest walk in this book. The fronds, usually less than twelve inches long, sprout singly along the rootstalk, which probes crevices and moss colonies for moisture. Rather than growing in the ground, licorice fern anchors itself to trees or rocks. It is not a parasite, however, because it steals nothing from its host, which is used solely as a means of physical support. The best time to see the fern is during the rainy season, from fall through spring. As the dry summer period approaches, the fronds wither away. New fronds take their place, however, with the first fall rains.

The trail now swings left amid a glorious fern garden, in which the slopes on either side are covered with sword fern and, in spring and summer, a smattering of lady fern. About eighty yards beyond the turn, come to a small bench on the left and beyond it a rail fence on the right, where a muddy path heads steeply uphill. Keep left, and as the trail rounds a bend gently to the right, look for California hazelnut on the left.

(16) In spring and summer the hazelnut can be recognized by its thin, papery-feeling, maple-shaped, light green leaves. In late winter, the shrub's yellow-green pollen-producing male flowers appear clustered in droopy catkins. Female flowers, which develop into nuts, are borne in pairs and may be recognized by the bright red-tipped pistils. Male and female flowers appear on the same plant.

In another sixty yards or so, as the trail continues winding upslope, it enters a stand of second-growth Douglas fir.

(17) Douglas fir requires mineral soil for germination and abundant sunlight for seedling growth. Since neither resource is widely available in old-growth forests, young Douglas firs are usually scarce even where mature firs are plentiful. Douglas fir grows rapidly and is often the first conifer to invade burned areas. Fire not only exposes mineral soil but contributes nutrients in the form of ash. The practice of burning logging slash following a clearcut is an attempt to emulate the post-fire habitat favored by Douglas fir. Where slash is left on the ground, red alder is likely to replace Douglas fir as the most abundant pioneer tree.

The trail switchbacks right, then bends left, and then parallels a rail fence. About forty yards beyond the fence, the trail passes a path on the right and skirts a gate meant to exclude trail bikes or aberrant autos. Beyond the gate the trail emerges onto the great lawn surrounding the old seminary building. The route back to the parking area is obvious.

12

O. O. Denny Park

Distance: ¾ - mile round trip
Season: all year
Highlight: largest Douglas fir in King County
Metro: 260

Located northwest of Juanita, on the eastern shore of Lake Washington, O. O. Denny Park combines a small but lovely beach, a well-groomed picnic area, and perhaps the most impressive big trees of any park in this book. Among the folks who throng the beach on warm summer weekends, few even realize that the forest exists or that the park extends up the ravine on the other side of Holmes Point Drive.

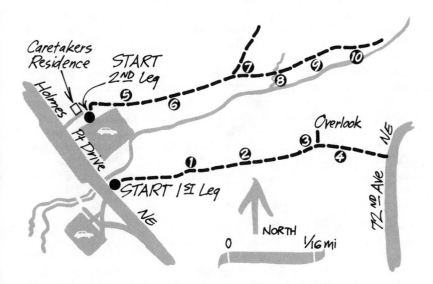

King County's largest Douglas fir in O. O. Denny Park

There are two trails in the park, one extending up each side of the canyon. Both are brief; both are worth taking; both may be combined into a single, leisurely, hour-long walk.

The park also offers a fine view across the lake to Seattle and southward to Cougar Mountain (Walk 19). Rest rooms and picnic tables are located near the lake. O. O. Denny Park has one other distinction: It is a Seattle City Park located outside Seattle. The property was purchased as a summer retreat by Seattle's pioneer Denny family, who later turned it over to the city.

From Seattle, drive I-90 or SR 520 east to I-405. Drive north on 405 to exit 20A, N.E. 116th Street. Drive west on 116th to 98th Avenue N.E. in Kirkland. Cross the intersection and continue on Juanita Drive. In about two miles turn sharply left on 76th Place N.E., which drops steeply down to the lake. Holmes Point Drive begins where the road turns sharply right to parallel the shore. The entrance to O. O. Denny Park is on the left (west), about one mile from Juanita Drive.

From the main parking lot, cross the road and find the first trail on the right-hand (south) side of a culvert. The trail climbs moderately through second-growth forest of fair-sized western red cedar and Douglas fir. Sword fern and Oregon grape are thick beneath the trees. The trail swings left, then right, coming shortly to a Douglas fir leaning out over the ravine.

(1) Heavy winter rains saturate the soil and lubricate soil particles, causing them to slide past one another more easily. The resulting soil creep causes trees on steep slopes to lean outward at increasingly precarious angles until, finally, they topple. Where the root ball is torn out of the ground, the exposed soil erodes more quickly than on the plant-covered slopes nearby, and runoff channeled into the depression begins to cut away a gully. Plant roots anchor the soils of steep slopes. Where vegetation is removed or drainage altered by roads or other development, slides are frequent. Each winter, Puget Sound residents read of someone's home, or sometimes even an entire street, slipping downhill. This is regrettable for those involved but also inevitable given the region's unstable slopes and heavy rains. Such is the real price of a hillside lot.

The trail now skirts the left side of a downed log, then passes through a portal consisting of a red cedar on the right and Douglas fir on the left. Look for Oregon grape, salal, false Solomon's seal, California hazelnut, red huckleberry, vanilla leaf, and trail plant. Pass under a fallen red cedar suspended more than a dozen feet above the path. Just beyond, look for wild roses on both sides of the trail.

(2) Three species of wild rose grow in the Puget Sound region: Nootka rose, little wild rose, and this one, baldhip rose. In addition, there are garden escapees, old-fashioned European varieties that are not unlike our wild native species. The baldhip rose has two distinguishing features: First, its stems are covered with small, straight, delicate thorns; second, its small, red, pear-shaped fruits, or hips, are free of sepals.

Detail of salal leaves

Just beyond the roses, come to a mossy log with foamflower growing on it, after which the grade begins to ease. Pass through a corridor of red cedar and Douglas fir and come to a junction. The left-hand trail leads to an overlook. Since there is no guard rail, children should be closely watched here.

(3) Throughout the Puget Sound region, ravines have served as forest sanctuaries because in the early days of logging it was too difficult to drag the trees out. And why bother when more accessible timber was so readily available? As a result, most of the best remaining old trees in the region are found in narrow ravines such as this one. Even where ravines were too wide to exclude loggers, they were subsequently ignored by home builders, so that second-growth woods quickly sprang up in the wake of logging. It is therefore not surprising that most of the region's parks are located in ravines.

Beyond the junction the trail continues through well-developed second-growth forest with trees up to three feet in diameter.

(4) In late spring this entire area is covered with the tiny seedlings of bigleaf maple. The maple seeds sprout readily, but most of the seedlings will die for lack of light or water.

The trail emerges from the forest at a paved road. Retrace your steps to Holmes Point Drive and walk east along the highway to the overflow parking lot, just across the creek.

The second leg of the walk begins just behind the house on the far (north) side of this dirt parking lot. A sign excludes trail bikers. The path runs along the fence, then turns right into the greenery. Maples and alders are overhead. There is a red cedar on the left. Indian plum, salmonberry, and California hazelnut are the most obvious shrubs. Sword fern, candyflower, bleeding heart, and waterleaf grow along the trail.

Much of this trail follows planks and boardwalks across poorly drained ground. After passing summer growths of lady fern and skunk cabbage on the left, come to the first of these walkways and, nearby, the first sign that this forest has something a little different to offer.

(5) The large conifer on the left side of the trail is western red cedar, which is highly prized for the beauty and durability of its wood. This tree is about five feet thick near the base and is free of branches for the first twenty feet or so above the ground. Continuing on, pass an even larger red cedar, with a secondary trunk fused with the main one near the base. Both trees date back to a fire that swept through this forest a century ago, elminating cedars but scarcely charring the thick bark of giant old Douglas firs. The large size of these "young" cedars attests to the excellent conditions for growth found in this ravine—namely, ample moisture and shelter from high winds. Near the base of the second tree, look for sword fern, bracken fern, bedstraw, Pacific blackberry, candyflower, fringecup, and bigleaf maple seedlings.

Not far beyond is an old stump with a young western hemlock growing from the top and red huckleberry from the base.

(6) Here, on the right side of the trail, is one of the largest black cottonwoods to be seen on any of the walks in this book. The trunk is about five feet in diameter at the base and retains that thickness for perhaps thirty or forty feet. The cottonwood is a close relation of Lombardy poplar, a common street tree throughout the Northwest, and of quaking aspen, which in our region grows mainly east of the Cascade crest. The leaves of all three trees turn brilliant yellow in autumn.

Pass summer growths of lady fern on the left and arrive at a fork in the trail. The left fork winds uphill amid big trees to an overlook perched high above the ravine. The trail, however, is often muddy and overgrown. Here at the junction is a bench.

(7) The dead tree at the junction is bigleaf maple. Note how licorice fern, which most commonly grows on live maples, persists on this dead one. The snag attracts the probings of woodpeckers, whose holes are in evidence, and provides perches from which birds such as the western flycatcher may sally forth to capture insects on the wing.

Cross another plank walk and pass a fair-sized Douglas fir on the left. A little way beyond, on the right, is a huge fallen log, which angles down into the ravine.

(8) This is a classic nurse log—that is, one that supports a nursery of young plants on its back. The little tree growing on it is western hemlock, which often begins life on such fallen giants. Red huckleberry, sword fern, and California hazelnut, along with the usual complement of mosses, also grow on the log. Each of these plants was probably established here in a different way. A bird very likely deposited the seed of the red huckleberry here in its droppings. A squirrel probably carried hazelnuts here but overlooked one. The spores of ferns and mosses were wafted here by breezes.

Pass a large red cedar and cross a boardwalk lined with large lady ferns, water parsley, and youth-on-age. Just beyond the planks, on the left, is another large red cedar and a multi-trunked bigleaf maple. This is a good spot to look for bleeding heart, candyflower, and Pacific blackberry. From there, enter a tunnel formed from the overarching boughs of California hazelnut.

(9)   The nut of the California hazelnut is very similar in appearance and taste to the domestic variety, or filbert. Anyone who has either type of hazelnut growing in the yard at home knows how greedily the local eastern gray squirrels devour the nuts, eating them while still green. The small, wild, Douglas squirrels, or chickarees, do the same. Mice, jays, and crows also relish hazelnuts.

Step onto another plank walkway. In spring and summer, especially on warm days, the heavy smell of stink currant, which grows abundantly here, is noticeable. On the left is a fire-scarred Douglas fir at least five feet in diameter. Another big fir grows on the right and a few yards uphill. But these trees scarcely prepare you for the one growing just ahead: a Douglas fir of Olympian proportions.

(10)   A bronze plaque at the base of the tree proclaims it to be "King County's Largest Douglas Fir." Although there are trees left in the Cascades that rival this fir in size, it surely is monarch of the greater Seattle metropolitan area. The plaque says the tree is 255 feet tall, 26.5 feet in circumference (8.5 feet in diameter), and 575 years old. To metropolitan walkers who have had their fill of alders and second-growth conifers, this fir and its companions in O. O. Denny Park are a boon. This is what Seattle and suburbs were like before they became Seattle and suburbs.

The trail continues only a short way beyond the fir. Near its end, however, there is a side trail leading down to the creek. The junction is marked by a big upturned red cedar stump, which was sawed to make way for the trail. The red cedar hedge on the left sprouted from a secondary trunk that branched off the tangle of roots.

From this point return to the parking area.

13

EASTSIDE/REDMOND

Farrel-McWhirter Park

Distance: ½ - mile loop
Season: all year
Highlights: woods, children's farm
Metro: 251 (½-mile walk to trailhead)

Farrel-McWhirter Park is a sixty-eight-acre woodsy-pastoral oasis on the outskirts of ever-growing Redmond. A large, open central green, with orchard and model farm, is surrounded by second-growth forest. Two miles of trails explore the peripheral woods, and Charlotte's Trail, an asphalt path that is perfect for wheelchair-bound visitors, travels the length of the park. The walk featured here is along the Mackey Creek Watershed Trail, a self-guided nature loop.

An equestrian trail forms a 1.5-mile loop along the edge of the park. This trail is popular with local riders, who are legion, with the result that during the rainy season it quickly degenerates to muck. At the north end of the park, however, the equestrian trail links up with the Puget Power/City of Redmond Multi-Use Trail, providing access to the park from the Metro bus stop on Avondale Road. The distance from Avondale Road to the park is about one-half mile.

There are picnic tables, cooking shelters, swings, and plenty of room for play and exploration. Rest rooms are located in the farm area in a converted silo, the top of which is a lookout that most children will find irresistible. Nearby is a restored barn with old farm implements and, best of all, numerous animals, including pigs, rabbits, goats, ponies, ducks, and chickens.

The land occupied by the park was purchased in the 1930s by the McWhirter family of north Seattle, who built the farm as a summer home. Elise Farrel-McWhirter, who had trained horses here, willed the property to the city of Redmond for use as a park. It was turned over to the city following her death in 1971.

Spotting mushrooms among young forest of Farrel-McWhirter Park

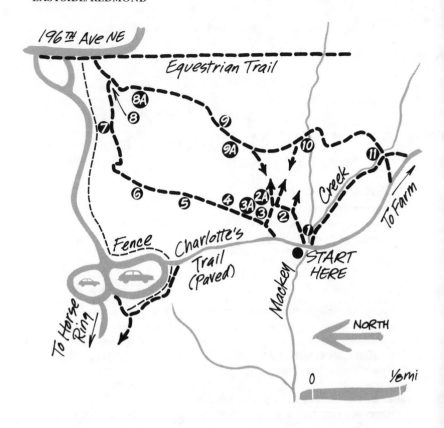

Farrel-McWhirter Park is open every day year-around from 8:00 A.M. till dusk. Brochures describing park programs are available at operations building, which is located next to the barn. Report emergencies to the park staff, either at the farm office or at the adjacent caretaker's residence. For further information on park programs, or to reserve one of the cooking shelters, call the Redmond Parks and Recreation Department (882-6401).

From Seattle drive SR 520 east, past Marymoor Park (Walk 14), to the signal at Redmond Way. Cross Redmond Way and drive just over one-half mile to Avondale Road. Turn right and in three-fourths mile turn right again on Novelty Hill Road. Drive about a quarter mile to Redmond Road; turn left and proceed another half mile to the park entrance, on the left.

Either turn in here and park at the south parking lot or continue to the north parking lot, which is smaller but closer to the beginning of the Mackey Creek Watershed Trail. On weekends, however, it may be crammed with horse trailers. To reach the north parking lot, continue on Redmond Road to N.E. 116th Street. Turn left and, in just under one-half mile, left again on 196th Avenue N.E. Drive about a quarter mile to the park entrance, on the right. Metro riders can reach this point by walking east from Avondale Road.

From the south parking lot, walk to the farm. Near the silo-turned-rest room pick up the paved Charlotte's Trail and follow it to the trail sign at the Mackey Creek crossing. From the north parking lot follow Charlotte's Trail southeastward to the trailhead. Interpretive booklets are available at the trailhead or from the park office. The following discussions attempt to complement, rather than replace, those in the booklet. The Mackey Creek Watershed Trail begins on the north side of the creek, across the bridge from the trail sign. The trail is easily recognized by its carpet of wood chips.

Along the trail are numbered signposts that correspond to discussions in the interpretive booklet. The following discussions are keyed to them as well. In addition, discussions of features located between the signposts are designated by a number and letter. For example, "(2A)" refers to a feature located along the trail at some point between signposts 2 and 3.

From near the stream, follow the wood-chip trail into the woods. Signpost 1 is located on the right, about twelve yards from Charlotte's Trail.

(1) In natural watersheds, runoff is filtered through the soil, which removes most or all of any pollutants it may contain. In urban and suburban areas, extensive areas of pavement not only increase the rate of runoff and prevent the water from soaking into the soil, but also contribute large amounts of surface pollutants from road oil, garden chemicals, and other sources. The watershed of Mackey Creek here in Farrel-McWhirter Park is largely natural, though the paved areas of nearby roads and even Charlotte's Trail increase runoff and pollution of the stream.

About twenty yards beyond signpost 1, where a faint side trail heads right, the main route turns left. Almost immediately come to signpost 2 on the left.

(2) The forest canopy here is made up of Douglas fir and bigleaf maple. Elsewhere in this forest, the canopy may also include red alder, western hemlock, or western red cedar. The canopy profoundly affects the forest environment in several ways. First, by blocking sunlight, it reserves the forest understory for plants that are adapted to varying degrees of low light. Second, it helps to shelter forest plants from the destructive effects of high winds and heavy rain or snowfall. Third, by lowering daytime temperatures within the forest compared to those outside, it inhibits the evaporation of moisture from both soil and plants. Fourth, by inhibiting the loss of heat at night, the canopy helps protect forest plants from hard frosts. Fifth, the dense foliage of the forest canopy traps fog droplets, which drip to the lower levels of the forest and help to supplement rainfall during the drier summer months. Sixth, the canopy provides habitat for numerous insects, birds, and mammals.

Ten yards beyond, the trail makes a sharp left turn. Two side trails enter here on the right. At the junction with the second side trail, look straight ahead and a little to the right for the exposed root mass of a fallen Douglas Fir.

(2A) Although trees greatly reduce wind speed within the forest, exceptionally high winds, combined with gaps or other irregularities in the canopy, can produce blow-downs such as this. Fallen logs, however, are essential to forest health, mainly through the recycling of nutrients bound up in them. The upper surface of the Douglas fir's exposed root mass, which provides a foothold for seeds, now supports several different kinds of plants. Among them are the evergreen blackberry, an aggressive vine imported from Europe, and the native Pacific blackberry, whose fruit is far superior. The stems of both species can be seen dangling from the roots.

Turn left and in several yards come to signpost 3 on the right.

(3) This fair-sized Douglas fir is one of many that have grown up here since this forest was logged a century ago. Next to it grows a shrubby western red cedar, the type of tree that once dominated this ground and whose giant stumps are still scattered through these woods.

Where the trail turns right, look for buttercups and violets in season. A few steps beyond, on the right, is a fine, airy vine maple, which begins to change color in late September.

(3A) Vine maple is one of the few plants that grow well either in deep shade or full sun. In the forest understory vine maples are typically like this one—open crowned, with elegantly contorted branches and flattened sprays of leaves angled to receive maximum sunlight. Some specimens, however, are small trees with single erect trunks. In openings, such as recently logged or burned areas, however, vine maples usually form medium to large, compact shrubs.

The vine maple grows next to an old fire-blackened red cedar stump with red huckleberry growing on top. Look for signpost 4 on the right, by another large red cedar stump about thirty yards up the trail.

(4) This old stump, and the many others like it found in this forest, are all that remains of the giant red cedars that once grew on this moist slope. The forest was logged about 100 years ago, and at the turn of the century the Peterson Sawmill, one of the largest in the region, was located on the site now occupied by Farrel-McWhirter Park. Growing atop this stump are three young western hemlocks, whose seeds were probably carried here by the wind. Other stumps in the forest host such diverse plants as red huckleberry, western red cedar, sword fern, and salal, as well as mosses, lichens, and fungi. Stumps that foster young plants in this way are appropriately called "mother" or "nurse" stumps; similarly, fallen trees upon which young plants grow are called "nurse logs." Both are commonplace in the cut-over forests of the Puget Sound region.

The trail ascends gently but steadily, passing between two large red cedar stumps. The lush growth of ferns indicates that this is a well-

New growth of western red cedar

watered area. Scattered among the ferns are Indian plum, red elderberry, and red huckleberry.

(5) Shrubs such as red huckleberry, Pacific blackberry, and salal are important in the diet of the Columbia black-tailed deer, which has frequented this park in the past and which still visits from time to time. The foliage of Douglas fir and red cedar is also important. In summer the deer feed as well on a wide variety of herbaceous plants. The black-tailed deer, a geographic race of the mule deer, is adapted to living in the humid coastal forest zone of the Pacific Northwest. Mule deer also occur in Washington, but mainly east of the Cascades.

The next signpost on the left is number 6.

(6) Here, red alders are part of the canopy, while young red cedars grow beneath. Because alders require full sun at all stages of life, seedlings are unable to thrive in the shade of their parents. Individual alders may grow up in sunny places created by a fallen conifer, but large stands of alders invariably spring up on lands where the original forest has been removed by fire, logging, or other disturbance. For that reason, stands of red alders usually consist of trees about the same age.

From signpost 6 the trail climbs gently, turning right, then left, before leveling out. In about twenty yards, look on the left for a small alcove in the undergrowth. Nearby is a bare snag riddled with woodpecker holes.

(7) Downy and hairy woodpeckers both frequent this forest. Black-capped chickadees are also common, particularly among the deciduous trees. In winter, mixed bands of chickadees, bushtits, red-breasted nuthatches, kinglets, and other songbirds work their way through the forest, searching for dormant insects, seeds, and other food. Winter wrens, which do not migrate south for the winter but remain active on their summer grounds, favor conifer stands with old logs and stumps, where they scout for insects. In spring and early summer, when the males are staking out nesting territories, their lively musical song fills the woods. Among the more common mammals of the forest are squirrels and raccoons. Coyotes also frequent the park. Look for their feces, or "scat," along the trail.

Back on the trail, come to signpost 8, on the right, in about fifteen yards. The post marks a so-called "dog hair" stand of young Douglas fir.

(8) Like alder, young Douglas firs require full sunlight for growth, which is why they are uncommon beneath mature Douglas firs. Where local seed sources and other conditions permit, Douglas fir rather than alder may be the first kind of tree established following fire or clearcutting. Dense stands such as this one, in which all the trees are the same age, represent just such an event.

Just beyond the signpost, come to a junction and a bench. The trail left leads to the equestrian trail and 196th Avenue N.E. To continue on the Mackey Creek Watershed Trail, keep right.

(8A) The trail winds through an area overgrown with bracken fern, with scattered smaller amounts of lady fern and sword fern. Bracken fern is easily told by the huge branched fronds. (Lady fern and sword fern, the only other types nearby, both have simple, unbranched fronds.) Bracken is among the first plants to colonize disturbed ground but is also able to persist in later communities, where competition for space, moisture, and nutrients is keen.

Look for signpost 9, on the left, which marks a Douglas fir toppled by the wind in 1981.

(9) Fallen logs serve to channel the movement of ground-dwelling animals within the forest. Some function as bridges for animals across ravines and streams or as elevated highways through dense tangles of vegetation. The same logs, however, pose obstacles for animals unable to climb over or around them.

(9A) On the right side of the trail, across from the signpost, look for trail plant. Just beyond, notice the huge cedar stump with a springboard notch. In the early days of logging, large trees such as this were felled by teams of two men, one on each end of a saw. To avoid the flaring pitch-filled base of the tree, loggers cut notches in the trunks deep enough to insert sturdy boards to stand on. From here to the end of the trail, large red cedar stumps, all with springboard notches, are numerous.

As the trail begins to drop more steeply, sword fern replaces bracken fern as the most abundant understory plant. Pass a side trail and continue downhill to the bridge over Mackey Creek. Signpost 10 is located near the creek.

(10) The most abundant fish in Mackey Creek is coho salmon, which returns to this stream each fall to spawn. The young spend a year or two in fresh water before returning to the ocean. Mackey Creek cohos enter the ocean by way of the Sammamish River, Lake Washington, and the fish ladder at the Ballard locks. The best time to see the spawning is, depending on weather and other circumstance, late September through early October.

Come shortly to a second bridge, this one crossing a smaller tributary to Mackey Creek. Signpost 11 marks this stream.

(11) The surface features of a stream depend mainly on the contours of the streambed. Steeper, shallower stretches are marked by riffles. Pools form as rushing water scours out a depression in the streambed. Fish lie at the head of pools, facing upstream, to await food washed down by the riffles.

From here, you can see the paved Charlotte's Trail. To visit the farm or park office turn left. To return to the beginning of the Mackey Creek Watershed Trail, turn right.

14

EASTSIDE/REDMOND

Marymoor Park

Distance: 2¼ - mile loop
Season: all year
Highlights: Lake Sammamish viewpoint, freshwater marsh, bottomland woods
Metro: 251, 253, 254 (½-mile walk from bus stop on West Lake Sammamish Parkway)

Marymoor Park, at the north end of Lake Sammamish, is the second largest in the King County park system, covering 520 acres. Well known for its extensive picnic area, athletic fields, and bicycle track, Marymoor is crowded most weekends of the year.

Many people who seek natural settings and quiet places to walk avoid Marymoor because they are unaware that one of its features is an informative nature trail that leads through bottomland woods and marshes to a panoramic overlook of Lake Sammamish. Families who come here to picnic can use the trail to walk off overdoses of potato salad.

James W. Clise, a Seattle banker, purchased the land now occupied by Marymoor Park in 1904 for use as a bird-hunting preserve. He began building a lodge, which evolved into the twenty-eight room mansion that now houses the Marymoor museum. Originally named Willowmoor, the property was later developed into a model farm, where the family raised Morgan horses and Ayrshire cattle. The Clises moved to California in 1917 and sold the farm in 1928. Under the name Marymoor, the farm was operated as a dairy from 1941 to 1956. King County purchased the land for a park in 1963.

From Seattle, drive SR 520 east to West Lake Sammamish Parkway in Redmond. Turn right and shortly come to the park entrance on the left. From the entrance drive past the large main parking area on the left and the Willowmoor Farm Historic District and picnic grounds on the right. In

Along the Sammamish River in Marymoor Park

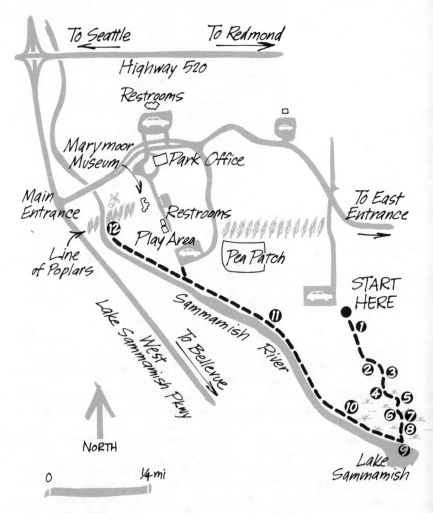

another 0.6 mile turn right on an unpaved road leading to a dirt parking lot in an open field. The paved trail heads south from the lot.

A sign identifies the track as the Marymoor Interpretive Trail and gives its total length as 4800 feet—just under a mile. This is the distance to the Lake Sammamish overlook. From the overlook, however, it is also possible to return along the Sammamish River trail and complete the loop described here by walking across open fields back to this parking lot, for a total distance of just under 2 miles.

A second sign announces that the area is a wildlife preserve. Visitors are urged to stay on the trail and refrain from picking vegetation. Dogs are forbidden. The interpretive signs along the trail are not numbered, and the following discussions complement the information given on the signs.

The trail heads south through an open field past a sign marking the border of the wildlife area. Not far beyond come to an interpretive sign on the left.

(1) Among the birds frequenting this field are savannah sparrow, American goldfinch, kildeer, ringneck pheasant, and common yellow-throat. Small mammals include voles, shrews, and moles. These tiny denizens in turn attract red-tailed hawks, northern harriers, and American kestrels, all of which patrol the fields for dinner. Coyotes and bobcats also patronize this cafeteria.

The trail crosses a wooden bridge over a small creek and turns left. On the right is a second trail sign.

(2) The sign identifies the tree as Piper's willow, one of thirty different kinds growing in Washington. Willows are readily distinguished as a group from other trees, but individual specimens can be difficult to identify, even for trained botanists. There is considerable variation in leaves and other characteristics within single species. Moreover, hybrid trees produced through cross-pollination among different willow species often have intermediate characteristics, making reliable identification futile for all but the experts. All willows belong to the genus *Salix,* from Celtic roots meaning "near water." It is true that most willows either thrive in or require damp, poorly drained soils, where they help to stabilize the banks of lakes, ponds, and streams. Although willow seeds must germinate within twenty-four hours or die, willows are also able to sprout freely from roots and stumps. Moreover, they produce an enormous amount of seed each year, which increases the chance that at least a few seeds will settle in a suitable spot and germinate.

The trail bends right and comes to the next interpretive sign, on the left.

(3) The open fields of Marymoor Park are maintained by mowing, which is presumably done during the fall or winter, after the nesting season is finished. Even so, hardhack and willows are invading the fringes of the field. These shrubs will be replaced in turn by the same trees that grow in the woodlands along this trail—Oregon ash, black cottonwood, and red alder. Ultimately, western red cedars and western hemlocks will replace the deciduous trees in all but the most poorly drained sites. In primeval Washington, before the coming of white settlers, almost all the land was covered with a blanket of conifers. Deciduous woods were restricted largely to the shores of lakes and streams, while prairies such as this were rare and local. Commercial logging and clearing the land for settlement increased the amount of open land and helped deciduous trees invade many areas formerly occupied by conifers.

The trail enters the woods and comes to another interpretive sign.

(4) The sign introduces walkers to this woodland and, through questions, points out that it is cooler, darker, and quieter beneath the trees than in the open. Cottonwoods are readily identified by their heart-shaped leaves and deeply furrowed gray bark. The black cottonwood, which is the largest species of poplar in the world, ranges along the Pacific slope from southern California to Alaska. The largest specimens may be as much as five feet in diameter and more than 150 feet tall. Cottonwoods provide nesting sites for a number of different kinds of birds and in western Washington are favored by beavers for food and building materials.

Several yards beyond, another interpretive sign, on the left, marks a large Oregon ash.

(5) Oregon ash reaches the northernmost limit of its range here in the Puget Sound region, from where it extends southward through western Oregon to central California. Among local deciduous trees it is readily distinguished by its leaves that consist of five to seven leaflets. In fall the leaves, like those of the cottonwood, turn bright yellow, making this a golden woodland. Oregon ash is prized for firewood and was used by early settlers for making tool handles, boxes, barrels, and furniture. In open areas, Oregon ash develops a broad, open crown, whereas specimens such as this one, that grow in dense woods, are tall and narrow. Because the trees are intolerant of shade, when crowded they sacrifice lateral growth for height, reaching sixty to eighty feet.

Just beyond the ash tree the woodland gives way to freshwater marsh. Another interpretive sign marks the transition.

(6) The marsh is a transitional community between the bottomland forest and the submerged aquatic communities in the shallow waters along the shore of Lake Sammamish. The most conspicuous marsh plants are either grasses or grasslike—common cattail, bulrush, sedges, and rushes. Willows, hardhack, red osier, and skunk cabbage are also common. Fresh-water marshes provide critical habitat for numerous aquatic creatures as well as for birds and mammals. Mallard, pintail, green-winged teal, northern shoveler, and American wigeon are among the ducks that find food and cover during the winter in the fresh-water marshes of the Puget Sound region. Unfortunately, many of the finest wetlands have been, and continue to be, lost to urban development.

The pavement ends as the trail follows an elevated boardwalk through the marsh. In spring listen for the scolding chatter of marsh wrens and the "kon-ka-reee" cry of red-winged blackbirds.

(7) Red-winged blackbirds nest in large colonies among cattails and other marsh plants. The males arrive in spring to establish nesting territories, which they defend vigorously against one another. The male's striking red epaulettes apparently function to warn off neighboring males and to attract a mate. During the nesting season, squadrons of red-winged blackbirds aggressively chase away hawks and other predators.

In a few yards come to another interpretive sign, on the left.

(8) The sometimes rank odor associated with marshes comes from gases such as hydrogen sulphide and methane, which are by-products of

the decomposition of marsh vegetation. Decomposition is slow and incomplete in these cold northern waters. As a result, partially decomposed vegetation settles to the bottom, forming layer after layer of peat. (According to the sign, the peat at this location is twelve feet deep.) As peat builds up along the shore, the overlying waters become shallower. Eventually, shrubs such as willow, red osier dogwood, and hardhack, which tolerate high water levels, are able to colonize newly emerged areas. At the same time, as peat and silt continue to accumulate along the lake margins, the marsh and shoreline push outward. (The sign includes a cross-sectional diagram showing the spatial relationship of lake, marsh, and woods.) Given enough time, the process of filling and expanding will completely fill in a pond or lake, forming first a bog, then perhaps a meadow, and finally, a forest. Given the size of Lake Sammamish, however, this successional sequence is unlikely to preclude water skiing any time soon.

The final interpretive sign announces the edge of the lake. Proceed to the Lake Sammamish overlook.

(9) Lake Sammamish, like Lake Washington to the west, occupies a former glacial valley carved out by the Vashon ice sheet, which 15,000 years ago covered the entire Puget Sound region south to Olympia. Like active glaciers today, the ice quarried channels in bedrock and piled the accumulated debris in heaps alongside and at the ends of the channels. Most of the hills scattered about metropolitan Seattle are made up of loosely consolidated glacial debris. The major exception is the range of high hills visible to the south. Known as the Newport Hills, or Issaquah Alps, this range consists mainly of volcanic and sedimentary rocks that predate the continental ice sheet.

Backtrack from the observation deck to where the boardwalk forks. From this point you have two choices. You can turn right and retrace your steps back to the parking lot. Or you can take the left route to follow the boardwalk north along the Sammamish River. The walk is pleasant except on weekends, when hordes of people, most walking their dogs, make this a crowded thoroughfare. In addition, winter flooding may block the trail.

People who elect to walk back along the river follow the boardwalk into a dense and soggy bottomland thicket, where willows, red osier and other plants grow in standing water. The boardwalk ends and the trail enters a small clearing before plunging back into the woods.

(10) This bottomland woodland, growing in a backwater of the lake, represents a transitional stage between the marsh and the drier, more open, and better developed deciduous forest through which the trail passed earlier. Look for skunk cabbage, water parsley, willows, and red osier in the wetter areas; Indian plum, sword fern, red elderberry, evergreen blackberry, red alder, cottonwood, and even young western hemlock, in the drier places.

In just over a quarter mile the trail emerges from the river-bottom thicket and follows the Sammamish River dike through open fields, with

Douglas fir cones

views of the Cascades to the east. In various places the river is lined with alder, willow, or red osier.

(11)   From 1964 to 1970, archaeologists from the University of Washington identified four pre-Columbian sites, two in Marymoor Park and two more just outside the park along the Sammamish River. Excavation of one of the sites yielded a variety of tools made from basalt, obsidian jasper, quartz, chert, and chalcedony. The tools included spear and arrow heads, scrapers, choppers, and small blades. The oldest tools were made about 6,000 years ago, the rest about 3,000 years ago. The artifacts now rest at the Thomas Burke Memorial Washington State Museum on the University of Washington campus.

As you approach the Douglas fir grove that marks the formal picnic and play area, look for a path on the right that leads to a parking lot. From here, you can follow the line of trees eastward across the open fields back to the parking area.

Or continue on the riverside path to the Willowmoor Farm Historic District and picnic grounds for a visit to the museum, rest rooms, drinking fountains, swings, picnic tables, or some combination of the above. At the edge of the picnic area come to a line of stately Lombardy poplars.

(12)   The poplars line what was once the formal drive leading to the mansion. The continuation of these poplars on the opposite side of the river shows that the Clise's bridge across the torrent was located precisely here. The Dutch windmill just north of the poplars is a slightly reduced model built from plans of an actual mill in Holland.

From the Clise museum, you can either follow the park road eastward back to your parking lot. Or you can strike out across the open fields. There is no path, but the way will be obvious to most people.

15

EASTSIDE/BELLEVUE/KIRKLAND

Bridle Trails State Park

Distance: ¾ - mile loop
Season: best summer
Highlight: conifer forest
Metro: 251 to N.E. 70th Street (¾-mile walk to park
entrance)

Bridle Trails State Park features more than 480 acres of wild forest
and some twenty-eight miles of trails, all just a couple of hundred yards
east of I-405. The forest itself is pretty much like any other in the region,
but its size, location, and trail density are remarkable.

As the name of the park suggests, it is dedicated mainly to pursuits
equestrian. There is a training and show arena, complete with judging
stand and bleachers, near the park entrance. And, of course, the trails owe
their existence and maintenance largely to the wanderlust of devoted

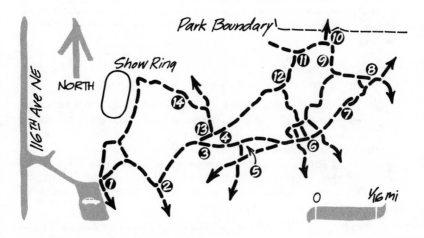

Among the tall trees in Bridle Trails State Park

riders. Even so, two-legged pedestrians are welcome, so long as they are well mannered. That means standing to one side to let horses and riders by.

It would be a mistake, however, to assume that the trails are overrun with horses. At any time of year it is possible to take the walk described below and not meet a beast any larger than a squirrel. The main inconvenience to hikers is that horses can churn large sections of trail into boot-sucking mire, especially during the fall-winter-spring drizzle fest. That's why the best time to walk in the park is during the usual prolonged dry spell of late summer and early fall. Mud-friendly footwear is recommended any time of year.

Rest rooms, drinking fountain, and picnic tables are all located near the show area by the parking lot.

From Seattle drive east on I-90 or SR 520 to I-405. Drive north on 405 to exit 18, N.E. 70th Place. At the stop sign, turn right on 116th Avenue N.E. and drive just over three-fourths mile to the park entrance on the left. Park as close to the northeast corner of the parking lot as possible. There is a choice of three paths: Take the middle one, straight ahead.

(1) Bridle Trails State Park features second-growth Douglas fir forest with a smattering of other conifers and deciduous trees. The park is located on a plateau with porous, sandy soil that dries out during the summer. Deciduous trees and other plants requiring reliable moisture during the growing season are largely restricted to poorly drained areas or shallow draws.

Come to a T junction with a broader path. The way left descends to the equestrian arena. Turn right and in a few yards come to a side trail leading left. Take this path.

(2) The stand of young western red cedars on the right is so shady that few plants are able to grow beneath the trees. Just across the trail, on the left, however, shrubs and wildflowers grow more thickly in the sunny opening.

The trail bends right and comes to a Y junction. Keep right. A couple of yards beyond the junction on the right side is a bracken fern garden with scattered sword fern, Oregon grape, and red huckleberries.

(3) The tender young shoots, or fiddleheads, of bracken fern have long been used as edible greens. Recent research, however, has shown them to contain carcinogens. Although local Indian tribes ate bracken, and though it might be necessary to consume enormous amounts to experience any ill effects, prudence suggests not using the fern for food. In any event, uprooting or cutting plants is forbidden in all public parks.

Not far beyond, the trail tops a gentle rise. On the left are a number of large, lacy, light green shrubs growing in a row.

(4) These are among the largest red huckleberry bushes encountered along the trails in this book. Growing in a line, they appear to have

Oregon grape with berries

sprouted along a fallen log that has long since decayed away. These plants must be twelve feet tall, an exceptional height for this species.

Pass a small side trail on the right. At the junction there is a large, spreading vine maple.

(5) While walking through the park, keep an eye and ear out for the chestnut-backed chickadee. The bird resembles the familiar black-capped chickadee of backyards, but its back and sides are a rich brown, and its cap is dark brown rather than black. Both birds search among the foliage for insects, but they tend to restrict their activities to different types of trees. The black-capped chickadee prefers maples, alders, and other deciduous trees, while the chestnut-backed chickadee normally forages in conifers. In addition, black-capped chickadees forage lower on a tree and closer to the trunk, while chestnut-backed chickadees feed higher and farther out in the foliage.

Keep left at the junction. As the trail bends right, it comes to a long muddy patch. In winter this could be a real mess. Walk along the edge of the path where possible. Pass two more narrow trails heading off to the right.

(6) Notice the dead and dying salal along here. Salal is a drought-tolerant shrub whose leathery leaves help it to conserve moisture. In this part of the woods, at least, the combination of deep shade and rapid drainage seems to be more adversity than even salal can manage.

Not far beyond is another long muddy stretch. In all but the wettest times it is possible to avoid the mud by walking along the edges of the trail. Keep straight at a four-way junction. Just before reaching a small alternative path (which leaves and shortly rejoins the main trail), there is a damp hollow on the right that is lush with mosses and, in spring and summer, with forest flowers.

(7) This spot is just as shady as the one where the salal is dying. The difference is likely moisture. Few plants tolerate dense, continuous shade, but what often seems to be an intolerance of shade is sometimes rather an intolerance of low moisture levels. Forest trees demand—and get—a lot of water. The plants growing beneath them must make do with whatever is left. Where moisture is ample, plants seem able to tolerate more shade than otherwise.

The trail passes the other end of the alternative path, then a second path heading left. At the latter junction avoid the abundant stinging nettle. Then intersect a large track at a four-way intersection. Turn left and come to another muddy area.

(8) The most abundant mammal in this or probably any other forest in the region is the deer mouse. It nests in holes in trees, beneath logs and stumps, or amid dense shrubbery. Unlike other wild mice, it also enters houses and may nest in them as well. A large part of its diet consists of conifer seeds, and the rodent's population may fluctuate with the seed crops. Owls, weasels, coyotes, bobcats, foxes, and other predators help keep populations of the ubiquitous and prodigiously fertile deer mouse in check.

Pass a narrow trail heading left. The trail gradually ascends, curves right, and comes to a small sawed-off stump supporting moss and numerous shelf fungi.

(9) The competition among fungi for the nutrients bound up in dead wood is fierce. The first species to arrive gets the most and may succeed in repelling late arrivals either physically or through the release of toxic substances. This is why dead wood more often supports large growths of one species of fungus than smaller colonies of several.

As the trail curves left, note the slender trees with reddish, peeling bark and trunks that snake upward into the canopy.

(10) These trees are madronas, which favor dry or otherwise poor soils, where competition with conifers is reduced. In this instance, however, the madronas must fight for light and to that end have sacrificed both girth and lower branches in a headlong rush upward.

Come to a trail heading right to a private home and corral. Keep straight and just beyond, turn left at the junction. The understory is sparse, but in spring or fall you may notice some tan mushrooms with mottled white spots, or warts, on their caps.

(11)   The mushrooms are toxic panther amanitas, which cause more cases of mushroom poisoning in the Northwest than any other species. Fortunately, the poisoning is rarely fatal, and the symptoms normally disappear within twenty-four hours. But what a twenty-four hours! During that time, victims may experience delirium, hallucinations, raging, muscle cramps, loss of coordination, hyperactivity, and deep, comalike sleep.

Pass a low mound in the middle of the trail—all that remains of an old stump—grown over with bracken fern, salal, red huckleberry, and moss. As the trail turns right and heads downhill, look for starflower.

(12)   In winter Bridle Trails State Park is a haven for a bird that closely resembles a robin but has a dark band across its rusty orange breast, patches of the same color on the wings, and a stripe over each eye. this is the varied thrush, a bird rarely seen outside conifer forests. Like the robin, the varied thrush forages on the ground for worms, insects, and other small creatures, but also eats berries in season. Unlike the robin, however, the varied thrush is shy and retiring. When alarmed, it quickly seeks cover on high branches or amid thick foliage. The bird is so elusive that it is often hard to get a good look at it. The song, however, is haunting—a series of clear, deliberate single notes in a minor key, each one higher or lower than the one before and separated from it by a marked pause.

The trail passes another stump and side path, then bends left, enters a muddy patch, makes an S turn, and tops out on a gentle rise. After dropping into an even shadier part of the woods, it crosses another muddy patch and intersects a narrow trail heading right.

(13)   The tall, slender tree with the dark reddish bark is bitter cherry. Like the madronas earlier, it has put all its energy into keeping up with the conifers. It's a losing fight. Bitter cherries don't get much taller than this one, and the conifers have only just begun to grow.

Turn right onto the smaller trail and come to a T junction in a very shady, dry, barren part of the woods. Turn left. The trail bends right and leaves the barrens for lusher, more open forest.

(14)   Abrupt changes in vegetation are common on this plateau. Moisture is at a premium here during the summer months, and slight differences in light, soil, topography, or some combination thereof may be critical in determining the type and amount of plant cover growing from place to place. This slope, for example, benefits from both surface and subsurface drainage from the higher, drier section back up the trail.

The path begins to drop steeply, passing two old stumps on the right and a good-sized bitter cherry on the left. The grade steepens as the trail follows a gully downhill through the woods, emerging from the forest at the equestrian ring. Turn left and follow the fence to the drinking fountain. Turn left again and walk to the parking area.

16

Kelsey Creek Park

Distance: ¾ - mile loop
Season: best spring through fall
Highlights: mixed woods, model farm
Metro: 220, 920 Van

Two major themes in American history find expression in Bellevue's Kelsey Creek Park (as well as Redmond's Farrel-McWhirter Park, Walk 13). One is American pastoral: a storybook farm, complete with animals, set in a manicured pasture watered by a babbling brook. The second is American primitive: a miniature wild woods sandwiched between the rural dream on one side and suburban reality on the other. Standing as a symbol of the journey from primitive to pastoral to modern suburban is the old Fraser log cabin, which dates back to 1888.

Kelsey Creek Park is a great place for family in-town outings. Children will love the farm animals and the nearby play area so much that they may consent to let their parents drag them around the one-mile forest loop. Joggers have a long, pretty circuit of their own. Rest rooms are located between the Japanese garden and the farm buildings. Picnic tables are nearby, but the best tables are two found along the forest loop. The Bellevue Parks and Recreation office is also located in the eighty-acre park, just south of the farm buildings. Further information on this and other Bellevue city parks is available there.

The park is hidden away in the heart of a quiet neighborhood, well away from busy streets. From Seattle drive east on I-90 or SR 520 to I-405. Follow signs for Bellevue and leave the freeway at exit 13, S.E. 8th Street. Drive east beneath the railroad trestle (at which point the road becomes 132nd Place S.E.) and at the intersection with the Lake Hills Connector keep straight. The road turns right, then left, and straightens out to become a quiet, narrow residential street (S.E. 7th). At the stop sign turn left

California hazelnut leaves

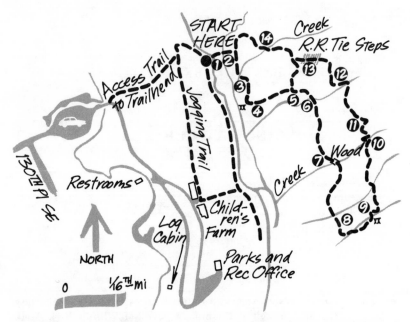

on 128th Avenue S.E., then right on S.E. 4th Place. Drive two blocks and enter the park and parking area.

Bus riders from downtown Seattle should take Metro 253 to the Bellevue Transit Center. Transfer to a Metro 920 *van* and get off at the intersection of the Lake Hills Connector and 132nd Place S.E. From there walk to the park, following the directions given above for automobiles. This walk adds about three-fourths mile each direction.

From the parking lot walk along the park road across the bridge over the west tributary of Kelsey Creek. Just beyond the bridge, follow the path on the left heading uphill through open woods. The path leads over the top of the hill and down the other side to a gravel service road now used primarily for jogging. Turn left on the road and follow it around to the beginning of the trail, on the left. To reach this trailhead from the farm buildings, begin between the two barns and cross the back pastures on the obvious path to the opposite side of the service road. Turn left and in a few hundred feet find the beginning of the trail on the right.

Cross the main branch of Kelsey Creek on a bridge.

(1) Kelsey Creek and tributaries drain sixteen square miles, including most of Bellevue and part of Kirkland. The creek begins at Larsen Lake, about a mile east of the park, but flows north for a mile to where Valley Creek joins Kelsey Creek. From there it turns south through the park, then swings west, picks up Richards Creek from the south, and empties into Mercer Slough. Cottonwoods, alders, and willows grow along the stream. Kelsey Creek supports a remnant of a once-great salmon fishery. Visit the park in late October and you may see a chinook, sockeye, or coho salmon on the last leg of its journey from the Pacific Ocean to its spawning grounds on this stream.

Follow boardwalk and trail through wet woods to a T junction and the loop proper. From here the trail can be walked in either direction. To follow the description below turn right.

(2) Here at the junction is a large bigleaf maple with ferns and fringecup growing on it, and Pacific blackberry crawling over its base. Maples and alders are the most common trees in this forest. Conifers are scattered and few in number. Of these, western red cedar is probably the most numerous. Judging by the stumps scattered through the woods, cedar appears to have been a prominent member of the original forest.

Walk through an open bigleaf maple woodland with an understory of vine maple. Common shrubs are salmonberry, Indian plum, California

Lush growth of vine maples and tall stinging nettles

hazelnut, and thimbleberry. The route then turns sharply left and follows a boardwalk across another wet area. Along this section look on the right for large, rangy shrubs with single stout spines growing at intervals along the stems.

(3) These shrubs are straggly gooseberry, one of several species of gooseberries and currants growing in the region. The black, sweet berries, which mature in late summer are relished by birds. Gooseberries and currants host white pine blister rust, a fungus that has caused serious losses among western white pines in the Northern Rockies. In an attempt to control the spread of the fungus, forestry officials have eradicated gooseberries and currants over large areas where white pines are important commercial trees. Since white pines are scarce in western Washington, however, this fungus is too, and eradication programs are unnecessary.

The boardwalk continues through the damp woods. Pass by large red alders and, where the walk turns sharply right, lady fern and skunk cabbage. Just beyond the end of the boardwalk, there is a red cedar on the left with a trunk nearly three feet in diameter. Vine maple is growing beneath it. On the right, at a sharp left turn, is a picnic table—the second best spot in the park to have lunch. The first lies up ahead.

The route passes a large bigleaf maple with a young Douglas fir leaning against it, then follows boardwalk again. Pass an uprooted tree on the right and, where the boardwalk jogs left, notice the large conifer, also on the right.

(4) This is Sitka spruce, the main tree in the Olympic rain forest. Though Sitka spruce normally grows within a few miles of the coast, it extends inland along rivers for distances of sixty miles or more. Sitka spruce once grew commonly in conifer swamps around Puget Sound but now is rather scarce in the region, thanks mainly to the draining of those swamps.

The boardwalk passes through another luxuriant lady fern garden. Not far beyond the boardwalk, the trail meets a path on the left. Across the main trail from the side path is a tall deciduous shrub whose pointed, egg-shaped leaves have prominent parallel veins that curve upward along the margins.

(5) This shrub is red osier, a species of dogwood. The flattened clusters of small, unadorned, greenish white flowers lack the ring of large, white, petallike bracts (modified leaves) that distinguish its showier cousins, the eastern and Pacific dogwoods. In fall and winter, however, the year's stems turn bright red, contributing a much-needed splash of color to the leafless woods. Red osier grows along streams and in damp bottomlands. The shrub spreads by layering—the sprouting of new plants wherever stems touch the ground.

The trail climbs gradually in open maple and alder woods, curving right and crossing a plank and a couple of small wooden bridges.

(6) Along the damper sections of trail you may see one or more light brown snails with shells whose shiny surface has partly worn away. These snails don't seem to have a common name, but they are known to zoologists as *Allogona townsendia*. Away from the coast they are largely restricted to damp places. They are abundant on this moist hillside.

The trail crosses another small bridge; a nicely shaped vine maple grows on the right. The trail drops again, bends left by a large bigleaf maple, and climbs gradually, passing among young red cedars growing up in the understory. In spring, the lavender-pink, heart-shaped flowers of western bleeding heart make an impressive display along here.

(7) Wherever you find bleeding heart you find bumblebees. The unusual shape of the flower proclaims the presence of nectar to the bees and prevents honeybees and other insects from getting at it.

The trail proceeds to an elaborate wooden bridge that crosses high above a small creek. The trail bends right, passes young cedars and alders, and drops to another short boardwalk over a small creek. Stinging nettle and hedgenettle both grow along the creek, as do water parsley and youth-on-age. The trail then turns right and descends a damp slope to a mossy alder in the middle of its path. Cross a muddy area (boots advised) and come to an old stump that is charred and disintegrating. Beyond the stump the trail levels out and, as it turns left, comes to a small, lively creek.

(8) The shrub on the left, at the creek, is Indian plum, or osoberry. The white hanging flowers appear in March. Their rank odor attracts flies and other insects, which pollinate the blossoms. The red berries appear in summer. Although local Indians ate the fruit, they apparently didn't relish it.

The trail now climbs gradually along the stream, then crosses over it and passes some young Douglas firs on the left. Not far beyond, near where the trail recrosses the stream, is the best spot to picnic in the park—a table set right beside the water.

(9) Vine maples are abundant in here, and the red alders are good-sized. Most of the alders and bigleaf maples on this hillside became established after the conifer forest that once grew here was logged. And since neither type of tree tolerates shade, both will one day be replaced by conifers. Gradually, the tall, straight needle bearers will shade the forest floor, thereby preventing young bigleaf maples and red alders from becoming established. Vine maples, however, do tolerate shade. They were probably present in the old forest and will probably still be present in some future conifer forest, when most of the other deciduous trees on this slope will have long disappeared.

As the trail recrosses the creek, it begins the backstretch of this loop. For the next third of a mile or so the path traverses the steep hillside, rising and dropping, ducking back into shallow gullies, and emerging on the other side. Ignore all side paths.

The trail climbs steeply but briefly, then more gently, and drops down to a small creek, where it turns left. Continue traversing the slope, ascending gradually before dropping once again to another creek, this one with a small bridge.

(10) There is a large cedar stump here with red huckleberry growing on it. The bright red berries, which appear in late summer and early fall, were prized as food by all the local Indian tribes. Rather than picking the berries one by one, the Indians combed them from the shrubs. In addition, some tribes used the leaves to brew a tea.

After crossing the creek, the trail switchbacks, squeezes between a couple of maples, climbs a bit more, then drops and turns right and left. Where the trail gradually descends, look on the left for a large maple with a spacious hole in the trunk.

(11) Holes in trees both living and dead are among the most critical needs of animals living in the forest. Holes not only serve as nests for birds and mammals but provide shelter during fierce storms or spells of frigid weather. This hole is big enough to accommodate raccoons or great horned owls.

The trail crosses another small creek—this time on but a single plank—and continues a descending traverse of the slope amid a jungle of stinging nettle.

Nettle leaves

(12) In and around Seattle, stinging nettle is nearly ubiquitous in cultivated areas, second-growth woods, and damp open places, as well as along roads and highways. It tolerates a wide range of light conditions but requires moist soils, especially those that are rich in nitrogen. Nettle is rare in undisturbed old-growth conifer forests, where the dominant trees hog most of the nitrogen, but it flourishes beneath red alders, which increase soil nitrogen through the action of bacteria in their roots.

The trail curves right and comes to another boardwalk, which crosses a damp slope lush with sword fern, lady fern, gooseberry, youth-on-age, Indian plum, and red osier. Pass a path on the right and come to a set of steps made from railroad ties. The stairway drops steeply among young red cedars. Growing between the ties are fragrant bedstraw, enchanter's nightshade, candyflower, and fringecup.

(13) Since butterflies and bees are not abundant in dark forests, shade plants often rely on flies or other insects to perform pollination. Like many forest plants, those growing between the ties have white flowers, which stand out against the dark background. Visible to all pollinators, white flowers are meant to attract the insect masses. Green or brown flowers are also common among forest plants. Such plants usually rely on strong, sometimes putrid, scents to attract pollinators such as flies and beetles.

After leaving the stairway, pass a trail on the left and come to a plank bridge. Not far beyond, the trail passes a large old bigleaf maple on the right, its trunk hollowed by fire and disease. The way then enters a damp area and crosses a second plank bridge.

(14) Damp woodlands are prime habitat for Pacific treefrogs. These are the smallest and most common of local frogs. Less than two inches long, the tiny amphibians are usually bright green with a dark, white-bordered stripe across each eye. In spring they breed in shallow ponds and quiet streams but soon leave to return to the woods. At night throughout the breeding season, the high croaking chorus of countless male tree frogs fills the forest.

The route curves right, crosses another bridge, turns left, and follows a short boardwalk. After leaving the boardwalk, come full circle to the first junction along the loop. Turn right to leave the woods and return to the parking area.

17

Bellefields Nature Park

Distance: 1 - mile loop
Season: best spring through fall
Highlights: bottomland woods, Mercer Slough
Metro: 220 (¾-mile walk to trailhead)

Welcome to wild Bellevue. Located along Mercer Slough on the southern outskirts of town, Bellefields Nature Park preserves forty-eight acres of marsh and bottomland deciduous woods. Originally, much of this low-lying area was a shallow backwater of Lake Washington, fed by Kelsey Creek flowing in from the north. With the completion of the Seattle ship canal in 1916, however, the level of the lake was lowered nine feet, exposing land bordering the slough. Later, the area was further drained for the purpose of cultivating blueberries and other crops. The largest blueberry farm in Bellevue still operates across the slough from Bellefields Nature Park.

In the land of conifers Bellefields Nature Park offers a refreshing change. Instead of towering firs, hemlocks, and cedars—the usual coniferous fare hereabouts—there are willows, cottonwoods, alders, birches, ashes, crabapples, bitter cherries, maples, and cascaras. In fact, this park is so dominated by deciduous trees that winter, while interesting for textures and, perhaps, ducks, is the least attractive season for a visit. Better to come for the spring flowers, the summer greenery, or the fall color.

The park is crossed by a network of trails, but most of the interior trails are purposely being allowed to return to a natural condition. Signposts— or what's left of them—mark some of the junctions and name some of the paths. Unfortunately, vandalism, neglect, and decay have taken their toll, so that the signs now stand (or tip over) as forlorn reminders of the former maze of trails. The walk described below follows the popular perimeter route, which walkers have managed through persistent tramping and pruning to keep reasonably clear. Moreover, a 1986 volunteer

A tall western red cedar marks the exit of Bellefields Nature Park loop trail

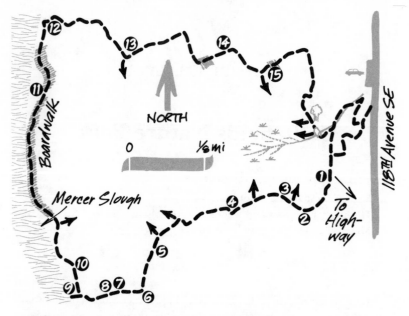

work party rebuilt some of the boardwalks and laid down new bark along the trail. The Seattle Audubon Society has adopted the park in recognition of its value as wildlife habitat. The society helps keep the perimeter trail open to walkers.

From Seattle drive I-90 or SR 520 east to I-405. Follow I-405 toward downtown Bellevue and get off the freeway at exit 12, S.E. 8th Street. Turn west on 8th and, at the first light past the freeway, turn left on 118th Avenue S.E. Drive about one-half mile to the small roadside parking area. The trailhead is along the road, about fifty feet to the south. Follow the fence line into the woods.

The trail heads downhill through woods of bigleaf maple and red alder. Descend to a small stream, cross a bridge, and enter an open area that once served as a pistol range. The trail leading straight ahead toward the odd covered bridge is the return route. For now, turn left and walk to the far (south) end of the area. Here a trail and an old road both head uphill to the highway. The trail to the right of the old road is the one to take. A large sign on the right says:

> This park is a living museum of natural history. Here you are a guest in a plant and wildlife community which is preserved so that you and many others may understand and enjoy it. Your wise use and cooperation are essential to protection of its features.

The sign stands in a small grove of western red cedar.

(1) These trees mark the former shoreline of Lake Washington. Though able to thrive in wet, mucky soils, red cedar has yet to establish itself in the swampy heart of the park. Here, the trees grow at the somewhat drier wetland fringe.

The trail is named Nightshade Avenue for the garden weed that here climbs over and through the shrubbery. Beyond the sign, come to two totem poles and, nearby, six benches arranged in a semicircle, which serves as place for school groups to gather before they enter the wetlands. Push onward into the dense deciduous tanglewood.

(2) The woods and thickets of Bellefields Nature Park comprise one of the region's most varied deciduous woodlands. In the coastal Pacific Northwest, deciduous trees have difficulty competing with conifers because moisture is normally most abundant during the winter, when deciduous trees are dormant, and scarcest during the summer, when they are active. Evergreen conifers, however, are able to assimilate water and nutrients during mild winter periods and become dormant, if necessary, during extended periods of summer drought. Because of their competitive disadvantage, deciduous trees are largely restricted to habitats where human intervention or natural conditions tilt the balance in their favor. Wet bottomlands such as this are one such habitat. Few conifers tolerate the cold, saturated muck, while deciduous trees have a reliable source of moisture throughout the summer growing season.

Pass an obscure, overgrown path on the right and, next to it, a wooded alcove with another, small, hand-carved totem pole.

(3) A narrow strip of herbaceous plants forms a green border on each side of the trail. Here, stinging nettle, fireweed, creeping buttercup, large-leaved avens, and water parsley enjoy the added sunlight along the trail corridor without having to compete with the shrubs and trees of the interior.

Pass by another side trail on the right, as the main path jogs left. Amid the tangle of shrubs and trees lining the trail, look for a small shrub with deeply divided maple-shaped leaves and a few stout spines at the bud nodes along the stems.

(4) This is straggly gooseberry, which bears small, sweet black fruit resembling commercial currants. Also look for swamp gooseberry, whose leaves are similar but whose stems are densely covered with sharp spines. Birds and rodents relish the berries, and deer favor the foliage over that of many other shrubs in the region.

The trail passes yet another side path on the right. Here cascara trees grow among the red alders. After crossing a couple of small bridges the trail enters an open area bordered by dense hedges of wild blackberries. Pass a path heading right and cross a small bridge between two clumps of black cottonwood.

(5) Black cottonwood is the largest deciduous tree in the United States, reaching heights of 150 feet or more, with a trunk up to five feet across. The trees here, though not that large, are impressive nonetheless. Cottonwoods are named for the cottony hairs that cover the seeds, enabling them to catch and ride the slightest breezes. Black cottonwood is common in bottomlands and near lakes and streams throughout the region. The tree's triangular leaves and deeply furrowed bark are distinctive. Like quaking aspen, the black cottonwood is a species of poplar.

The trail crosses another wooden bridge, turns right and enters a small grove. A large old Pacific crabapple is on the left.

(6) Pacific crabapple has egg-shaped leaves, some of which are usually lobed on one or both sides. They turn bright orange or red in the fall. Typical apple blossoms appear in spring, followed in summer by small, red, sour fruit. Pacific crabapple ranges from northwestern California to south-central Alaska and is generally restricted to wetland woods and thickets such as this.

Opposite the crabapple are several bitter cherry trees. Leave the grove and enter a clearing where the trail is lined with tall, coarse shrubs.

(7) These shrubs, called hardhack, are common in wetlands throughout the region. In summer they sport showy pyramid-shaped clusters of pink blossoms. These quickly turn brown and persist through much of the fall and winter. Hardhack is a species of spiraea, some of which are grown as ornamentals.

Growing among the shrubs are a few slim paper birches.

(8) The birches are the trees with the white trunks. Paper birch closely resembles the widely planted European white birch, a common yard, street, and park tree throughout the Puget Sound region. Individual specimens may be difficult or impossible for the casual observer to distinguish. Generally, however, the leaves of paper birch are somewhat longer, and more rounded at the base. Those of European white birch tend to be more triangular, with a flattened base. Paper birch grows abundantly across Canada and in the woods of the north-central and northeastern United States. Scattered groves occur in western Washington—mainly along major streams—southward to the Seattle area. The Bellefields stand may be the southernmost paper birches along the Pacific Coast. Paper birch is named for its thin bark, sheets of which were used by Indians in the Far North and Northeast to cover their canoes.

About thirty yards beyond the birches, the main trail turns north (right). Before making this turn continue ten yards straight ahead to Mercer Slough.

(9) Mercer Slough is a 1½-mile waterway that connects Lake Washington, to your left, with Kelsey Creek, to your right. The slough is lined with willows, red osiers, alders, Himalaya blackberries, and cattails. The path following the edge of the slough is a good place to find Puget Sound garter snakes, which feed on fish, tadpoles, frogs, and other aquatic creatures, as well as toads, tree frogs, birds, and other small land animals. Although the snake is harmless, it may bite or defecate if handled. Mercer Slough also hosts a variety of waterfowl and marsh birds. Look for mallards, coots, great blue herons, red-tailed hawks, and kingfishers year-

Birdwatching in Bellefields Nature Park

around. Green-backed herons and bitterns are summer residents. A good selection of ducks may be found here during the winter months.

From the slough, backtrack to the main trail, turn left, and follow it north along the slough. Thirty yards from the junction, around a small bridge, look for commercial blueberry plants growing among the hardhack, red osier, and willows.

(10) This clearing was once part of an active blueberry farm like the one to the west, across the slough. On the right keep a lookout for some of the old blueberry bushes, which still bear fruit in summer. In winter the bare twigs are conspicuously reddish bronze, while those of nearby red osier are a brighter, truer red.

At the next opening onto the slough, look for a picnic table tucked out of sight around the corner of brush on the left. At a junction with a trail heading right, keep left on the main trail. Beyond the junction, the route bends left and follows a long, winding boardwalk that runs alongside Mercer Slough. Just beyond the end of the boardwalk is a small, isolated grove of trees.

(11) These trees are Pacific willows, which are readily told from other local willows by their dark, furrowed bark and slender, dark green leaves, which have warty glands at their bases. In winter, willows as a group can be recognized by the single scalelike cap covering each bud.

The route continues along the slough on a second, long boardwalk passing willows, red osier, hardhack, lady fern, and cattails. Leaving the boardwalk the trail comes to another opening on Mercer Slough before plunging back into the woods through a winding corridor of alders and shrubs. During spring and winter, these woods and thickets are alive with birds.

(12) The deciduous trees and shrubs of Bellefields Nature Park attract a number of birds that are rarely seen in conifer forests. These include red-eyed vireo, yellow warbler, and willow flycatcher. In spring, listen for the drumming of ruffled grouse, which is largely restricted to deciduous woods and in our region is replaced in conifer forests by the more common and widespread blue grouse.

After passing through a soggy tangle of willow, cherry, and crabapple, the path enters an opening with picturesque crabapple snags. Leaving the snags, the trail zig-zags through damp woods. Just beyond a junction with a side trail on the right, the main trail angles sharply left. About ten yards beyond the turn look on the left for small, straggly shrubs with whorls of droopy, leathery leaves with the margins rolled under and lower surfaces matted with rusty hairs.

(13) The shrubs are Labrador tea, a member of the heath family, along with huckleberry, rhododendron, madrona, and many other local shrubs. Certain Indian tribes steeped the leaves to make a strong tea, which served as a laxative or "blood purifier." The effective ingredient is the toxic compound ledol, which apparently was not present in dangerous concentrations in the Indian brews. Nevertheless, attempting to steep your own Indian tea is not recommended.

The trail continues to alternate between soggy ground, short boardwalks, and little bridges. Where the boardwalks finally end, there are two low signs, one on each side of the trail. (The one on the left warns quite rightly that the boardwalks are very slippery when wet. The one on the right says that the trails are for feet only.) In back of the left-hand sign, look among the red alders for some tall, slim treelike shrubs with small, round leaves.

(14) The shrubs are swamp, or bog birches, which are relatively common in the mountains but rather unusual in the Puget Sound lowlands. Normally, swamp birches are six feet tall or less, but here in Bellefields taller specimens, such as the ones here, are commonplace. Swamp birches are easily identified in spring and summer by their shiny, toothed, fan-shaped leaves, which are about the size of quarters. In fall the leaves turn gold. The sticky, warty twigs are also distinctive. As the name and this location suggest, swamp birch is a plant of wet bottomlands, bogs, and damp meadows.

The trail turns right, angles left and passes a side trail on the right. Keep left and in ten yards come to a wooden bridge.

(15) Numerous skunk cabbages grow in the damp ground on either side of the bridge. In early spring they are recognized by their green club-shaped flower spikes, each partly enclosed by a large, bright yellow bract (modified leaf). Later, the huge, broad leaves—the largest of any plant in our region—are unmistakable. The plant is named for the fetid odor of the flowers, which to many noses does indeed resemble essence of skunk. Others deny the alleged similarity. In either case, the aroma serves to attract various insects, which pollinate the flowers.

The trail crosses a second bridge, then makes a sharp right turn and climbs out of the wetland to a many-branched red cedar, which survives even though its trunk has been hollowed out by fire. Continue to the covered bridge, with its adolescent grafitti and benches. Cross the creek and follow it upstream to retrace your steps up the hillside to the highway.

18

EASTSIDE/BELLEVUE

Lake Hills Greenbelt

Distance: 1½ miles
Season: all year
Highlights: lake, wetlands, shore pines
Metro: 252 (½-mile walk to trailhead on S.E. 16th)

Walk through fields, wetlands, conifer woods, and a working blueberry farm to a small lake, all in the heart of Bellevue. The paved trail is for hikers, cyclists, and joggers, but offers plenty of attractions for just plain old nature lovers. This is an excellent trail as well for the handicapped as it permits wheelchair access.

The Lake Hills Greenbelt is a wetland corridor owned by the city of Bellevue. Located in the Robinswood district, about a mile west of Lake Sammamish, the green belt links Phantom Lake in the south to Larsen Lake in the north. The first section of trail, from S.E. 16th St. to Larsen Lake, was built in the winter of 1986–1987. A second section, from S.E. 16th to Phantom Lake will be completed by the spring of 1988.

From Seattle drive I-90 east to exit 11B, 148th Avenue S.E. Drive past the Mormon temple and Robinswood Park to S.E. 16th St. Those who wish to begin this walk from Larsen Lake should keep straight here, arriving at the trailhead in just under ¾ mile. Park on the shoulder. To follow the trail in the order described below, turn right on S.E. 16th Street and drive ½ mile to the entrance to the pea-patch parking lot, on the left, just before reaching 156th Avenue S.E. Turn left into the parking lot and park here. From the parking lot follow the short, paved path down to the trail.

(1) Here, at the current beginning of the trail, an old house is visible to the east, on the other side of 156th Avenue N.E. This house, built in 1890, was the home of the first farmer to work the land between Phantom Lake and Larsen Lake. Originally, the two lakes were more or less con-

Larsen Lake from the Lake Hills Greenbelt Trail

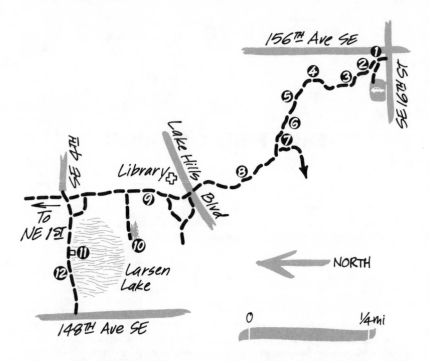

nected: more during high winter runoff periods, less during the drier summer months. Drainage was northward, from Phantom Lake to Larsen Lake, the headwaters of Kelsey Creek. In order to drain the land for crops, a farmer cut a new outlet from the south end of Phantom Lake to nearby Lake Sammamish. When the drainage of Phantom Lake was diverted, the water level in the lake lowered several feet, and the land between Phantom and Larsen lakes was left higher and drier than before. The diverted water also washed out several farms downstream, along Lake Sammamish.

Turn left on the paved trail, which makes a broad S turn through a corn field on the right and a wet thicket of willow and red osier on the left.

(2) Most of the trail crosses a peat bog, where partially decomposed plant remains have piled up over thousands of years. In order to disturb as little as possible the natural flow of water through the peat, a new type of trail construction was employed. A heavy-duty black plastic was laid on the ground and covered with eighteen inches of wood chips. The plastic was then folded over the top of the chips and the flaps sewn together. This flattened tube was then covered with gravel and paved. The trail literally floats on top of the peat bog.

As the trail curves left, notice the blue spruces, a tree native to the Rocky Mountains, on the right. Farther on, where the trail turns right, look for young grand fir growing among the spruces.

Needles of the Grand Fir

161

(3) Although grand fir is native to lowland valleys of the Pacific Northwest, these young trees, along with the spruces were planted by a commercial daffodil farmer. In spring the beautiful yellow flowers, volunteers from bulbs left behind, are much in evidence. Among the first farmers to cultivate the greenbelt were Japanese immigrants, who settled in the area between 1915 and 1920.

The trail turns sharply right, then makes a broad sweeping curve to the left. On the right is a corn field. To the south is a fine view down the greenbelt to the old farm house and, in the distance, cougar and Squak mountains in the Issaquah Alps.

(4) The field and others nearby are leased by the City of Bellevue to a local farmer, who raises corn and other vegetables on the land. He sells his produce each summer from the stand on the corner of S.E. 16th Street and 156th Avenue S.E. In winter, the fields attract flocks of Canada geese, who forage for seeds and small creatures among the stubble.

The trail straightens out and crosses an open field where the most conspicuous plant is hardhack, a member of the rose family and an aggressive invader of damp areas.

(5) Most of the greenbelt has been subject to intense cultivation, and parts still are. The rest is slowly reverting to natural vegetation. Among the first plants to have invaded fallow areas are reed canary grass, which is everywhere abundant, evergreen blackberry, and hardhack. This large, dense stand of hardhack provides food and shelter for some wildlife but greatly reduces the diversity of habitats that might otherwise or eventually occur in this area. The Bellevue park department plans to enhance habitat diversity in the greenbelt by clearing certain areas of hardhack and replanting them with native grasses, shrubs, and trees.

The hardhack gradually gives way to deciduous woods of red alder, willow, bitter cherry, and cascara. Beyond the woods come to an open corridor and a bench on the right.

(6) This corridor was hacked through the wetland two years ago by Metro in order to lay a four-foot diameter sewer pipe along this line. The agency took care to restore the topsoil removed in the course of the project, and the corridor has since grown up to reed canary grass and scattered clumps of Scotch broom. This is a good place to see ring-necked pheasants, which nest and forage among the tall grasses, and California quail, which feed in the grassland but find cover in the woods on each side. Because of the close proximity of deciduous woods, conifer forest, shrub thickets, and grassland in this one small area, it comes alive with birds in late spring and early summer.

The trail enters the conifer forest, which is a mix of native and planted trees. As the trail bends slightly right, begin to look on both sides of the trail for tall, slim conifers with flaky bark and needles attached to twigs in bundles of two.

Himalaya blackberry leaves

(7)   The trees are lodgepole pines, which grow abundantly on the east side of the Cascades but are only locally common west of the mountains. The coastal form of the lodgepole pine is the so-called shore pine, which frequents wetlands and coastal bluffs. Although shore pines grow along this trail (see discussion 10 below), the pines growing in these woods resemble the mountain variety of lodgepole, which differs from shore pine in being taller and slimmer, with a more regular growth habit and lighter green needles. At one time, a nursery backed up on these woods, and these pines may have originated as nursery stock. This is not certain, however. Other nonnative plants growing in these woods include laurel and Norway spruce, both of which are found on the left side of the trail as it leaves the woods up ahead.

The trail passes a neighborhood access trail, leaves the woods, and does a broad S curve through another open field.

(8)   The Lake Hills Greenbelt Trail roughly follows the route of an old Indian trail that led from Phantom Lake to what is now Kirkland. A branch headed west from near Larsen Lake to Mercer Slough, where there was a winter encampment. Other trails headed from Phantom Lake east to near the present site of Fall City and south over Naches Pass, near Mount Rainier, to the Yakima Valley. The Yakima Indians use the latter trail as a trading route. Local Indians used controlled burning to create and maintain open prairies for attracting wildlife and encouraging the growth of valuable bulb plants such as camas.

The trail passes between a Little League field on the left and a softball field on the right, crosses Lake Hills Boulevard (crosswalk), and in fifty yards comes to a neighborhood access trail on the left. The Lake Hills Library is on the right.

Beyond a path heading right to the library parking lot, the trail enters the blueberry farm surrounding Larsen Lake.

(9)   This land has been in blueberry cultivation for about sixty-five years. In fact, the city first purchased the land primarily as a way of preserving Bellevue's agricultural heritage. The current grower leases the land from the city and hopes to bring the plants back after several years of neglect by his predecessors.

Tract homes are now visible on the right, though not so close as to intrude. Come to a grassy path heading left to an open, isolated stand of conifers at the south end of Larsen Lake. The path runs alongside a wire fence erected by the city to keep visitors out of the choicest blueberry plants remaining. The conifer stand is perhaps 200 yards from the trail and is noteworthy because it contains several shore pines.

(10)   The shore pine is a coastal race of the lodgepole pine. Shore pines favor wetlands and sea bluffs and range along the coast and west of the mountains from northern California to southeastern Alaska. Like lodgepoles that grow east of the Cascades, shore pines have only two needles per bundle. The only other native pine found widely west of the

Cascades—the western white pine—has five needles per bundle. All other needle-bearing conifers in the region bear their needles singly.

In about eighty yards the trail forks. The trail straight ahead leads to a shopping center parking lot on N.E. Main Street. Turn left toward Larsen Lake. Keep left again at a second junction and in about 100 yards come to an access path heading left to an observation platform on Larsen Lake.

(11) Since the greenbelt is essentially a long strip, waterfowl, bald eagles, and other birds use it for commuting between Lake Sammamish and Larsen Lake. There are a pair of eagles nesting at Lake Sammamish, and their hunting territory includes the south end of the lake and northward through the greenbelt to Larsen Lake. Canada geese also use the corridor, along with wigeons, gadwalls, mallards, and other species of ducks. Waterfowl are attracted not only by the lakes themselves, but also by the small ponds and drainage ditches scattered through the wetland. Red-tailed hawks nest in adjacent woodlands and hunt in the open fields, as do several species of owls.

Return to the main trail and turn left. In twenty yards come to a wooden bridge over a creek.

(12) This is the beginning of Kelsey Creek, which drains most of Bellevue and the southern portion of Kirkland. From here the creek empties into a control pond at the northern end of the greenbelt. During periods of high runoff, water is backed up into the wetland and released gradually downstream. This protects the lower stream from flood erosion and purifies the water by filtering it through the wetland muck. The new trail should remain elevated above the flood. Beyond the control pond, Kelsey Creek flows north to near Bel-Red Road, then swings south through Kelsey Creek Park (Walk 16) and enters Mercer Slough.

From the bridge, it is another 150 to 200 yards to 148th Avenue S.E., where parking exists on the shoulder along the highway. Since the rest of the way differs in no important respect from much of what has gone before, most visitors will retrace their steps back to the pea patch parking lot on S.E. 16th Street.

A.A. RIDGE TRAIL
← COUGAR PASS
CLAYPIT PEAK

LOST BEAGLE TR
KLONDIKE SWAM
NIKE PEAK →

19

EASTSIDE/ISSAQUAH

Cougar Mountain Regional Wildland Park: Three Snag Loop

Distance: 1½ - mile loop
Season: best spring and summer
Highlights: huge snags
Metro: None

Cougar Mountain Regional Wildland Park is the only large wilderness park in the Seattle-Tacoma metropolitan area. Established in 1984, the newest and largest King County park currently covers 1700 acres of ridges, canyons, streams, waterfalls, ponds, forests, meadows, and swamps—all within twenty minutes of downtown Seattle. Plus it's got bears.

The park isn't untouched—or even slightly touched—wilderness of the Cascade-Olympic backcountry variety. No, Cougar Mountain has been used—and in places, used hard. Coal operations began in what were known as the Newport Hills in the nineteenth century. Logging began then too and continued right up to the present. Following World War II, the military installed rockets and radar on the summits. Road builders envisioned throughways for the canyons. Home builders crept up the hillsides and skinned nearby ridge tops to open up the views. Developers even proposed to build a community of 10,000 people in the heart of the wildland.

The movement to set aside Cougar Mountain as a park began in the late 1970s with the establishment of the Issaquah Alps Trails Club. This informal but dedicated coalition of hikers, naturalists, conservationists, and local residents built trails, led hikes to show people what was there, formulated a park plan, and pleaded, cajoled, persuaded, and harassed

Trail markers in Cougar Mountain Regional Wildland Park

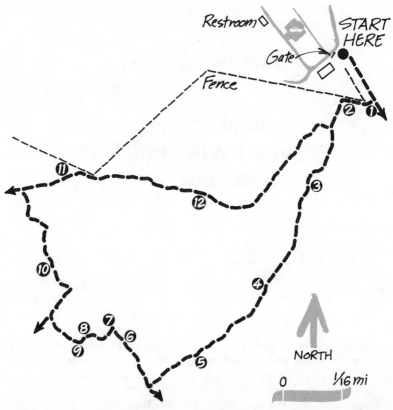

local officials into agreeing that a Cougar Mountain Regional Wildland Park was a fine idea indeed. Thanks to these same hiker-conservationists, more than twenty-five miles of signed and unsigned trails wind through the park.

The loop described here is merely a sample of what awaits hikers in Cougar Mountain Regional Wildland Park. Also see Walk 20, Lakemont Gorge, which lies just outside the park but within the trail network. For additional hikes in this great urban wilderness, see Harvey Manning's *Footsore 1*, second edition (The Mountaineers, 1983) and *50+ Trails of Cougar Mountain Regional Wildland Park, Squak Mountain State Park, Lake Sammamish State Park, Coal Creek Park, May Creek Park* (Issaquah Alps Trails Club, 1985).

From Seattle, drive I-90 east to exit 11A, 150th Avenue S.E. Keep right where the exit forks and turn right at the stop sign. Drive about one-half mile south to S.E. Newport Way. Turn left and, in one mile, right again on 164th Avenue S.E. In just under two miles this winding road straightens out and becomes Lakemont Boulevard. At just over two miles turn left on Cougar Mountain Way. In a little over a mile the road turns sharply right and becomes S.E. 60th Street. (All this sounds more confusing than it really is.) Just beyond, turn right on Cougar Mountain Drive and continue three-fourths mile to a gate. Proceed through the gate and drive uphill to Radar Park. Park here. (If the gate is closed, park along the road and continue on foot the last quarter mile to the trailhead.)

Radar Park is a flat, open grassy area, bounded by woods but offering a panoramic view of the Sammamish valley and the Cascades north to Mount Baker. Before or after doing this walk, be sure to stroll to the north side of the park to take in this fine view. The park is also an excellent spot to picnic, toss frisbees, or just lie about. Here too are the only rest rooms in the area. Near the rest rooms is a sign with a map of the park and a brief history of coal mining in the area. Four photographs by early-day Seattle photographer Asahel Curtis show mining activities in the first decade of this century. According to the sign, some 150 million tons of coal and waste rock were removed from Cougar Mountain between the discovery of coal in 1868 and the closing of the last mine in 1963. Nearly twice that much remains.

Backtrack to the parking lot gate. The trail is marked by two signs. The smaller one shows a profile of a hiker and an arrow pointing the way. The larger one warns hikers to stay away from mine openings, which may emit toxic gases. There are no open shafts, however, along the short loop described below. Proceed straight ahead between the signs (ignore the small sign reading "To foot trails," which is nailed on an alder a few yards left of the official trailhead signs). The trail parallels the chain link fence and turns right (another sign marks the turn) when the fence does. At the corner is an old, charred red cedar snag.

(1) Western red cedar is easily damaged or killed by fire, but flames seldom sweep the damp habitats preferred by this tree. When conditions are dry, however, as in the summers of 1984 through 1986, fires pose a severe danger to red cedar stands.

The trail sign, on a young western hemlock, points to Anti-Aircraft Peak trailhead, Clay Pit Peak, Anti-Aircraft Peak Trail, Lost Beagle Trail, and Klondike Swamp. The trail continues along the fence.

(2) Look for swamp gooseberry on the left. The plant is readily identified by the numerous sharp spines that cloak the stems like hairs. Wild gooseberries and currants are important to wildlife throughout the western United States, where these shrubs are particularly numerous. Some thirty species grow in Washington alone.

The path turns left away from the fence and, not far beyond, passes an unsigned trail heading off to the right. This is the other end of the Anti-Aircraft Peak loop. You can take either path to complete the loop, but since the route is described here in clockwise direction, keep left.

The trail crosses a flat, poorly drained area dominated by red alder, with sword fern and salmonberry in the understory.

One of many burned snags hosting new growth

(3)   Red Alder is the most common and widespread hardwood both in western Washington and along this trail, often forming dense thickets in habitats where conifers do poorly. This slender deciduous tree is characteristic of damp, poorly drained places and recently burned or logged areas. All three types of habitat are found along this trail. Alder is probably the most abundant tree on the heavily logged lands of Cougar Mountain Regional Wildland Park.

The trail gradually enters pleasant, open, second-growth forest. Alders are still the overwhelmingly dominant tree, but among them are scattered western hemlocks, red cedars, and Douglas firs.

(4)   This forest's most distinctive feature is an abundance of giant charred snags, some more than thirty feet tall, which stand as ghostly reminders of past glory. Some of the snags are topped with "sky gardens" of red huckleberry and salal. The first of the snags is on the right side of the trail—blackened by fire, full of woodpecker holes, and rotting in place. Such snags provide wildlife with food, nesting places, and temporary shelter. The pileated woodpecker, a crow-sized bird with a flaming red crest, is rarely found except where snags occur. Pileated and hairy woodpeckers excavate holes for nests and probe the rotting wood for insects. Abandoned woodpecker holes are used in turn by other creatures, including squirrels, raccoons, and hole-nesting birds such as owls and chickadees. Snags are also nutrient reservoirs, which enrich the soil as they decay. In today's clearcut logging, snags are cut down and burned as slash. How much better to leave them, as was done here, for animals to use and humans to admire.

Next to the first snag is a huge fallen log (obscured by rank brush in summer), with sword fern, red huckleberry, coast red elderberry, and western bleeding heart growing on it. Just beyond, on the left, is the number-one monster snag of the forest, a massive pillar of a trunk measuring some six feet in diameter and more than thirty feet tall. Just beyond, notice the young conifers scattered among the alders. These are western hemlocks.

(5)   Western hemlock is more tolerant of shade than any other tree in our region and commonly lives to be 300 to 400 years old. Red alder, however, is among the least shade-tolerant and rarely lives past 100 years. As a result, young hemlocks can grow in the shade of mature alders, but young alders cannot grow in the shade of mature hemlocks or even mature alders. As the alders die, the young hemlocks shoot upward and replace them until, finally, there are few or no alders left in the forest.

In a few yards is a second junction where signs point left, downhill to Cougar Pass and right, uphill, back to Anti-Aircraft Peak. Keep right to continue the Three Snags Loop. For the first time, the trail begins to climb, though not steeply and only for a short distance.

(6)   About halfway up the slope the dominant plant in the understory changes from sword fern to Oregon grape, which is easily recognized by its shiny, dark green, hollylike leaves. Sword fern does not disappear; it just becomes less common. Many factors may contribute to such shifts in vegetation, but the most important one in this instance is probably moisture. Sword fern is a reliable indicator of moist, well-drained soils. Oregon grape typically prefers drier habitats within the forest.

Just at the point where the trail turns sharply left there is a big old stump crowned with red huckleberry.

(7)   In September the small red berries resemble tiny Christmas ornaments. The birds eat the berries and plant the seeds when they deposit their stool atop logs and stumps. Red huckleberries are also a favorite food of bears and small mammals, as well as humans. Indians ate the berries both fresh and dried, and brewed tea from the leaves.

The trail crosses two fallen logs, one lying across the other. Both are covered with dense growth of red huckleberry, lady fern, sword fern, coast red elderberry, and various mosses.

(8)   A variety of animals depend on fallen logs for food and cover. Wood-boring beetles, carpenter ants, termites, and wood-tunneling mites eat the fallen tree, exposing its insides to the elements and thereby initiating the recycling of nutrients bound up in the wood. Spiders, centipedes, salamanders, and other carnivores feed on animals living in and on the log. Still other animals, such as earthworms, mites, millipedes, and earwigs, feed on dead tissues and feces of other organisms. Shrews and shrew-moles in turn devour virtually all animals frequenting fallen logs. The Trowbridge shrew in particular is closely associated with large, rotting logs.

Beyond the logs, the trail turns sharply right. Here by the trail is one of several bigleaf maples growing in the vicinity. The trunk is covered with a thick, luxurious moss coat that feels like the soft fur of an animal.

(9)   Mosses are spore-producing plants whose life cycle comprises two distinct generations. The familiar, leafy moss plant is the sexual generation, which produces microscopic eggs and sperm. These unite to form the second, or spore-bearing, generation, which consists of tiny capsules on stalks that rise from the leafy green mat. When the spores are mature, the capsules flip open and release them to the wind, which may carry them great distances. Spores that alight on a suitable surface absorb moisture and develop spreading threadlike mats, from which the leafy green moss plant arises.

At an unsigned junction, keep right, passing between a couple of fallen logs. Where the trail turns sharply left, notice the large red huckleberry bushes growing from the top of the old stump. Common snowberry and coast red elderberry grow nearby. Soon the trail leaves the mixed conifer-deciduous woods for a dog-hair stand of red alder.

(10) Dog-hair stands are so named because the trees seem as thick as the hairs on a dog. Nearly pure alder stands such as this one are usually even-aged, that is, the trees spring up all at once in the wake of clearcutting or fire. That conifers once grew here is evident from the giant cedar stumps scattered through the area. Look at the girth of the stumps and imagine what that forest of giants must have looked like.

After passing a couple of large fallen logs, come to a signed junction. The left fork heads steeply downhill for about a half mile to Klondike Swamp—in spring a good side trip for birders. To return to Radar Park, turn right and come to the chain link fence encircling the old installation.

(11) Near the fence and left of the trail is a nurse log supporting swamp gooseberry, sword fern, and red huckleberry. Nearby is a red-flowering currant, a thornless cousin of the gooseberry and one of our loveliest native shrubs. In late March, when the undergrowth is still sparse and the currant is in bloom, this shrub is conspicuous. By midsummer, however, some searching may be needed to find it in the tangle of greenery.

At the fence the trail turns right and in a few yards passes between a couple of western hemlocks. The trail gently winds through mixed woods. Along this final leg of the loop keep a lookout for false lily of the valley and coltsfoot.

(12) Cougar Mountain is perhaps Seattle's closest remaining stronghold of the black bear. From here to the Cascades, the peaks of the Issaquah Alps provide a wild corridor along which large mammals can move back and forth, having to cross highways in only a couple of places. A mother bear and cub were seen along this trail in 1985.

In about one-quarter mile rejoin the beginning section of the trail. Turn left and retrace your steps to Radar Park.

20

EASTSIDE/ISSAQUAH

Lakemont Gorge

Distance: 1¼ - mile round trip
Season: best summer and fall
Highlights: ferns, creek
Metro: 210

From a trailhead at the very edge of I-90, plunge into a moss-padded, fern-choked gorge—well, a deep ravine, really—where trees blot out highway noise, and eternal dampness quickly reduces human artifacts to moldering rubble. There are no facilities here—no rest rooms, picnic tables, or interpretive signs; just jungle and a trail. There are also no guarantees: This lovely canyon is privately owned and earmarked for development. As of now, however, walkers are allowed access to the gorge.

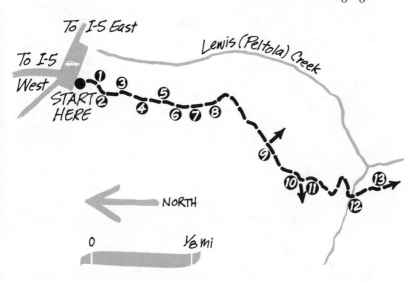

Thickly covered trail in the Lakemont Gorge

The price of lushness is goo. Abundant precipitation, low evaporation rates, spring-loaded slopes, and saturated soils not only promote jungle but guarantee that portions of this trail will be mucky most of the time. Boots are highly recommended.

To reach the trailhead, drive I-90 east to exit 13, W. Sammamish Road S.E., Newport Way. Turn right and immediately come to a stop sign at Newport Way. Cross the road and park. The trail takes off straight ahead, across a small, damp field and into the woods. A sign here—courtesy of the Issaquah Alps Trails Club—reads "Lakemont Trailhead-Cougar Mountain Park-Precipice Trail-Bear Orchard-Peggy's Trail."

(1) Lewis (Peltola) Creek has cut Lakemont Gorge back into the steep slope that runs along the northern base of Cougar Mountain, paralleling I-90 from Eastgate to Issaquah. This steep slope, informally known as "The Precipice," was quarried more than 15,000 years ago, as the continental ice sheet, coming down from the north, slammed into and scraped along the hard rock of the Issaquah Alps. Later, streams draining the uplands cut narrow slots into The Precipice on their way to Lake Sammamish.

As the trail enters the woods, look on the right for a tree with a reddish brown trunk that noticeably flares at the base. The tree is growing next to the trail on a slope mostly covered with sword fern.

(2) This tree is a western red cedar. The reddish bark and flat sprays of scalelike leaves are characteristic. Red cedars are shallow-rooted yet typically grow in unstable, saturated soils. As a result, they are prone to being blown down by wind, or undermined through erosion or the gradual downward creep of soil due to gravity. Buttressed trunks provide a measure of stability and support in this environment. This and other red cedars along the trail have grown up since the area was logged earlier in the century. Old red cedar stumps along the trail dwarf the youngsters and show what the forest was like once upon a time. Today, bigleaf maple dominates the forest canopy along this first section of trail.

The path climbs over a small hump, then descends gently as it traverses the slope amid sword fern and red huckleberry. Step over roots and look on the left side of the trail for an old bigleaf maple stump with three young maples growing on it. Look for banana slugs browsing the moss on this stump... and everywhere else along this trail as well.

(3) The banana slugs of Lakemont Gorge are pale greenish yellow with black spots. Elsewhere they may be olive, yellow, or brown, with or without spots. Banana slugs grow to six inches or more in length. They occasionally feed on foliage but more commonly forage in the damp forest duff. They rarely venture into gardens, but the voracious brown garden slug, a European import, has invaded suburban woods such as this and may also be encountered along this trail.

Beyond the maple stump, pass a young western red cedar growing from a huge old red cedar stump. Step over a few small logs, after which the trail turns right, then left. Come to another red cedar stump, on the

Forest floor detail

right, with a young western hemlock growing on it. In spring and fall, look here and elsewhere along the trail for mushrooms.

(4)   Among the mushrooms that may be found along the trail are amanitas, boletus mushrooms, questionable stropharia, orange fairy cup, oyster mushroom, and others. Mushrooms are merely the spore-producing organs of fungi that live either in the soil or in the dead or living tissues of plants. Fungi lack chlorophyll and therefore are unable to carry out photosynthesis. Instead, they obtain nutrients directly from organic materials. Parasitic fungi feed off the tissues of living organisms, including forest trees. The majority of fungi, however, are beneficial. Saprophytic fungi decompose dead plant and animal matter, thereby recycling nutrients back into the environment. Micorrhizae are fungi that form symbiotic associations with forest trees and other plants by sheathing the roots of host plants. The fungi, in effect, expand the hosts' root systems, increasing their ability to obtain moisture and nutrients. In return, the host plants provide the fungi with essential carbohydrates that they cannot produce themselves.

The trail passes still another red cedar stump, then drops to a little muddy bottom. On the left notice the plants with large maplelike leaves perched atop long, thorny, spindly stems. These plants are devil's club.

(5)   The presence of devil's club indicates that this slope is saturated with moisture all year long. The shrub's large leaves are held horizontally to receive the maximum sunlight available in its shady habitat. The small white flowers appear atop the stem in June and develop by August into tight pyramidal clusters of red berries. Devil's club is commonly found beneath red cedars . . . or where red cedars once grew.

The trail begins climbing, passes a red cedar on the left, and enters an area where maidenhair fern is abundant.

(6)   Many people consider maidenhair ferns to be among the loveliest of the clan. Several species of maidenhair are native to North America. Our Northwestern representative—the northern maidenhair, or five-finger fern—is perhaps the most elegant. Its fingerlike leaflets and black, wiry stems are unmistakable. Northern maidenhair favors damp, mossy banks, often near waterfalls, or any place where humidity remains high throughout the largely dry growing season.

The trail passes between two low, eroding banks, remnants of an old road cut. Leaving the cut, it continues on the level and passes another bank on the right, where maidenhair fern, sword fern, lady fern, and wood fern all grow together.

(7)   Growing atop the bank, its foliage nearly obscured by the canopy of maples, is cascara, a slender tree whose leaves are fine-toothed and have prominent, straight, parallel veins. Cascara bark is the active ingredient in most commercial laxatives, a use Northwest Indians were the first to discover.

Bracket fungi

Just beyond the bank is a snag about twelve feet tall, with red huckleberry growing on top. The trail narrows, passing between dense hedges of salmonberry, coast red elderberry, and ferns. On the left is a picturesque fire-scarred stump. The trail widens as it joins an abandoned dirt road. On the right, parallel to the trail, is a fallen log supporting a rich nursery of young plants.

(8) Lady fern, wood fern, sword fern, red elderberry, and red huckleberry grow abundantly from the top of the log. All these plants may also be found growing in the ground, but they flourish atop logs or stumps, where they are assured an ample supply of moisture and nutrients during their fomative years. "Nurse logs" such as this are characteristic of the Northwest coastal forest and are encountered again and again on the trails described in this book.

The track ascends gently and bends to the right. Pass by the first Douglas firs encountered along the trail, as well as an uprooted red cedar wedged between two maple trunks. The trail bends left at this point and continues climbing through a corridor of salmonberry, stink currant, and red elderberry. The trail then passes through stands, first, of pole-sized, then of mature red alders. Come to a bigleaf maple log lying across the trail.

(9) Clustered atop this log are licorice ferns, which are seen most frequently growing on the mossy bark of standing bigleaf maples. The fronds are similar to those of sword fern but are easily distinguished from them by the way the leaflets are attached to the stem. Leaflets of the common sword fern are attached at a single point while those of licorice fern are attached along the entire lengths of their bases. Young licorice fern "fiddleheads" uncurl after the first rains of fall and persist through the winter. They wither in late spring and early summer with the onset of drier weather.

Come to a junction, with a sign pointing left to Peggy's Trail and Cougar Mountain Park

(10) Here at the junction the underbrush has changed somewhat in composition. Clumps of salal and Oregon grape are conspicuous on the right, marking a gradual shift toward relatively drier conditions than existed downhill. The leaves of both plants are thick and coated with a varnishlike substance called cutin (the same substance coats the leaves of conifers as well). The coating, a device to reduce moisture loss through evaporation, is characteristic of drought-tolerant plants.

The trail leading straight ahead climbs rather steeply through alder woods and salmonberry jungle to a road on the plateau above The Precipice. From there it is possible to piece together a loop that links up with Peggy's Trail on the opposite side of Lakemont Gorge. It is also possible to wander almost endlessly on a maze of old logging roads that crisscross the plateau. Our route turns left on Peggy's Trail, which descends beneath a canopy of alder and vine maple to a small, seasonal creek.

(11) In middle to late October vine maples put on a fine show of color both here and on the plateau above. Vine maples that grow beneath the forest canopy usually turn pale yellow, while those in the open usually turn fiery shades of red and orange. The difference lies in the production of anthocyanin, the main pigment responsible for red coloration in leaves.

Anthocyanin functions mainly as a sun screen (plant PABA, so to speak) and apparently is not produced in quantity by vine maples growing in the shade.

From the small creek, the trail climbs briefly, then turns right and left beneath a canopy of red alder. Crossing a rise, it turns left, enters shadier woods, and begins to descend to the creek bottom. Just beyond a triple-trunked maple, the trail turns sharply right, then right again, and parallels Lewis Creek. Bigleaf maples and alder form the canopy; vine maples line the creek. Come to a rude bridge that arches the flood.

(12) Notice the rocks in the creek bottom. Along with the sedimentary and volcanic rocks native to these hills are granite cobbles that were transported southward from Canada by the continental ice sheet and deposited here and elsewhere in the Issaquah Alps in mounds and ridges of glacial debris. Later, weathering exposed the rocks, and stream action carried them downhill to their present positions. Rocks such as these, which have been transported and deposited by glaciers far from their places of origin, are called erratics. The granite cobbles in the creek bed are easily distinguished by their large crystals and salt-and-pepper color from the other rocks.

Cross the plank bridge and immediately begin climbing, as the trail bends toward the left up the steep slope. The trail passes a fallen log, jogs right and left, and continues its climbing traverse along the side of a narrow slot carved into The Precipice by Owens Creek. On the left, pass a cedar stump with a young cedar growing on top. Turn right and left one more time and enter an opening that provides a good view down into the narrow gorge.

(13) The vegetation in this damp side canyon is lush. Both slopes are mantled with ferns. Huge moss-covered maples lean out over the gorge. Hemlocks and red cedars rise from the opposite bank. The lush vegetation found here and in the main branch of Lakemont Gorge is due partly to the ravine's position on the northern flank of Cougar Mountain. In the Northern Hemisphere, northern exposures usually receive less sunlight than slopes facing in other directions. As a result, temperatures are lower, moisture evaporates more slowly, and humidity within the forest remains at higher levels year-around. Moreover, since storms generally strike from the south, trees growing in this gorge are largely sheltered from damaging high winds.

Beyond this point the trail steepens and becomes more slippery and therefore cannot be recommended for parties with small children. Finish the walk by returning the way you came.

Ambitious hikers, however, can climb Peggy's Trail all the way to Radar Park (Walk 19). Or, upon gaining the plateau just above the gorge, they can turn right and walk the loop through the Bear Orchard and back down Lakemont Gorge (See *Footsore 1*).

21

EASTSIDE/MERCER ISLAND

Pioneer Park

Distance: ¾ - mile loop
Season: all year
Highlight: mixed forest
Metro: 202

Pioneer Park consists of three adjacent quarter-mile-square sections separated by Island Crest Way and S.E. 68th Street. The northwestern and southeastern sections are crisscrossed by equestrian trails. The northeastern section features a self-guided nature trail and is reserved for walkers. The following account covers only the nature trail; for walks of two or three miles, link up trails in either or both of the other sections. An interpretive booklet is available from the Mercer Island park department office (address in Seattle directory blue pages). The following discussions are meant to complement rather than replace those in the booklet.

Pioneer Park is Mercer Island's "wild" park and as such it contains neither rest rooms nor picnic facilities. Both can be found, however, a quarter mile north, on Island Crest Way, in Island Crest Park.

To reach Pioneer Park from Seattle, drive I-90 east to Mercer Island. Exit at Island Crest Way and drive south 3.2 miles to S.E. 68th Street. A single parking space is available on the southeast corner of the intersection. Other parking spaces are located along Island Crest Way just before this intersection. If these are all taken, turn right onto 68th and in one-eighth mile left into the shopping center parking lot. Park as near to the intersection as possible. Normally, there should be no problem parking here, as the number of spaces far exceeds current demand. Because the parking area is private property, however, park visitors who park there do so at their own risk. It is also possible to park at Island Crest Park, located 0.6 mile north of 68th on Island Crest Way, and walk back to the trailhead.

Salal at the forest's edge, Pioneer Park

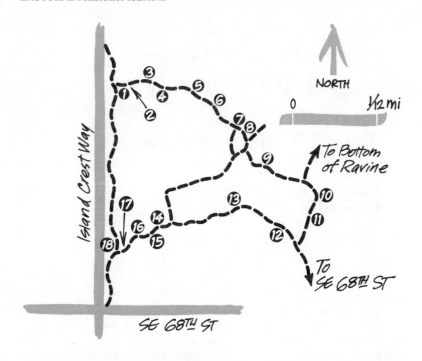

At the intersection of Island Crest Way and S.E. 68th, cross to the northeast corner and follow the paved walkway north along Island Crest Way. Pass signpost 19 on the left and come to a "Nature Trail" sign on the right where the nature loop emerges from the woods. Continue on the paved walkway another eighth of a mile to a second path entering the woods. Several upright green posts set across the trail are meant to keep out horses. This trail is for walkers only! Signpost 1 is on the right, at the very start of the path.

(1)   The small tree directly in front of the signpost is a young Douglas fir. The ground cover here is Oregon grape, whose shiny, spiny leaflets resemble those of English holly, which can be found directly opposite the signpost. Oregon grape is a native shrub that thrives in shade as well as sun. English holly is a native of Europe that has become naturalized in many of the urban and suburban parks in the Puget Sound region.

About ten yards beyond the upright posts, signpost 2 is on the right.

(2)   The western red cedar to the left of the post is perhaps three feet in diameter. Western red cedars are actually not cedars at all but a species of arborvitae. True cedars of the genus *Cedrus* grow naturally only in the Old World. Easterners may also confuse our local red cedars with the

A sign marks the exit of Pioneer Park's nature trail

common eastern red cedar, which is found east of the Mississippi River. The eastern red cedar, however, is also not a true cedar, but a species of juniper. To further confuse matters, the incense cedar of Oregon and California is neither a true cedar nor related to any of the other "cedars" mentioned above. This confusion of common names is why scientists and serious students of nature rely on scientific names, which indicate the evolutionary relationships of plants and animals. For example, the name *Thuja plicata*, the scientific name for the western red cedar tells us that this tree is a distinct species from the northern white cedar (*Thuja occidentalis*) of northeastern North America and the Chinese arborvitae (*Thuja orientalis*) of Asia, but that all three trees evolved from a common ancestor.

In some forty yards come to signpost 3 on the left. Directly in front of it is a multi-trunked bigleaf maple. To the left of the signpost is a red alder; to the right, a young Douglas fir. And a few yards down the trail, on the right, is a western hemlock.

(3) Bigleaf maple and red alder are the most common deciduous trees occurring in the conifer forests of the Puget Sound region. Red alders pioneer disturbed sites where conifers have been removed by logging, fire or other disturbance. Bigleaf maples also require forest openings in order to regenerate and grow. Thanks to human alteration of the landscape, alders and maples have both greatly increased in the Puget Sound region.

From signpost 3 the trail makes an S curve between a young Douglas fir and red cedar and in about twenty yards comes to signpost 4 on the right.

(4) The young trees growing hereabouts are competing for limited supplies of water, space, and nutrients, Eventually, the slower growing, the weaker, and the poorly positioned trees will die, and their decaying remains will release nutrients to the soil that will nourish the continuing growth of the survivors. The resulting forest will be more open and consist of fewer, larger trees.

The trail bends right then left and in some forty yards comes to signpost 5 on the left. There is a good-sized red huckleberry bush just left of the post. To the right are a pair of slender red alders. Oregon grape, salal, and sword fern, all evergreens, are the most prominent understory plants. Directly ahead, in some alders, are the remains of an old tree house.

(5) A song bird that commonly makes its home in red alders is the warbling vireo, which may also be found nesting in cottonwoods, willows, and other deciduous trees. It suspends its woven nest from the fork of a twig. The first warbling vireos generally arrive in the Seattle area in April, but the bulk arrive in May. From then until early July, when nesting is largely complete, the male's persistent, wandering, rough-edged warble is one of the most common bird songs in deciduous and mixed forests in the region. The bird itself is hard to locate because it is a nondescript grayish color and spends most of its time foraging for insects in the upper branches of deciduous trees.

The trail passes a Douglas fir on the left, then bends right and in about thirty yards arrives at signpost 6 on the left. To the right of the post is a "nurse log" that supports a variety of shrubs and ferns.

(6) The plants most often found growing atop fallen logs or stumps fall into two categories. The first category consists of plants with conspicuous berries that attract birds and mammals. Examples include red huckleberry (which is the most conspicuous plant on this particular log), evergreen huckleberry, salal, and coast red elderberry. Animals eat the berries of these plants and deposit the seeds, often well above the ground, in their droppings. The second category consists of spore-bearing plants such as ferns, mosses, and fungi (mushrooms), whose spores are borne to lofty perches by the wind. Sword fern, wood fern, and several types of moss are all found on this log.

The trail bends left and enters a bare, open area, where a trail branches right. (This trail winds about one-eighth mile south to the southern leg of the loop, between signposts 13 and 14.) Signpost 7, on the left, opposite the side trail, overlooks a lush ravine.

Overlooking the forest ravine in Pioneer Park

(7)   The forest of the upper ravine is a mixture of red alder, bigleaf maple, western red cedar, and western hemlock. Old red cedar stumps, such as the one on the left, are relics of the earlier old-growth forest, as are a few large conifers growing in the bottom of the ravine. This is a good place to search for birds of the forest canopy, which are often difficult to spot from below. These include band-tailed pigeon, golden-crowned kinglet, Swainson's thrush, vireos, and warblers. Ravines also provide refuge for coyotes and raccoons, which venture forth at night to forage in neighborhood backyards.

Do not take the side trail. Instead, continue along the edge of the ravine and in some fifteen yards come to signpost 8.

(8)   The ravine bottom is cooler, moister, and more protected from wind than the upper forest. In the upper forest the understory is relatively sparse and consists mostly of sword fern in the moister spots, such as here, and salal and Oregon grape in the drier ones. In the ravine, however, the understory is lush and various, with abundant ferns, devil's club, elderberry, skunk cabbage, rushes, horsetails, and young alders, to mention only the most common plants. The luxuriant ravine vegetation shows that low light is not the only factor determining the composition and structure of the forest understory. Moisture is also critical, and given enough of it many plants are able to tolerate a greater degree of shade than otherwise.

About seven yards beyond signpost 8 the trail turns right, at which point a side trail on the left drops steeply into the bottom of the ravine. The main trail in five more yards comes to an unsigned junction with a side trail heading right. (This side trail shortly meets up with the one opposite signpost 7; see above.) The main trail turns left here, and in about twenty yards returns to the edge of the ravine, where signpost 9 sits in an opening among a number of storm-battered maple.

(9)   Note the broken trunks and branches of many trees in this area. There is also a fallen red alder about ten yards to the right. Although wind speeds are generally much lower within a forest than they are on the outside, trees that are diseased, old, shallow-rooted, or growing in steep or otherwise precarious locations are vulnerable wind damage. By breaking branches and even toppling trees, winds open up the canopy and allow sunlight to penetrate to the forest floor. Such openings provide opportunities for a variety of plants that are rare or absent in the shade. In this way, winds initiate change within the forest and increase the diversity of plants, and therefore animals, that occur within it. Winds also help to reinvigorate the community by removing old trees so that new ones can take their places.

The trail passes between a couple of maples and in about sixty-five yards turns right as it passes a leaning Douglas fir. As the trail moves away from the edge of the ravine, which it has followed from the outset, the composition and appearance of the forest begin to change. In another ninety yards, where the trail turns right rather sharply between two Douglas fir, signpost 10 is on the left.

(10) Notice how the maples and alders that grew commonly along the edge of the ravine have gradually been replaced by Douglas firs on this higher, drier ground. The types and relative abundance of shrubs have also changed. Along the ravine the most common plants growing beneath the trees are sword fern and elderberry; after signpost 9 salal and ocean spray gradually increase in numbers. Farther along the trail, they are even more predominant. This shift in vegetation is a response to a change in soil. The soil along the ravine is relatively rich and holds enough moisture during dry summer months to support deciduous trees. On higher ground away from the edge of the ravine, however, the soil is less fertile and more sandy. It drains rapidly and dries out during the summer. Trees and shrubs that grow in this soil must be able to withstand anywhere from two to four months of little or no rainfall. Salal, Oregon grape, and the conifers all have thick, leathery or waxy leaves designed to retard water loss. In addition, they are all evergreen, which means that they can remain active during the wet season and reduce operations—and therefore water consumption—during periods of drought, which in this region usually come in the summer.

Beyond signpost 10 the trail turns left. In another twenty yards, look for signpost 11 on the left.

(11) The signpost is located in a second-growth stand of Douglas fir in which the largest trees are about two feet in diameter. Most of this area was logged about fifty years ago, and these trees date from that time. They are competing for limited supplies of water, space, and nutrients. Eventually, the slower growing, the weaker, and the poorly positioned trees will die, and their decaying remains will release nutrients to the soil that will nourish the continuing growth of the survivors. The resulting forest will be more open and consist of fewer, larger trees.

The trail winds back and forth across the flat and arrives at a T-junction about 160 yards past signpost 11. Here a white arrow painted on a post points the way. Take its advice and turn right. Signpost 12 is on the left about fifty yards beyond the junction.

(12) In spring and summer this damp clearing supports a thick growth of stinging nettle, which is an indicator of moist, poorly drained soil. Notice, however, that nettle and other plants sharing this opening give way abruptly to a dense cover of salal on the higher, drier ground upslope from the signpost. Farther on, when the trail leaves the damp clearing to enter the drier woods, the transition to drier, sandier, upland soil is complete, and salal reigns supreme in the understory.

From signpost 12 the trail meanders through an open alder woodland. About twenty yards beyond the signpost the trail swings to the left and in another ten to fifteen yards turns even more sharply left and enters conifer forest. Signpost 13 is on the right. A fallen log extends along the trail to the left of the signpost.

(13)   Many decades will pass before this log is reduced to forest litter, and two or three centuries may pass before mature fallen trees entirely disintegrate. The job of decomposing the woody tissue is carried out primarily by various species of saprophytic fungi, whose networks of threadlike mycelia even now have spread throughout its woody heart, releasing chemicals that dissolve the tough fibers. In the deciduous forests of eastern North America, the primary agents of decomposition are bacteria. In the West, however, fungi are more important because they are better able to process the more acidic plant materials found in conifer forests.

From signpost 13 the trail meanders through open, mixed forest with fair-sized Douglas firs, western hemlocks, red cedars, red alders, bigleaf maples, and madronas. Salal and Oregon grape dominate the understory. In eighty yards the trail meets a side trail, which heads right for about one-eighth mile to signposts 7 and 8 on the northern leg of the loop. Keep left; from the junction the main trail curves left then right and in fifteen yards comes to signpost 14 on the right.

(14)   The dead branches on the trunks of these young Douglas firs are not victims of disease but of a natural self-pruning process whereby the trees rid themselves of unproductive limbs. The lower branches, deprived of sufficient sunlight by the ones above, as well as by the foliage of neighboring trees, gradually lose their needles and eventually fall to the ground. In this way the trees reduce the amount of tissue that must be maintained with water and nutrients without significantly reducing the production of carbohydrates through photosynthesis. Long, clear trunks also help to protect the tree from fire.

The trail bends left and in about ten yards comes to signpost 15 on the right.

(15)   Directly in front of and about ten yards from the signpost, look for three slim, leaning trees, with smooth, peeling, reddish bark and waxy evergreen leaves. These are Pacific madronas, or madrones. Madrona is another plant well adapted to drier soils within the forest. Notice how some of the branches have died, a condition common to madronas throughout our region. This is caused by a canker fungus, which girdles year-old stems and kills the leaves. The presence of the fungus is indicated by black or purplish areas in the bark.

The trail bends left, then right, and in thirty yards comes to signpost 16, which is located on the right.

(16)   Right in front of the signpost is a western hemlock that is perhaps three feet in diameter. Western hemlock is perhaps the most abundant conifer in western Washington, growing in all but the wettest and driest places from sea level to 3500 feet elevation. Because it is more tolerant of shade than any of its companions, seedlings and saplings are usually the most common conifers in the forest understory. An immature western hemlock can exist in a suppressed state for decades, until wind or disease creates an opening in the forest canopy. Then the tree shoots upward rapidly to claim its place in the sun. In this way, western hemlock eventually replaces other conifers, which are less tolerant of shade. The process is rarely completed, however, because over the course of centuries enough openings are created in the canopy to allow other species to become established.

The trail bends left, then right, and passes through a stile designed to keep out horses. Immediately beyond the stile, look for signpost 17 on the right. The small broadleaf tree nearby is Pacific dogwood.

(17) In spring Pacific dogwood is conspicuous for its large white "flowers." Actually, the flowers are greenish and rather small. What appear to be white petals are actually large bracts—modified leaves that create a foil or setting for blossoms that otherwise might go unnoticed by insects. Some dogwoods also put on a second, smaller crop of flowers in the fall. One of the few butterflies to frequent the damp, shady forests of western Washington is the spring azure, whose larvae feed on the leaves of dogwood.

Signpost 18 is located directly across the paved walkway from signpost 17.

(18) The Mercer Island park department maintains these islands of natural vegetation as landscape elements in a sea of manicured lawn. Note the density and variety of plants growing here—a tangle composed of salal, Himalaya blackberry, sword fern, bracken fern, and several other less conspicuous species. The small deciduous tree to the left of the signpost is alder; the three broadleaf evergreen trees directly in front of the signpost are Pacific madronas. There is room and moisture and sunlight enough for all, here at the edge of the forest. But look in vain for the delicate shade plants of the forest floor: vanilla leaf, western trillium, candyflower, red huckleberry, lady fern, wood fern, and many others.

Retrace your steps southward along the paved walkway to the junction of Island Crest Way and 68th. The Pioneer Park nature trail has ended, but you need not stop walking here. You can cross 68th Street and enter the southeastern section of the park, or cross Island Crest Way to explore the northwestern section. Both tracts are much like the one you have just traversed, and the same ecological processes are working in all three.

22

SOUTH COUNTY/AUBURN

Great Blue Heron Marsh

Distance: ½ - mile round loop
Season: best spring through early summer
Highlights: great blue heron rookery, pond
Metro: 194 and 181

Come for the spectacle of great blue herons nesting and raising their young in the tops of red alders. Stay to enjoy the easy quarter-mile path meandering through lush bottomland woods. This walk can also be combined with Walk 23 for a longer day in the wetlands of southern King County.

Among the numerous small wild places tucked among the homes and highways of the Puget Sound region, Blue Heron Marsh is unusual for existing *because* rather than in spite of human activity.

Thirty years ago there were no herons or pond or marsh—only an abandoned gravel pit collecting debris. As water from Mill Creek and hillside runoff gradually filled the pit, cattails, willows, and other marsh plants began to grow in the damp soil. The herons apparently discovered the spot in 1968 and have nested there every year since. In the mid-1970s the state Department of Transportation planned to reroute Peasley Canyon Road directly through the young marsh but were convinced by local residents to follow the highway's present route alongside the marsh instead. Although highway noise is inescapable along this walk, the great birds, the lovely setting, and the knowledge that this special place stands as a monument to the recuperative powers of nature and the dedication of concerned citizens—they all help visitors forget the whine of engines and the hum of tires.

Be sure to bring binoculars or, better yet, a good tripod-mounted telescope. The path is often wet or muddy, so boots are recommended. There are no rest rooms or formal picnic facilities, although there is a decrepit old picnic table in the orchard at the end of the trail.

Birdwatching at Great Blue Heron Marsh

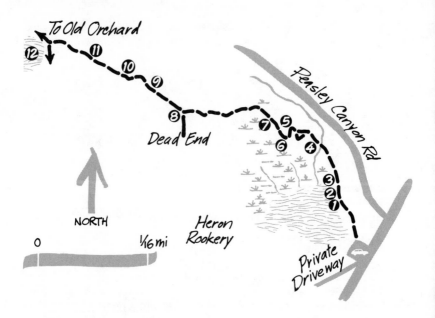

From downtown Seattle drive I-5 nineteen miles south to exit 143, S. 320th Street, in Federal Way. Leave the freeway and turn left (east) on 320th. After crossing Military Road, the street becomes Peasley Canyon Road. In just under three miles from I-5, come to the junction with West Valley Highway. Turn right and then immediately right again into the small gravel parking lot at Blue Heron Marsh. On a clear day the view eastward across the valley to Mount Rainier is dramatic.

Bus riders from Seattle should take Metro 194 to Federal Way and transfer to the 181 going to Auburn. Get off at West Valley Highway, across from the marsh.

Follow the gravel path leading from the north end of the parking area back toward Peasley Canyon Road and come to an overlook of the pond and cattail marsh. The heron nests are located in the tops of the trees growing on the hillside across the pond.

(1) The nests—visible to the naked eye—are bulky stick platforms about four feet across. They are located here in the very tops of red alders, but elsewhere other types of trees may be used. The great blue heron is born blind and naked, and the young remain in the nest for as long as two months. Treetop nests afford the young herons a good measure of protection from predators during this period. Nearby ponds, streams, and valley wetlands provide excellent places for adult herons to hunt for fish, frogs, snakes, rodents, and insects.

The pond was created inadvertently when fill dirt dumped here dammed Mill Creek.

(2)   Ponds are bodies of fresh water that are usually no more than ten to fifteen feet deep. That is shallow enough for the temperature of the water to be more or less uniform throughout and for aquatic plants to grow on the bottom. A mature pond, such as this, consists of several zones, each with its own distinctive plants and animals. The littoral zone is the shallow-water area adjacent to the shore. Here, plants such as cattails, sedges, and willows are distributed according to water depth. The water surface is called the neuston zone. It is the realm of floating plants such as duckweed and white pond lily and of small creatures that take advantage of the water's surface tension. Water striders skate across the surface; mosquito larvae, snails, leeches, and other creatures live on the underside of the surface. The limnetic zone is the area of open water. It is frequented by microscopic plants and strong swimmers such as fish, tadpoles, and diving beetles. The benthic, or profundal, zone is the pond bottom, home to worms, snails, and various insect larvae. Of course, many animals frequent more than one zone, depending on time of day, water temperature, and light levels.

From the overlook the narrow path skirts Peasley Canyon Road and comes to an information sign on the left. The sign gives the history of Great Blue Heron Marsh and information about the breeding habits and schedule of the resident herons. It also includes lists of plants and animals found in the sanctuary. The map showing locations of different kinds of plants has long faded.

(3)   Immediately to the left of the sign is western serviceberry, which is covered with showy, fragrant white blossoms in April and May. The berries, which ripen in August, are favored by birds and small mammals. Though not to most people's taste, the berries were eaten both fresh and dried by Indians throughout the West. The foliage of serviceberry is an important food for deer.

Continue along the path and come to a set of steps leading down into the bottomland woods. Cross a plank bridge over a shallow pool of standing water.

(4)   This bottomland forest is dominated by red alder and Pacific willow. Most of the trees are leaning because their shallow roots are poorly anchored in the mucky soil. The unstable footing makes them vulnerable to being thrown down by high winds. When the prostrate Pacific willow directly ahead toppled during a storm, the trail had to be rerouted around it.

Follow the right-hand path around the fallen tree and arrive at a wooden bench at a sharp turn in the trail. Take care to avoid the stinging nettle along the path. You may also want to check around the bench before sitting down.

(5)   The burning sensation that follows contact with the leaves of stinging nettle is caused by formic acid, the same substance injected by biting ants and stinging bees and wasps. When you brush the leaves, tiny

hairs containing the acid are broken off and become embedded in the skin. The irritating sensation lasts several hours and may cause children significant discomfort. Applying meat tenderizer or a baking-soda paste to the afflicted area brings some relief.

From the bench walk a few yards to a trail sign, where the route turns right as it rejoins the old trail now blocked by the fallen willow on the left.

(6) In winter there are few signs of life in these woods. The trees and shrubs are without their leaves, which form a dense, sodden mat on the forest floor. As fungi and bacteria decompose this litter, nutrients contained in the leaves are liberated to the soil, where they contribute to the profusion of greenery in spring and summer.

The path follows a series of short boardwalks—some new, some decrepit—as it wanders through the most beautiful section of the bottomland, one marked in spring and summer by lush growths of shrubs, ferns, and skunk cabbage. The abundant vegetation and well-layered structure of these woods indicate that conditions of soil and moisture are optimum for supporting the maximum variety of plants. For a good look about, stop at the third boardwalk.

(7) Abundant lady ferns, great masses of common horsetail, and the huge, bright green leaves of skunk cabbage, create an almost tropical effect. The woods seem primordial, like an oil deposit in the making, a place where some great lumbering proto-frog might haul itself up out of the ooze. The actual amphibian residents of this bottomland include red-legged frog, rough-skinned newt, long-toed salamander, and ensatina (or Oregon salamander). All four amphibians breed in the sanctuary's two ponds but spend most or all of their adult lives out of water. Outside the breeding season, even the red-legged frog may be encountered well away from the ponds.

After leaving the bottomland, the path crosses a sluggish creek and climbs a short set of steps to a junction with a side trail on the left. Keep right.

(8) The bank on the left is completely covered with Pacific waterleaf, which grows by late summer to three feet tall. The rounded clusters of small white, greenish, or dull purple flowers appear in late April and May, but the plants are most attractive in March, when the plants are small and the new leaves are still fresh and bright green. Later they become coarser and somewhat ragged, as hungry insects take their toll.

Although the path is now elevated only slightly above the wet bottomland, plants requiring drier soils begin to appear, including bigleaf maple and common snowberry, both on the right-hand side of the trail, near the junction. From there, cross another damp flat shaded by red alders. After yet one more boardwalk, come to a small opening in the woods.

(9) Tall salmonberry shrubs flourish in the sunny opening, while in the deep shade of the alder woods the scant understory vegetation consists mainly of waterleaf and stinging nettle. Shade, moisture, soil conditions, or some combination thereof probably accounts for this abrupt change in vegetation.

The trail now climbs for the first time, though not steeply and not too far. In March, look for trillium along the trail. At the top of the rise there is an old hollow stump on the right. The stump is an old western red cedar, which may well have dominated the forest that once grew here. Next to the stump is a multi-trunked bigleaf maple.

(10) When fully formed, the leaves of bigleaf maple measure eight to twelve inches across, with stalks up to six inches long. A few yards to the left is vine maple, whose leaves are more or less round, divided into seven to nine pointed lobes, and only three to four inches across. The large leaves of bigleaf maple represent an adaptation to shade shared by a number of other forest plants, including devil's club and skunk cabbage. A few large leaves are able to intercept as much light as smaller leaves of comparable total surface area. The bigger leaves are a more efficient response to low light, however, because they require less energy to produce than more numerous smaller leaves of equal area.

The trail descends to another damp flat, which is crossed by means of ramshackle boardwalks.

(11) The boardwalk is lined on both sides by thick growths of grass and sedge, perfect habitat for one of the most common but least seen mammals in the Puget Sound region—Townsend's vole. Voles are also called meadow mice, though they are quite unlike the common house mouse. Voles have rounded or blunt snouts and hairy rather than naked tails. Townsend's vole feeds mainly on the succulent stems of grasses and sedges. It is, in turn, an important food source for predators such as owls, weasels, coyotes, and garter snakes, all of which help to keep the vole population down.

The trail comes to a track leading left and just beyond it a pond ringed with willows and alders.

(12) The surface of the pond is green, not from algae scum but from duckweed. Each tiny, roughly oval "leaf" (actually a structure called a *thallus*, which combines all the functions of leaf, stem, and flower) is a single flowering plant, one of the smallest annd most primitive in nature. The flowers, which appear rarely, are microscopic. Each thallus has a single hairlike root that extends an inch or so below the water surface. As the name indicates, duckweed is eaten in great quantity by ducks.

The trail continues to a long-abandoned orchard, where there is a quaint old picnic table. To reach the orchard, pick your way over the fallen cottonwood on the right and follow the path (often wet here) for just a couple of dozen yards. Otherwise, retrace your steps to the parking area.

$\mathcal{23}$

West Hylebos Wetlands State Park

Distance: 1 - mile loop
Season: all year
Highlights: diverse wetland communities, old-growth Sitka
    spruce
Metro: 174 to S. 348th Street

The wetlands of West Hylebos (pronounced *hile-boss*) Creek is hidden at the edge of booming Federal Way, just ten blocks from I-5 and a mere stone's throw from the strip development along Pacific Highway S. The West Hylebos Wetlands are probably the wildest, most diverse, least disturbed headwater swamp in King County. It's a jungle in there, with giant spruces, cedars, and Douglas firs towering over impenetrable thickets of deciduous trees and shrubs. Winding through it all is a one-mile nature trail so packed with wonders that all day will not be long enough for some people to make the trip.

As of fall 1986 the park is still in the planning stage, but construction of visitor facilities, including an interpretive center, is scheduled for 1987. That the park exists at all is due to the foresight, generosity, and hard work of Ilene and Francis Marckx, who recognized the value of the wetland and launched the park process in 1981 by donating 24.5 acres of land to the state. The park will eventually be of about 100 acres, of which sixty-nine have already been committed.

Access to the park will eventually be via S. 356th Street, where a parking lot and visitor center will be located. From there a trail will have to be built to link up with the existing loop. Until then the Marckx family, who live in the northwest corner of the wetlands, have provided parking next to their home. Although the wetland is now open to the public, visitors are asked to call ahead. The Marckx's phone number is (206) 838-0951.

Old alder trees in West Hylebos Wetlands

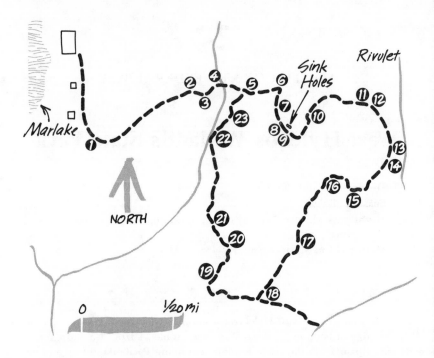

Of all the walks in this book, this is the one farthest from Seattle. Even so, at freeway speed the trip takes only a half-hour from downtown. And it's worth every minute! Drive I-5 south to exit 142B, S. 348th Street, in Federal Way. Leave the freeway, drive west on 348th, and cross Pacific Highway S. About one-half mile beyond, turn left onto 4th Avenue S., which looks like a driveway. The Marckx home sits at the end of the blacktop, on the right. Parking is permitted on the grass south of the house (there is a sign here) or directly across the driveway in a field.

The large pond in back of the Marckx home was created by Francis Marckx by damming a tributary of West Hylebos Creek. To the north of the house is an arboretum containing three specimens of every conifer found in Washington state.

From the parking area, follow the gravel driveway past a small white house, shed, gardens, and work areas—all part of the Marckx's remarkable homestead. At the end of the drive, only a few yards off on the right, is their young "living fossil" grove and a pictorial display map of the wetlands.

(1) The young trees in the grove (donated by local service clubs) are coast redwood, giant sequoia, dawn redwood, and gingko. All were common in the lush semitropical forest that covered North America during the Tertiary Period, some thirty million years ago. Today, of course, the coast redwood is found only along the northern California

coast and an adjacent corner of southwestern Oregon, while the giant sequoia is confined to the Sierra Nevada. The dawn redwood was unknown to western science until only a few decades ago, when it was discovered in a remote section of China. The gingko survives in cultivation but no longer grows in the wild. Gingko Petrified Forest State Park, near Vantage, Washington, preserves the world's only known petrified gingko forest.

From the end of the gravel drive, continue on a grassy track, which bends left past stacks of railroad ties and lumber—the stuff of future trail and other improvement projects. The track enters a stand of red alder and bigleaf maple, then re-emerges into the open and tops a gentle rise. There is a sheltered bench on the left here.

(2) This rise is a glacial drumlin, a low, elongated hill, or ridge, consisting of unsorted rock deposited between 10,000 and 15,000 years ago by the retreating Vashon ice sheet. A series of drumlins in the area accounts for the wavy topography along 348th Street. As the ice sheet withdrew, meltwater collected in the depressions separating the drumlins. Gradually, these depressions were filled with sediments and the pioneer wetland plants such as sedges and rushes invaded the area. Shrubs and trees followed, as ponds evolved into marshes, marshes into bogs, bogs into forested swamps, and swamps into bottomland woods and thickets. Today, the West Hylebos Wetlands contain samples of all of these vegetation types.

From the rise, the track descends into the wetland proper. Just before the track narrows to a trail, there is a signed red alder on the right.

(3) Red alder—without question the most abundant and widespread deciduous tree in western Washington—grows in a variety of situations, but it prefers damp bottoms such as this, where moisture is abundant through the summer and competition from conifers is minimal. In such situations it commonly grows with willows, black cottonwood, and Oregon ash.

The trail crosses planks over a low wet area. A few steps beyond the planks, on the right, a small sign set in the ground reads: "Flooding to this side of tree, January 18th, 1986." A yard beyond that, another sign marks the flood line of the winter of 1981–82. (Other floods were not marked.)

(4) West Hylebos Creek drains many square miles of Federal Way. Flooding in the wetland was rare before 1978 because undeveloped lands were able to soak up normal precipitation. As the area of pavement has steadily increased, however, so has surface runoff. As a result, wetland floods have become annual affairs, with several occuring each winter. After forty-eight hours of rain, the small creek just ahead on this trail becomes a spreading torrent. Two days later the flood has passed. Such rapid runoff sweeps surface pollutants into local streams, and ultimately into Puget Sound before they can be filtered out by percolation through the soil.

Step onto planks and cross a small wooden bridge over First Stream. In a few yards, on the left, there is a sign pointing out a coyote trail. As the trail bends left, a large conifer with dead lower limbs grows left of the trail.

(5) This is Sitka spruce, which flourishes along the Pacific Coast from northern California to south-central Alaska. Sitka spruce is the principal tree of the Olympic rain forest. Picturesque, wind-battered spruces adorn the headlands and sea stacks along the Washington and Oregon coasts. Though fairly common in the area before development, it is now rare throughout the Puget Sound Lowland. It is still common, however, in the West Hylebos Wetlands. Shallow roots make Sitka spruce vulnerable to wind as the fallen spruce here demonstrates. In the moist habitats favored by Sitka spruce, expending energy to grow a deep tap root—whose only function would be to serve as an anchor—is apparently a poor investment of scarce resources. The largest Sitka spruces exceed ten feet in girth and are some 300 feet tall.

The trail on the right is the end of the loop. To continue, keep left and step onto a boardwalk about thirty feet long. (There are plans to lengthen it.) At the far end, a good-sized Douglas fir grows on the right. Beyond a second, shorter boardwalk, come to a ninety-degree right-hand turn.

(6) The tree leaning over here is western hemlock. It has been gradually falling since the mid-1970s. Sometimes, such a tree will right itself. Western hemlock is Washington's state tree.

Continue straight, passing a pair of fine, old western hemlocks. On the left, a few yards past the hemlocks, a sign points out Labrador tea.

(7) This low, spindly member of the heath family is common in conifer swamps and a reliable indicator of acid soils. In fact, ion exchange in the root hairs of Labrador tea helps the plant to create its own acid environment. Acid tolerance is a trait shared by many members of the heath family, including rhododendron, azalea, salal, huckleberry, and swamp laurel, all of which grow in the woods or wetlands of the Pacific Northwest.

Step onto planks as the trail curves back and forth. Come to a hemlock grove where understory vegetation is scant and the forest floor is a springy carpet of conifer needles and layers of dried moss below. On the right, where the trail turns left, is a sign describing soil corings that were taken at this site.

(8) Most of the wetlands are underlain by deep deposits of peat. In cool northern wetlands such as those in the Puget Sound region, the decomposition of dead plants proceeds slowly and is often incomplete. Plant materials, often mixed with silt deposited by streams, pile up layer by layer, gradually creating new land by filling in lake margins and bottomlands. These partially decomposed and carbonized materials are called peat. In the British Isles, peat has long been used as fuel (and as a flavoring for whisky). Coal deposits are thought to develop where buried

Wooden plank walkway in West Hylebos Wetlands

peat has become completely carbonized over the course of millions of years. Local businesses mine and sell peat for soil improvement.

Directly across the trail, behind a wood fence, are two innocuous-looking holes filled with water.

(9) These are sink holes, each about seventeen feet deep. Their cause is uncertain. Some scientists believe that these are simply two deep springs. Others have suggested that the sink holes may be all that remains of a shallow lake that once covered this area. Most have declared that they don't know the origin of these "deep sinks." Even after a prolonged dry spell, the water level in these holes never falls more than fourteen inches below the surface.

The trail turns sharply left. Just beyond a short boardwalk, enter another grove in which there are almost no plants growing in the dense needle litter on the forest floor.

(10) Several of these barren forest "islands" are scattered through the wetlands. It isn't known why these groves are nearly devoid of understory plants while adjacent areas, which are sharply divided from them, may be overgrown with shrubs, ferns, wildflowers, and mosses. The "islands" do

Handwritten nature signs in West Hylebos Wetlands

not seem to be any higher than surrounding areas. Nor do they seem any shadier than nearby groves that have lush understory vegetation. No one knows what goes on below. Many questions about this wetland await future research for answers.

The trail leaves the forest barrens and turns ninety degrees left. It then curves left again and enters another barren grove. At the opposite side of the grove, a plank marks where the trail leads abruptly into rank growths of lady fern and coast red elderberry. The boundary here is very sharp . . . and that too is a mystery.

The trail curves right amid alder, hemlock, spruce, and cedar. Come to another boardwalk, which becomes a bridge across Second Stream. Step off the bridge and onto a short boardwalk. Several yards beyond the boardwalk look on the left for a nurse stump with western hemlock and red huckleberry growing on it. Here too is a clump of wood fern.

(11) When bracken and lady fern have turned brown and died back in the fall, look-alike wood fern, an evergreen, comes into its own. Growing only on dead wood, wood fern is abundant in the especially wet eastern side of the wetland.

Just beyond the stump, on the left, is a short side trail leading to a small rivulet, one of many that carry water through the wetland. Turn left here and walk until you meet the tiny stream.

(12) Everywhere in this headwater swamp, water moves in a general north-to-south direction, in small streams above the surface and along sand seams below. Together, seams and streams make up the "plumbing" of the wetlands. The water gathers at the south side of the wetlands, flows through a culvert, and becomes West Hylebos Creek. The creek flows into the saltwater Hylebos Waterway in Tacoma, a distance of six miles.

Return to the main trail and turn left. The trail begins to bend southward, though this is difficult to perceive at ground level. Step onto planks as the trail bends right through a salmonberry-lady fern thicket and crosses an area of standing water. Leaving the planks, the trail angles left, turns right past a signed elderberry shrub, and comes to an old stump on the left.

(13) A sign on the stump identifies the mosslike plant as the liverwort *Porella,* one of six species of liverwort growing in the wetland. Like mosses, liverworts have two distinct generations: an ongoing, asexual, spore-producing (sporophyte) generation, and a temporary, sexual, egg-and-sperm-producing (gametophyte) generation. The leafy plant growing on the stump is the latter. The sporophytes are tiny and lack chlorophyll. Many kinds of liverworts are found in the damp woods of the Pacific Northwest.

The trail now bends left, passes under a fallen hemlock, then comes to a Douglas fir on the right that is just over four feet in diameter.

(14) Douglas firs are uncommon in the wetland. Since they require mineral soil to germinate and full sun to grow, these must have been established when this area was more open and less overgrown.

The trail jogs left around the dishlike exposed root mass of the fallen hemlock and crosses Second Stream again on a cedar bridge. The tree growing in the stream on the left is Sitka spruce. The trail makes a series of S turns and crosses a wet area on buried cedar rounds, continues winding through woods and thicket, and comes to a large Sitka spruce on the left. Just beyond, on the right, are a pair of fire-scarred red cedars. The timing or cause of the fire is uncertain. Beyond the red cedars the trail winds through a dense deciduous thicket.

(15) The canopy is dominated by red alder and cascara. Oregon crabapple and bitter cherry are also present. The tall shrub layer contains red osier, red elderberry, salmonberry, black twinberry, straggly gooseberry and wild roses.

Shortly cross a fallen alder and turn left alongside the log. The trail bends left around a cascara tangle, follows planks, and comes to some buried cedar rounds.

(16) The low-growing plant with glossy kidney- or heart-shaped leaves is swamp violet. Both the leaves and the flowers grow directly from a creeping stem. Restricted to peaty soils, this violet is quite common along this section of trail.

The path continues winding through the thicket, then suddenly leaves it to enter another conifer barren. On the left is a sign pointing to a stump that was chopped down by a pileated woodpecker. The bird was after a bark beetle whose egg channels show in the exposed wood. On the right, just beyond, another sign points out the shelf fungus *Polyporus versicolor,* the so-called turkey tail.

(17) This fungus grows mainly on dead deciduous trees, less often on conifers. Unlike the parasitic fungi, which infect living trees, the turkey tail is one of the decomposers, which break down wood fibers into simpler substances that can be utilized by living plants. By contributing to the decomposition of fallen trees or old stumps, such fungi also make room for new plants.

As the trail leaves the conifer barren, it turns sharply right, then left, and plunges back into the thicket. It then comes to a red alder on the left with lichens conspicuously growing on the trunk.

(18) Lichens consist of two intimate partners: a green alga that carries out photosynthesis and a fungus that absorbs moisture and dissolved nutrients from the surface to which the lichens are attached. Most of the common types of lichen can be grouped into three physical types: crustose lichens, which form crusts on rocks and other surfaces; foliose lichens, which are leafy in appearance; and fruticose lichens, which have branching stalks. Still other lichens have a dusty appearance. Crustose and foliose lichens are both on this tree.

The trail bends right, then left, and then sharply right. Straight ahead is another conifer barren. Beyond it, the trail turns left around a lovely vine maple and enters yet another conifer barren. Within a few yards, at a group of hemlocks, the route turns ninety degrees to the right. (It is easy to miss this turn because the trail is faint in the needle duff. But should you come to a low sign pointing out the parasitic fungus *Fomes pinicola* growing on a downed limb, you have gone too far. Backtrack several yards and pick up the trail again.) This turn is known as "Amanita Corner" for the abundant seasonal growths of *Amanita* mushrooms.

Beyond Amanita Corner, on the west side of the conifer barren (a compass would help here), look for a small sign pointing the way. Beyond it, the trail is obvious, bending left and leaving the barren to enter a large, open area. Immediately look on the left, next to the trail, for the small sign pointing out swamp laurel, which is growing here beside a signed Labrador tea.

(19) Swamp laurel grows only in the damp, highly acidic soils characteristic of fens and bogs. Its lovely, simple pink flowers appear May through September. The leaves superficially resemble those of Labrador tea. The leaves of swamp laurel are sharp-tipped, shiny above, and dusty white beneath. Those of Labrador tea, however, have rounded tips, rolled margins, and a mat of fine rusty hairs beneath.

Just before the trail leaves the opening, a sign points right to swamp birch. These tall shrubs, located several yards away from the trail, can be picked out because they rise well above the bracken fern and lower shrubbery.

(20) Swamp birch is fairly common in mountain wetlands but rare in the Puget Sound region. The only other place in this book where this birch is known to grow is Bellefields Nature Park, in Bellevue. Swamp birch has small, round, shiny leaves and reddish brown bark.

The trail turns left, leaves the opening, and goes through a conifer stand where the ground cover is sparse but much better developed than in the barren groves encountered earlier. Leaving the grove, the trail crosses an opening with a number of wind-downed trees, passes around one of them, and enters a mixed woodland, with Pacific dogwood and cascara in the understory.

(21) Compare the broad, thin leaves of these deciduous trees with the relatively thick, heavily varnished needles of hemlock, spruce, and Douglas fir. The leaves of deciduous trees are broad to capture sunlight efficiently and thin because, like paper cups, they are disposable. Because of their thinness they decompose faster than do conifer needles. Therefore, rich soils—and lusher, more varied arrays of understory shrubs and herbs—tend to develop more rapidly beneath deciduous than coniferous trees.

The trail winds through the mixed woods, then enters a shady grove of western hemlock, some of considerable size.

(22) This grove contains a few old timbers (one is nailed to a small hemlock on the right side of the trail) that may be the remains of an old moonshiner's still from Prohibition days.

The trail turns sharply right, alongside First Stream, and comes to a fair-sized western red cedar.

(23) To the right of the cedar, and set back off the trail, are two black cottonwoods about as thick as the cedar. During a storm in October 1981, the upper section of the cottonwood on the left (a white sign with a black arrow is posted on the trunk) broke off and was hurled toward the earth. The force of the wind was so great that the trunk was driven several feet into the ground, where it remains today, just a few steps beyond the cedar, on the left side of the path.

The trail winds through the woods and comes to the loop's end at the first Sitka spruce encountered along the route. Turn left here and return to the parking area.

24

Saltwater State Park

Distance: ¾ - mile loop
Season: best fall through spring
Highlights: forest, streams
Metro: 130 (1-mile walk to trailhead)

Saltwater State Park in Des Moines features a quarter mile of sandy beach backed by eighty-eight acres of forested ravine and adjacent uplands. The ravine, originally known as McSorley's Gulch, was purchased for park purposes in the early thirties. The new park was dedicated in 1933. Today, it receives an astonishing 700,000 visitors a year, mostly because of the beach but partly because Saltwater has one of the few campgrounds in the Seattle–Tacoma metropolitan area. On warm summer weekends, thousands of people throng to the park. If you are part of the throng, this walk may offer a welcome change of pace from the frenetic beach scene. For a quieter walk, plan to come in midweek or between Labor Day and Memorial Day.

From Seattle drive south on I-5 to exit 149, SR 516, the Kent–Des Moines Road. Drive west on 516 to SR 509 in Des Moines. Drive south on 509 for just over a mile, to where it veers left. Keep right on 8th Place S. and shortly enter the park. The road drops down to a large parking area and picnic area next to the beach. At the stop sign cross the median, turn left, and park by the rest rooms. The trailhead is located immediately left of the play area next to the rest rooms.

At the edge of the parking strip cross a small creek lined with common horsetail. Creeping buttercup and large-leaved avens grow abundantly nearby. In winter, however, only the buttercup is evident.

(1) Creeping buttercup is an aggressive invader from Europe. It spreads by sprouting along its trailing stems. The flowers are shiny yellow

English ivy covering a tree trunk in Saltwater State Park

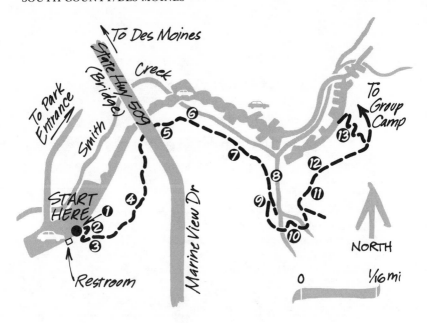

and usually about three-fourths inch in diameter. The leaves consist of three white-haired leaflets, each further divided into three toothed lobes. Large-leaved avens is a native that is easily identified by its leaves alone. The basal leaves consist of several leaflets arrayed along a common stem, with the one at the end several times larger than the others. The flower resembles that of the creeping buttercup except that it is paler yellow, not shiny, and only about five-eighths inch across.

To the right of the bridge is a large bigleaf maple with a vine maple growing beneath it. The trail turns left, then right and heads up the hill. Climb steps bordered by salmonberry and switchback up the slope. The trail climbs gently amid vine maple and Indian plum and in another thirty yards comes to a steep trail cutting across the switchbacks. Red alders are common here.

(2) Following fire, logging, or other disturbance, red alders are often among the first trees to colonize newly opened areas within the forest. Carried into openings by the wind, alder seeds germinate readily. The young alders grow faster even than Douglas fir seedlings, which may be shaded out and thereby largely excluded from the new forest. The shade-tolerant seedlings of western hemlock and western red cedar, however, normally thrive beneath alders, which shelter them from direct sunlight and enrich the soil by "fixing" atmospheric nitrogen in compounds that plant roots can absorb. Eventually, the young conifers replace the alders, which begin dying from heart rot, a fungus disease, after about sixty years of age.

210

Twenty yards beyond the steep, eroded cross path, the trail cuts back to the left, passes a bigleaf maple on the left, and continues to climb gradually, once again crossing the eroded switchback-shortcut trail. Ten yards beyond, on the right, come to a Douglas fir with a trunk nearly three feet in diameter. It is located opposite a rail fence. Several more fair-sized Douglas firs grow some twenty-five yards beyond, where the trail bends to the right.

(3) The ground beneath Douglas firs is often littered with cones. Look among the leaves and debris for small cones with three-pointed bracts extending from between the woody scales. These bracts provide an easy way to distinguish the cones of Douglas fir from those of other local conifers. Note how the scales of the cones are arranged in a spiral. The diameter of a conifer cone increases at a constant rate with each turn of the spiral. Mathematicians call this a logarithmic spiral, and it is found throughout nature—in spider webs, mollusk shells, the curve of a rams' horns or elephants' tusks, the disks of sunflowers or daisies, the galaxies of outer space. The logarithmic spiral allows a flower, or cone, or even the trunk of a conifer to retain its overall proportions while increasing in size.

The trail curves left, right and left again as it continues a gently ascending traverse of the wooded slope. Bigleaf maples, red alders, and scattered conifers form the forest canopy. Vine maple, red elderberry, salmonberry, and Indian plum are the most common shrubs. Trillium, sword fern, and wood fern line the trail. As the trail bends right one more time, stop to listen for the scolding call of Steller's jay.

(4) Steller's jay is the familiar "blue jay" of the Pacific Northwest. Like its cousin the crow, the jay is omnivorous and a habitual nest robber. A bold, noisy buccaneer of a bird for most of the year, Steller's jay becomes quiet and secret during the nesting season. Such stealth helps to keep its own nest concealed from predators and assists its predation on the nests of other birds.

The trail curves right, passing a fat, stumpy, moss-covered log. Fifty yards beyond, step over fallen alders lying across the path. The SR 509 bridge is visible just ahead. Where the trail passes under the bridge, you can look down to a picnic shelter in the bottom of the ravine. Beyond the bridge is a trio of old stumps. The second one on the right, some thirty yards from the bridge, has a European mountain ash, or rowan, growing from it.

(5) Stumps serve as moist, elevated nurseries for a number of native forest plants, most notably western hemlock, red huckleberry, salal, red elderberry, ferns, mosses, and mushrooms. The growth on this stump of European mountain ash, a widely planted ornamental tree, shows that, thanks to birds, garden escapees can also become established on stumps or logs. Robins and other birds feed on the bright red berries of mountain ashes growing in parks and gardens, then fly into nearby woods and deposit the undigested seeds in their droppings.

Detail of mossy ground cover

The ground cover here is mainly youth-on-age, with scattered fringe-cup, lady fern, waterleaf, enchanter's nightshade, and large-leaved avens. Thirty yards beyond the European mountain ash, the trail bends right and passes on the left a bigleaf maple with mosses, licorice fern, and English ivy on the trunk. The smaller trees in here are vine maple, which are inconspicuous in winter.

(6) The abundance of bigleaf maples and vine maples makes this a good park for fall color. When deciduous trees enter dormancy in the fall, water and minerals are cut off from the leaves. As a result, the production of the green pigment chlorophyll ceases, revealing other pigments beneath. The most important of these are the yellow carotenoids and the red pigment anthocyanin, which combine to give a range of colors from gold through deep red.

The path continues left and in thirty-five yards arrives at a large, knobby bigleaf maple on the right, with a thick cushion of moss growing on the trunk.

(7) After a rain, or when humidity is high, look for slugs grazing on the mosses both here and elsewhere throughout the forest. The two largest slugs are both familiar to most residents of the Pacific Northwest. The native banana slug only rarely enters gardens and even then is seldom a pest. The large brown or black garden slug, a highly destructive yard pest imported from Europe, has invaded suburban woods, where it causes little harm but adds little charm.

Fifteen yards beyond the maple, the trail swings left and, a few yards farther, skirts a damp area. The trail stays level and in thirty yards turns right. In another fifteen yards it bends right again and continues thirty yards to a steep track that drops to Smith Creek and the campground. A few steps farther, a second side trail heads right. In late spring the woods are alive with birds.

(8) Three types of warblers nest in the forest. The orange-crowned warbler frequents the forest edge, where it nests on the ground among dense ferns and wildflowers and forages in shrubs and understory trees. Wilson's warbler prefers similar habitat within the heart of the forest. The black-throated gray warbler usually nests ten to twenty feet above the ground but forages high in the canopy. By nesting and foraging in different areas, these three warblers are able to coexist with a minimum of direct competition. Such ecological segregation, as it is called, is common in nature and permits maximum diversity within a natural community.

The trail turns right and heads up a tributary ravine beneath a canopy of alders and maples. Fifty yards beyond the last side trail, pass another path heading down on the left. Keep on the main trail, avoiding turns left and right. In summer look for lady fern and maidenhair fern growing with evergreen sword fern on the bank bordering the right side of the trail.

(9) Lady ferns often grow in soil that is too wet and mucky for sword ferns. And while lady ferns are most commonly found in shady woods, they can tolerate full sun where moisture is plentiful. Sword ferns prefer shaded, moist, well-drained slopes and rarely grow in full sun. Maidenhair fern is most common on moist banks, often near streams where mists keep the nearby air perennially damp. This bank provides a compromise habitat suitable for all three ferns. In the winter only sword fern is evident here, for the other two are deciduous. Notice too how much coarser the fronds of sword fern are than the delicate foliage of lady and maidenhair ferns.

In 100 yards pass some fair-sized western hemlocks growing on the slope. In another seventy yards, come to the head of the ravine, where the trail crosses a small creek via a long wooden bridge. A house is visible atop the ivy-covered slope behind the bridge.

(10) With residential and industrial development of suburban areas, small streams like this are subject to increased pollution and runoff during the rainy season. As pavement proliferates, the volume of runoff increases because there is not enough vegetation to arrest the flow long enough for the ground to absorb it. As a result, water quality declines and erosion increases.

The trail leaves the bridge and bends back along the opposite side of the stream, then climbs gradually. Forty yards past the bridge, where the trail bends right to head up a seasonal tributary creek, look for western starflower. The trail then turns left to cross a bridge over a small creek. From the bridge the trail descends gradually along the opposite side of the ravine.

Thirty yards beyond the small creek, come to a junction; keep left and enter a stand of tall, straight hemlock and maple. The most common understory shrub on this drier slope is salal. Twenty yards from the junction the trail turns left and crosses a small seasonal creek. Sword fern and elderberry are abundant.

(11) Bewick's wren and the song sparrow are both common residents of thickets and forest shrubbery. Although a good deal of mutual aggression occurs during the nesting season, these two small brown birds are able to coexist because they occupy different *niches* within their shared habitat. That is, they utilize the same broad habitat in different ways. The wren nests in crevices and small holes near the ground, and its diet consists almost entirely of insects and other small animal life. Song sparrows, however, build nests on the ground and feed mainly on seeds, though insects are fed to nestlings. Creatures occupying the same habitat do not need to have totally different niches, merely ones where the overlap does not produce critical shortages of shared resources.

In twenty yards the trail again curves right, passing on the left an old red cedar stump with young hemlocks growing on it. Look for large false Solomon's seal on both sides of the path. Fifteen yards beyond the stump the trail turns left, then right, where there is a fallen tree partly covered with dirt. The work of bark beetles is evident in the exposed wood.

(12) The wandering channels in the surface of the wood are the work of bark beetles, which feed on the live green tissues of the inner bark and adjacent cambium layer. The beetles inhabit both living and dead trees but move on when their food source is exhausted. Tree bark poses a formidable barrier to insects and other organisms. By boring through the bark, these beetles connect the interior of a tree to the outside world. Fungi that enter through these openings cause disease in living trees and start the process of decomposition in dead ones. Both processes are vital to the ongoing cycle of life and death in the forest.

The trail crosses a muddy patch and in twenty-five yards swings left. Fifteen yards beyond, it comes to a four-way crossing. Turn left here and follow the path winding downhill along the ravine. In forty yards, where the trail turns right, there is a small cedar snag that has been hollowed out by fire.

(13) Snags such as this one, along with the remains of ash in the soil, help researchers construct the fire history of the region. Cool, humid summers tend to inhibit the incidence and spread of wild fires in the coastal forests of the Pacific Northwest. Fires generally break out during

Lacy fronds of the maidenhair fern

unusually prolonged periods of hot, dry summer weather. Historically, such fires have often been catastrophic. One of the worst in the Northwest was the Tillamook (Oregon) burn of 1933, when some 250,000 acres of old-growth timber were lost. Before the coming of whites to the region, large fires generally occurred every 300 to 400 years in a given place. Indian tribes also set fires to certain areas for the purpose of maintaining habitat for deer, elk, and wild huckleberries.

The trail winds downhill to a gravel service road through the walk-in campground. Turn left, passing the tent campsites, and cross Smith Creek on a wooden bridge. Follow the paved campground road back to the trailhead. For a longer trail walk, turn right on the gravel service road. Keep right at the junction with the main access road to the walk-in campground and just after crossing the creek, turn left and find a trail heading into the woods. This trail loops back along the north side of McSorley's Gulch to the parking area.

25

SOUTH COUNTY/BURIEN

Ed Munro-Seahurst County Park

Distance: ¾ - mile loop
Season: all year
Highlights: big trees, stream
Metro: 136

Ed Munro-Seahurst County Park occupies a deep, forested ravine emptying into Puget Sound. The park features a half mile of beach and more than two miles of trails that wander through the forest. Although the woods are mostly second-growth, some good-sized Douglas firs and western red cedars remain. As elsewhere, this wild corridor owes its existence to the difficulty posed to developers by ravines. King County purchased the land for a park in the 1960s.

The loop described below explores the forest. It can be combined with a picnic or a walk along the beach or both. Rest rooms and picnic tables are located in the grassy area near the beach.

From downtown Seattle, drive highways 99 and 509 south to Burien. Exit the freeway at highway 518, the airport exit. At the stop light, turn right and drive to Ambaum Boulevard S.W. Turn right again. In a couple of blocks turn left on S.W. 144th Street, which is marked by a park sign. In three blocks, at another park sign, turn right on 13th Avenue S.W., which changes to S.W. 140th Street as it winds down to the park.

Two-tenths of a mile beyond the park entrance gate, come to a stop sign. On the left is the entrance to the upper parking lot, where the trail described below will emerge from the forest. Continue on the park road another two-tenths mile to the lower parking area, at the beach. Park on the left as soon as possible after entering the parking area. (Bus riders face a walk of about a mile from the bus stop on Ambaum at 144th Street to the beach parking lot.)

Cross the footbridge and just beyond, leave the brick walk and follow either of two narrow, unmarked paths heading uphill on the left. Climb

Detail of wood fern

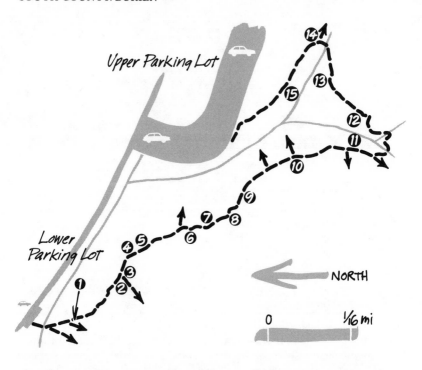

steeply but briefly to a fork. One trail heads right, climbing steeply up the nose of the ridge. The left trail continues straight ahead and traverses the slope above the creek. Growing between the two trails is a large bigleaf maple in the process of shedding its lower branches.

(1) The forest of Ed Munro-Seahurst County Park consists mostly of bigleaf maples and red alders, but also contains large Douglas firs, western hemlocks, and western red cedars. This mix of conifers and deciduous trees is typical of forests throughout the Seattle-Tacoma metropolitan area. What is not typical, however, is the large size of the conifers.

From the junction take the left trail, which climbs gradually for some twenty yards, then levels out as it traverses the side of the densely wooded ravine. In another thirty yards pass a second large bigleaf maple on the left. From here the trail drops slightly and crosses a muddy area. Look for a large fallen log blocking an obscure path heading upslope on the right.

(2) Scattered through the undergrowth along this damp stretch, as well as elsewhere farther along the trail, are a number of tall, rangy shrubs with dark green, smooth, maplelike leaves on long leaf stalks. This shrub is stink currant, which is named for its rank odor. Stink currant is common in damp, shaded places throughout the region. Its large, dark green leaves grow in whorls and are held horizontally, presumably to intercept the maximum amount of sunlight. The greenish-white flowers are inconspicuous. The rough, blue-black berries have an objectionable flavor, though not to hungry birds.

A few yards beyond the side path, pass what at first appears to be two large bigleaf maples leaning out over the trail.

(3) One of these trees has a trunk shaped like an inverted Y or wishbone and may have begun as two separate trees that at some point fused together above their bases to form a single trunk. Regardless, moss and licorice fern grow abundantly on the trunks of these maples. Licorice fern was used for medicinal purposes by Indian tribes throughout western Washington. Its root stalk, or rhizome, was chewed as a cough medicine and used as an ingredient in a tonic for measles.

The trail jogs left and right, and about fifteen yards beyond the maples passes between a pair of trees—on the left another maple and on the right a young western hemlock growing atop an old red cedar stump.

Low tide at Ed Munro-Seahurst County Park

(4)   These trees represent three stages in the ongoing history of this forest. The old red cedar stump is the ghost of forest past. Along with western hemlock and Douglas fir, it dominated the lush conifer forest that once grew on this slope. The maple represents the present forest, which evolved on the site in the wake of logging. The young western hemlock represents the future forest, when conifers, having shaded out the deciduous trees, will regain their dominant status on this slope.

Cross a log with a step cut out of it. Then step over another log and about five yards beyond, where the trail levels out at the top of a short rise, notice a bigleaf maple growing in front of a Douglas fir about three feet in diameter. To the right of the fir is a hemlock growing out of an old stump. To the left of the maple is another stump, this one with red elderberry, sword fern, wood fern, and several other types of plants growing on it.

Western hemlock cones

(5)   The fallen logs and old stumps scattered through this forest, along with the large conifers still remaining, are reminders of what these woods were once like. When Seattle's first settlement was established at Alki Point in 1851, a thick luxuriant conifer forest mantled western Washington from the Cascades to the sea. Deciduous trees such as bigleaf maple and red alder, which are so common and widespread today, were much less common then. They occurred sparingly within the forest itself and flourished only in special habitats where conifers fared poorly. All this changed, of course, following settlement.

The trail crosses another log and, about fifteen yards beyond, curves right as it continues a gentle ascending traverse of the slope. The vegetation is extremely lush on this damp slope, and the principal shrubs are mainly salmonberry and coast red elderberry. In another twenty-five yards pass a side path heading down to the stream. A dozen yards beyond, the trail turns right and climbs to a Douglas fir snag on the right.

(6)   Douglas firs are among the largest trees in the world. This dead one is perhaps seven feet in diameter at the base. Its swollen base, which is typical of old Douglas firs, probably provided stability in high winds. The current champion Douglas fir is a tree in the Queets River rain forest of Olympic National Park. The Queets fir is more than fourteen and a half feet thick, with a trunk broken off 221 feet above the ground. The former champion was Oregon's Clatsop fir, which was more than thirteen feet thick but had an unbroken top 302 feet tall!

The trail continues the traverse. Downslope on the left, about ten yards past the snag, there is a smaller but still living Douglas fir. Beyond it, the trail climbs and turns left, as larger firs come into view upslope on the right. Across from where a small side trail enters on the right are a couple of Douglas fir snags, one of which is perhaps fifty feet tall.

(7)   Large numbers of standing dead trees are characteristic of old-growth forests in the Pacific Northwest. These snags, like the large trees hereabouts, are residual from the old-growth forest that once grew here. Research in Oregon forests has shown that Douglas fir snags usually remain intact for fifty to seventy-five years before breaking off at somewhere below the thirty-five foot level. Western red cedar snags may persist up to 125 years. Snags appear to decompose more rapidly than fallen trees and therefore release bound-up nutrients back into the soil more quickly.

The forest becomes more impressive, as Douglas firs and western hemlocks that are three or four feet thick become more common. The trail climbs gently as it traverses the slope.

(8)   In summer look for a variety of ferns along this section—sword fern, lady fern, wood fern, maidenhair fern, and licorice fern. In winter, however, the deciduous maidenhair and lady ferns are not apparent, having died back to underground root stalks. Licorice fern, in contrast, is most conspicuous in winter but turns brown and dies back in summer. Evergreen sword and wood ferns are evident year-around.

Lush licorice ferns

Western trillium

The trail is blocked by another log, into which a step has been cut. Beyond it the trail continues its gradually ascending traverse. In another twenty yards it passes several western hemlocks and, fifteen yards beyond them, comes to a large Douglas fir that is growing upslope on the right. The fir is located only a few yards before the trail comes to a huge fallen red cedar.

(9) Douglas fir requires mineral soil for seed germination and abundant sunlight for seedling growth, neither of which are commonly available in old-growth forests. It is able to maintain its presence by being long-lived. That is, over the many hundreds of years of its life span, the chances are good that fire, wind, or some other force will open up the forest. This Douglas fir, like all others, began in such an opening.

There is just enough room to duck under the fallen cedar lying across the trail. On the right are several more large Douglas firs. Step over or go under one more log and pass a small stand of western hemlocks whose boughs overhang the trail. In thirty to forty yards from the fallen cedar pass two side trails, one after the other, head down to the small creek. Opposite the second side path is a stump with western hemlocks (one of which is about one foot in diameter and forty feet tall) growing on it. The undergrowth along this section is lush because moisture is abundant and the open forest canopy allows more sunlight to penetrate. Look for a variety of ferns, as well as bedstraw, sweet cicely, candyflower, youth-on-age, and western trillium.

(10) The lovely western trillium, or wake robin, is among the earliest spring wildflowers. Leaves, sepals, and petals are normally in threes. The petals are white when they open but fade first to pink and then to deep rose. Ants carry off the seeds to feast on their oily coating. In the process the insects serve to disperse the plant through the forest.

Fifteen yards beyond the second side path, the main trail passes a snag on the left, then descends gradually and levels out. In another thirty-five yards it veers right and gently climbs to another side trail. Fifteen yards more and the trail arrives at an overlook of the small creek, which consists of small pools and riffles. The pools are dammed behind woody debris.

(11) Fallen logs and branches help determine the shape, stability, and aquatic habitats of small forest streams. Pools that form behind large woody debris create critical habitats for fish and other aquatic life. The deposition of sediments in these pools slows down the removal of nutrient-rich debris from the forest, allowing decomposing organisms time to work on the materials before the latter are washed downstream and lost to the community. The characteristic stepped stream profile of alternating pools and drops also stabilizes the streambed and reduces erosion.

At the next junction, turn left and wind down to the creek, an easy crossing on logs. The stream is only a couple of feet wide, and for most adults the crossing will be routine. Senior citizens, however, or parties with small children, may want to turn back here, especially if the logs are wet.

On the other side of the stream, climb steeply a few yards uphill to a prominent hemlock whose roots are exposed on the bare slope. The trail forks at the tree; take the left fork downhill. The obvious trail swings around to cross a second small creek, then climbs gently, curves right, and swings back toward the left. About forty yards past the last creek, pass a side trail on the right. Several yards beyond, notice a large red cedar stump.

(12) A log or stump such as this provides shelter for the ensatina, a small salamander that is common but seldom seen. The ensatina is a lungless salamander that "breathes" by means of gas exchange through its thin moist skin. Lunglessness would seem to have evolved as an adaptation to aquatic life. Yet the ensatina is rarely found in water. Instead, it carries the stream with it, so to speak, in the form of the moist layer of mucous covering its skin. The ensatina is active above ground mainly in spring and fall, when the earth is damp and the weather is mild. Then, it can often be found beneath leaf litter, rocks, logs, and loose bark. During cold or dry weather it retreats to underground chambers (often the tunnel or burrow of another animal), the interior of logs or stumps, or moist crevices in bark, rocks, or decaying wood.

Thirty yards beyond the stump, the trail turns a corner and begins to descend beneath alder, maple, and hemlock. Just a few yards beyond, on the left, is a giant cedar log with hemlock, red huckleberry, and wood fern growing on it.

(13) Among the liveliest and most characteristic of creatures frequenting fallen timber is the tiny winter wren, which always seems to be busy, scooting here and there among the underbrush. Although the wren is active year-around, it is most conspicuous in spring, when its high, rollicking, musical song—surprisingly loud for so small a bird—rings throughout all the forests of western Washington.

The trail drops to a log bridge across another small creek and comes to a side trail on the right. the junction is overarched with coast red elderberry.

(14) Coast red elderberry is one of the most common shrubs in damp lowland forests of western Washington. In early spring its plumes of creamy white flowers are among the first to appear in the forest. And by late summer the dense clusters of scarlet berries provide startling accents to the overwhelming forest green. Red berries are a sure sign that a plant species mainly or entirely relies on birds to disseminate its seeds. Band-tailed pigeons, grouse, robins, and cedar waxwings are among the birds that perform this service for the elderberry.

Keep left at the junction and in ten yards pass a second side trail on the right. The main trail descends gradually, and in about fifty yards passes a number of leaning and wind-thrown trees.

(15) Trees that grow in damp soils are usually shallow-rooted because water is available near the surface, so the roots don't need to search for it at lower depths. Because of their shallow roots, however, the trees are particularly susceptible to being toppled by wind or undermined by runoff. Although the ravine affords some protection from wind, little wind is needed to topple trees rooted in damp soil.

Where the trail levels out, pass another small side trail on the left. Just beyond it, the trail turns right and descends to the park's large, curving upper parking area. Turn left, follow the parking lot to the road, turn left again and walk along the sidewalk one-tenth mile back to the beach parking lot.

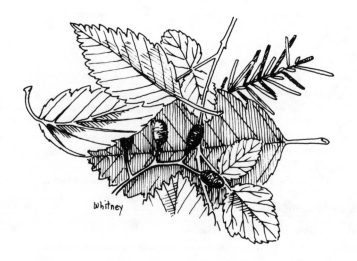

whitney

Appendix A. Selected Reading

FIELD GUIDES

The following books are recommended to readers who wish to identify the plants and animals mentioned in *Nature Walks in and around Seattle*.

General

Kozloff, Eugene N. *Plants and Animals of the Pacific Northwest.* Seattle: University of Washington Press, 1976. Good coverage but cumbersome to use in the field.

Ransom, J. R., ed. *Harper & Row's Complete Field Guide to North American Wildlife, Western Edition.* New York: Harper & Row, 1981. Good general guide.

Animals

Mammals

Burt, William H. and Richard P. Grossenheider. *A Field Guide to the Mammals.* Boston: Houghton Mifflin Company, 1964. The standard field guide to mammals.

Murie, Olaus J. *A Field Guide to Animal Tracks.* Boston: Houghton Mifflin Company, 1954. Interesting to read as well as use in the field.

Whittaker, John O., Jr. *The Audubon Society Field Guide to the Animals of North America.* New York: Alfred A. Knopf, 1980. Outstanding color photographs are the best feature of this guide.

Birds

Peterson, Roger Tory. *A Field Guide to Western Birds.* Boston: Houghton Mifflin Company, 1961. The long-time bible of western bird watchers. A new edition is expected sometime soon.

Robbins, Chandler S., Betel Bruun, and Herbert S. Zim. *Birds of North America: A Guide to Field Identification,* rev. ed. New York: Golden Press, 1983. A good all-purpose beginner's field guide to the birds of North America.

Udvardy, Miklos D. F. *The Audubon Society Field Guide to North American Birds, Western Region.* New York: Alfred A. Knopf, 1977. Valuable for its color photographs and expanded descriptions of each species, but rather difficult for novices to use in the field.

APPENDIX A: SELECTED READING

Reptiles and Amphibians

Stebbins, Robert C. *A Field Guide to Western Reptiles and Amphibians.* New York: Houghton Mifflin Company, 1966. A well-illustrated, authoritative guide.

Behler, John H. and F. Wayne King. *The Audubon Society Field Guide to North American Reptiles & Amphibians.* New York: Alfred A. Knopf, 1979. Excellent photographs and up-to-date species accounts.

Nussbaum, Ronald A., Edmund D. Brodie, Jr., and Robert M. Storm. *Amphibians & Reptiles of the Pacific Northwest.* Moscow, Idaho: The University Press of Idaho, 1983. Somewhat technical but the most useful guide to Northwest reptiles and amphibians.

Insects and Spiders

Borror, Donald J. and Richard E. White. *A Field Guide to the Insects.* Boston: Houghton Mifflin Company, 1970. A noble, if not entirely successful, attempt to reduce a vast subject to the confines of a pocket guide.

Christensen, James R. *A Field Guide to the Butterflies of the Pacific Northwest.* Moscow, Idaho: The University Press of Idaho, 1981. A useful guidebook with color photos of every species.

Milne, Lorus and Margery. *The Audubon Society Field Guide to North American Insects & Spiders.* New York: Alfred A. Knopf, 1980. Recommended for the excellent photographs.

Pyle, Robert Michael. *The Audubon Society Field Guide to North American Butterflies.* New York: Alfred A. Knopf, 1981. An excellent guide by a Northwestern lepidopterist.

Plants

General

Lyons, C. P. *Trees, Shrubs, & Flowers to Know in Washington,* second paperback edition. Toronto: J. M. Dent & Sons (Canada), 1977. The standard guide for the region, though outdated.

Trees

Brockman, C. Frank. *Trees of North America.* New York: Golden Press, 1968. A useful guide with color plates showing every species.

Little, Elbert L. *The Audubon Society Field Guide to North American Trees.* New York: Alfred A. Knopf, 1980. Excellent color photographs and text but not always the easiest guide to use.

McMinn, Howard H. and Evelyn Maino. *An Illustrated Manual of Pacific Coast Trees.* Berkeley: University of California Press, 1967. The standard work. Useful if somewhat technical.

Watts, Tom. *Pacific Coast Tree Finder.* A brief, truly pocket-sized guide.

Wildflowers

Niehaus, Theodore F. and Charles L. Ripper. *A Field Guide to Pacific States*

Wildflowers. Boston: Houghton Mifflin Company, 1976. An easy-to-use guide with species arranged by color and shape.

Spellenberg, Richard. *The Audubon Society Field Guide to North American Wildflowers, Western Region.* New York: Alfred A. Knopf, 1979. Most valuable for its color photographs.

Ferns and Mosses

Harthill, Marion P. and Irene O'Connor. *Common Mosses of the Pacific Coast.* Healdsburg, California: Naturegraph Publishers, 1975. The only pocket-sized novice's guide to mosses of the Northwest.

Keator, Glenn and Ruth M. Atkinson. *Pacific Coast Fern Finder.* Berkeley: Nature Study Guild, 1981. A brief, truly pocket-sized guide.

Mushrooms

McKenny, Margaret (revised by Daniel E. Stuntz). *The Savory Wild Mushroom.* Seattle: University of Washington Press, 1971. A classic guide to Northwestern mushrooms.

Lincoff, Gary H. *The Audubon Society Field Guide to North American Mushrooms.* New York: Alfred A. Knopf, 1981. Valuable for its fine photographs.

FURTHER READING

Arno, Stephen F. and Ramona Hammerly. *Northwest Trees.* Seattle: The Mountaineers, 1977.

Clark, Lewis J. *Wild Flowers of the Pacific Northwest.* Sidney, British Columbia: Gray's Publishing, 1976.

Cowan, Ian McTaggart and Charles J. Guiget. *The Mammals of British Columbia.* Victoria: British Columbia Provincial Museum, 1965.

Farrand, John, Jr., ed. *The Audubon Society Master Guide to Birding* (3 vols.). New York: Alfred A. Knopf, 1983.

Hunn, Eugene. *Birding in Seattle and King County.* Seattle: Seattle Audubon Society, 1982.

Ingles, Lloyd G. *Mammals of the Pacific States.* Stanford, California: Stanford University Press, 1965.

Larrison, Earl J. *Birds of the Pacific Northwest.* Moscow, Idaho: The University Press of Idaho, 1981.

Larrison, Earl J. *Mammals of the Northwest: Washington, Oregon, Idaho, and British Columbia.* Seattle: Seattle Audubon Society, 1976.

Larrison, Earl J., G. W. Patrick, W. H. Baker, and J. A. Yaich. *Washington Wildflowers.* Seattle: Seattle Audubon Society, 1974.

Morgan, Brandt. *Enjoying Seattle's Parks.* Seattle: Greenwood Publications, 1979.

Nehls, Harry B. *Familiar Birds of the Northwest.* Portland, Oregon: Portland Audubon Society, 1981.

Neill, W. A. and D. J. Hepburn. *Butterflies Afield in the Pacific Northwest.* Seattle: Pacific Search Books, 1976.

Pyle, Robert Michael. *Watching Washington Butterflies*. Seattle: Seattle Audubon Society, 1974.

Schwartz, Susan. *Nature in the Northwest*. Englewood Cliffs, New Jersey: Prentice-Hall, 1983.

Wahl, Terrence R. and Dennis R. Paulson. *A Guide to Bird Finding in Washington*. Bellingham: T. R. Wahl, 1977.

Whitney, Stephen R. *Western Forests*. New York: Alfred A. Knopf, 1985.

Whittlesey, Rhoda. *Familiar Friends: Northwest Plants*. Portland, Oregon: Rose Press, 1985.

Wydoski, Richard S. and Richard R. Whitney. *Inland Fishes of Washington*. Seattle: University of Washington Press, 1978.

Appendix B. Scientific Names

PLANTS

alder, red, *Alnus rubra*
amanita, panther, *Amanita pantherina*
arborvitae, Chinese, *Thuja orientalis*
ash, Cascade mountain, *Sorbus scopulina*
ash, European mountain, *Sorbus aucuparia*
ash, Oregon, *Fraxinus latifolia*
ash, Sitka mountain, *Sorbus sitchensis*
aspen, quaking, *Populus tremuloides*
avens, large-leaved, *Geum macrophyllum*

bedstraw, *Galium* species
birch, bog (see *birch, swamp*)
birch, European white, *Betula pendula*
birch, paper, *Betula papyrifera*
birch, swamp, *Betula glandulosa*
blackberry, evergreen, *Rubus laciniatus*
blackberry, Himalaya, *Rubus discolor*
blackberry, Pacific, *Rubus ursinus*
bleeding heart, western, *Dicentra formosa*
broom, Scotch, *Cytisus scoparius*
bulrush, *Scirpus microcarpus*
buttercup, creeping, *Ranunculus repens*

cabbage, skunk, *Lysichitum americanum*
candyflower, *Montia sibirica*
carrot, wild (see *Queen Anne's lace*)
cascara, *Rhamnus purshiana*
cattail, common, *Typha latifolia*
cedar, Alaska, *Chamaecyparis nootkaensis*
cedar, eastern red, *Juniperus virginiana*
cedar, incense, *Libocedrus decurrens*
cedar, northern white, *Thuja occidentalis*
cedar, western red, *Thuja plicata*
cedar, yellow (see *cedar, Alaska*)
cherry bitter, *Prunus emarginata*
chicory, *Cichorium intybus*

APPENDIX B: SCIENTIFIC NAMES

chinquapin, golden, *Castanopsis chrysophylla*
club, devil's, *Oplopanax horridum*
cottonwood, black, *Populus trichocarpa*
crabapple, Oregon (see *crabapple, Pacific*)
crabapple, Pacific, *Pyrus fuscus*
creambush (see *spray, ocean*)
currant, red-flowering, *Ribes sanguineum*
currant, stink, *Ribes bracteosum*

dewberry (see *blackberry, Pacific*)
dogwood, Pacific, *Cornus nuttallii*
dogwood, red osier (see *osier, red*)
Douglas fir (see *fir, Douglas*)
duckweed, *Lemna minor*

elderberry, coast red, *Sambucus racemosa*

fairy cup, orange, *Aleuria aurantia*
farewell-to-spring (see *candyflower*)
fern, bracken, *Pteridium aquilinum*
fern, deer, *Blechnum spicant*
fern, lady, *Athyrium filix-femina*
fern, licorice, *Polypodium glycyrrhiza*
fern, maidenhair, *Adiantum pedatum*
fern, sword, *Polystichum munitum*
fern, wood, *Dryopteris austriaca*
fir, Douglas, *Pseudotsuga menziesii*
fir, grand, *Abies grandis*
fir, Pacific silver, *Abies amabilis*
fir, subalpine, *Abies lasiocarpa*
fireweed, *Epilobium angustifolium*
fringecup, *Tellima grandiflora*
fungus, turkey tail, *Polyporus versicolor*

gingko, *Gingko biloba*
gooseberry, straggly, *Ribes divaricatum*
gooseberry, swamp, *Ribes lacustre*
grape, low Oregon (see *grape, Oregon*)
grape, Oregon, *Berberis nervosa*
grape, tall Oregon, *Berberis aquifolium*
grass, reed canary, *Phalarus arundinacea*

hardhack, *Spiraea douglasii*
hawthorn, Columbia, *Cratageus douglasii*
hazelnut, California, *Corylus cornuta* variety *californica*
hedgenettle, Cooley's, *Stachys cooleyae*
hemlock, mountain, *Tsuga mertensiana*
hemlock, western, *Tsuga heterophylla*
holly, English, *Ilex aquifolium*
horsechestnut, *Aesculus hippocastanum*
horsetail, common, *Equisetum arvense*
huckleberry, evergreen, *Vaccinium ovatum*
huckleberry, red, *Vaccinium parvifolium*

iris, European yellow, *Iris pseudacorus*

ivy, English, *Hedera helix*

lace, Queen Anne's, *Daucus carota*
larch, alpine, *Larix lyalli*
larch, western, *Larix occidentalis*
laurel, swamp, *Kalmia occidentalis*
lily, white water, *Nymphaea odorata*
loosestrife, purple, *Lythrum salicaria*

madrona, Pacific, *Arbutus menziesii*
madrone (see *madrona, Pacific*)
maple, bigleaf, *Acer macrophyllum*
maple, vine, *Acer circinatum*
milfoil, European water, *Myriophyllum spicatum*
mushroom, oyster, *Pleurotus ostreatus*

nettle, stinging, *Urtica dioica*
nightshade, enchanter's, *Circaea alpina*
nightshade, climbing, *Solanum dulcamara*

oak, Garry (see *oak, Oregon white*)
oak, Oregon white, *Quercus garryana*
ocean spray (see *spray, ocean*)
osier, red, *Cornus stolonifera*
osoberry (see *plum, Indian*)

parsley, water, *Oenanthe sarmentosa*
pea, purple, *Lathyrus latifolius*
piggyback plant (see *youth-on-age*)
pine, lodgepole, *Pinus contorta* variety *latifolia*
pine, ponderosa, *Pinus ponderosa*
pine, shore, *Pinus contorta* variety *contorta*
planetree, London, *Platanus acerifolia*
planetree, Oriental, *Platanus orientalis*
plum, Indian, *Oemleria cerasiformis*
poplar, Lombardy, *Populus nigra* variety *italica*

red cedar, western (see *cedar, western red*)
redwood, California, *Sequoia sempervirens*
redwood, dawn, *Metasequoia glyptostroboides*
rose, baldhip, *Rosa gymnocarpa*
rose, little wild, *Rosa pisocarpa*
rose, Nootka, *Rosa nutkana*
rowan (see *ash, European mountain*)

salal, *Gaultheria shallon*
salmonberry, *Rubus spectabilis*
sequoia, giant, *Sequoiadendron giganteum*
serviceberry, western, *Amelanchier alnifolia*
snowberry, common, *Symphoricarpos alba*
spray, ocean, *Holodiscus discolor*
spruce, blue, *Picea pungens*
spruce, Englemann, *Picea engelmannii*
spruce, Norway, *Picea abies*
spruce, Sitka, *Picea sitchensis*
starflower, *Trientalis latifolia*

APPENDIX B: SCIENTIFIC NAMES

stropharia, questionable, *Stropharia ambigua*
sycamore, American, *Platanus occidentalis*
sycamore, California, *Platanus racemosa*

tea, Labrador, *Ledum groendlandicum*
thimbleberry, *Rubus parviflorus*
trillium, western, *Trillium ovatum*
twinberry, black, *Lonicera involucrata*

vanilla plant, *Achlys triphylla*

waterleaf, Pacific, *Hydrophyllum tenuipes*
willow, Pacific, *Salix lasiandra*
willow, Piper's, *Salix piperi*
willow, Scouler's, *Salix scouleriana*

yew, western (see *yew, Pacific*)
yew, English, *Taxus baccata*
yew, Pacific, *Taxus brevifolia*
youth-on-age, *Tolmiea menziesii*

ANIMALS

aplodontia, *Aplodontia rufa*
bass, large-mouth, *Micropterus salmoides*
bear, *Ursus americanus*
beaver, *Castor canadensis*
beaver, mountain (see *Aplodontia*)
beetle, bark, *Phloeosinus* species
bittern, American, *Botaurus lentiginosus*
blackbird, red-winged, *Agelaius phoeniceus*
bobcat, *Felis rufus*
bushtit, *Psaltriparus minimus*

carp, *Cyprinus carpio*
chickadee, black-capped, *Parus atricapillus*
chickadee, chestnut-backed, *Parus rufescens*
chickaree (see *squirrel, Douglas'*)
chipmunk, Townsend's, *Eutamias townsendii*
coot, American, *Fulica americana*
cottontail, eastern, *Sylvilagus floridanus*
coyote, *Canis latrans*
creeper, brown, *Certhia americana*
crow, American, *Corvus brachyrhynchos*

deer, Columbian black-tailed, *Odocoileus hemionus*

eagle, bald, *Haliaeetus leucocephalus*
elk, *Cervus elaphus*
ensatina, *Ensatina eschscholtzi*

finch, house, *Carpodacus mexicanus*
finch, purple, *Carpodacus purpureus*
flycatcher, olive-sided, *Contopus borealis*
flycatcher, western, *Empidonax difficilis*
flycatcher, willow, *Empidonax trailli*

fox, red, *Vulpes fulva*
frog, red-legged, *Rana aurora*

gadwall, *Anas strepera*
goldfinch, American, *Carduelis tristis*
goose, Canada, *Branta canadensis*
grosbeak, black-headed, *Pheucticus melanocephalus*
grouse, blue, *Dendragapus obscurus*
grouse, ruffed, *Bonasa umbellus*

harrier, northern, *Circus cyaneus*
hawk, red-tailed, *Buteo jamaicensis*
hawk, sharp-shinned, *Accipiter striatus*
heron, great blue, *Ardea herodias*
heron, green-backed, *Butorides striatus*
hummingbird, rufous, *Selasphorus rufus*

jay, Steller's, *Cyanocitta stelleri*

kestrel, American, *Falco sparverius*
kildeer, *Charadrius vociferus*
kingfisher, belted, *Ceryle alcyon*
kinglet, golden-crowned, *Regulus satrapa*
kinglet, ruby-crowned, *Regulus calendula*

mallard, *Anas platyrhynchos*
mole, coast, *Scapanus orarius*
mouse, deer, *Peromyscus maniculatus*
muskrat, *Ondatra zibethicus*

newt, rough-skinned, *Taricha granulosa*
nuthatch, red-breasted, *Sitta canadensis*

pheasant, ring-necked, *Phasianus colchicus*
pintail, northern, *Anas acuta*
pipit, water, *Anthus spinoletta*
pumpkinseed (see *sunfish, pumpkinseed*)

quail, California, *Callipepla californica*

raccoon, *Procyon lotor*
rail, Virginia, *Rallus limicola*
robin, American, *Turdus migratorius*

salamander, long-toed, *Ambystoma macrodactylum columbianum*
salamander, Oregon (see *ensatina*)
salmon, chinook, *Oncorhynchus tshawytscha*
salmon, coho, *Oncorhynchus kisutch*
salmon, sockeye, *Oncorhynchus nerka*
sapsucker, red-breasted, *Sphyrapicus ruber*
shoveler, northern, *Anas clypeata*
shrew, Trowbridge, *Sorex trobridgii*
shrew-mole, *Neurotrichus gibbsii*
slug, banana, *Ariolimax columbianus*
slug, brown, *Arion ater*
snipe, common, *Gallinago gallinago*
sora, *Porzna carolina*
sparrow, fox, *Passerella iliaca*

sparrow, golden-crowned, *Zonotrichia atricapilla*
sparrow, savannah, *Passerculus sandwichensis*
sparrow, song, *Melospiza melodia*
sparrow, white-crowned, *Zonotrichia leucophrys*
squirrel, Douglas', *Tamiasciurus douglasii*
squirrel, Eastern gray, *Sciurus carolinensis*
squirrel, northern flying, *Glaucomys sabrinus*
steelhead, *Salmo gairdneri*
sunfish, pumpkinseed, *Lepomus gibbosus*
swallow, barn, *Hirundo rustica*
swallow, tree, *Tachycineta bicolor*
swallow, violet-green, *Tachycineta thalassina*

tanager, western, *Piranga ludoviciana*
teal, blue-winged, *Anas discors*
teal, cinnamon, *Anas cyanoptera*
teal, green-winged, *Anas crecca*
thrush, hermit, *Catharus guttatus*
thrush, varied, *Ixoreus naevius*
tortoiseshell, Milbert's, *Aglais milberti*
towhee, rufous-sided, *Pipilo erythrophthalmus*
treefrog, Pacific, *Hyla regilla*
trout, cutthroat, *Salmo clarki*

vireo, red-eyed, *Vireo olivaceus*
vireo, warbling, *Vireo gilvus*
vole, Townsend's, *Microtus townsendi*

warbler, black-throated gray, *Dendroica nigrescens*
warbler, orange-crowned, *Vermivora celata*
warbler, Wilson's, *Wilsonia pusilla*
warbler, yellow, *Dendroica petechia*
warbler, yellow-rumped, *Dendroica coronata*
wigeon, American, *Anas americana*
woodpecker, downy, *Picoides pubescens*
woodpecker, hairy, *Picoides villosus*
woodpecker, pileated, *Dryocopus pileatus*
wren, Bewick's, *Thryomanes bewickii*
wren, marsh, *Cistothorus palustris*
wren, winter, *Troglodytes troglodytes*

yellowthroat, common, *Geothylpis trichas*

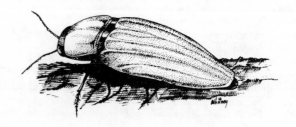

Index

Page numbers of photographs are in **boldface.**

Photo by James Hendrickson

Photo by Peter Damron

STEPHEN R. WHITNEY is author of seven books on natural history, including *A Field Guide to the Cascades and Olympics,* also published by The Mountaineers. He has worked as managing editor of *The Sierra Club Bulletin,* associate editor of *The Mother Earth News,* and consulting editor of *Backpacker Magazine,* and is now involved in book editing in the Northwest. He lives with his wife and son in the wilds of north Seattle.

JAMES HENDRICKSON has been involved in serious photography for six years (he built his own 4x5 camera to start). He has attended the Owens Valley (California) workshop taught by John Sexton, Oliver Gagliani's workshops in Nevada, and other workshops in Washington, all devoted to black and white photography. Hendrickson uses two cameras — an Olympus OM-4 and a 4x5 Wista field camera — and Ilford FP4 and Kodak T-Max film. His interest in landscape photography led to his participation in this book.